The Ambivalence of Form

The Ambivalence of Form
Lukács, Freud, and the Novel

Susan Derwin

The Johns Hopkins University Press
Baltimore and London

© 1992 The Johns Hopkins University Press
All rights reserved
Printed in the United States of America on acid-free paper

The Johns Hopkins University Press
701 West 40th Street
Baltimore, Maryland 21211-2190
The Johns Hopkins Press Ltd., London

Library of Congress Cataloging-in-Publication Data
Derwin, Susan.
The ambivalence of form : Lukács, Freud, and the novel / Susan Derwin.
    p.   cm.
Includes bibliographical references and index.
ISBN 0-8018-4381-2
1. Fiction—History and criticism.   2. Mimesis in literature.
PN3491.D4   1992
809.3—dc20   92-6557

Contents

	Acknowledgments	*vii*
	Introduction	*1*
One	Mimesis and Subjectivity in Lukács's *Die Theorie des Romans*	*7*
Two	Mimesis in a Two-way Mirror: Freud's *Totem und Tabu*	*35*
Three	Dreadful Discovery in Balzac's *La Recherche de l'Absolu*	*51*
Four	The Secret of the Third Story in Charlotte Brontë's *Jane Eyre*	*94*
Five	Domesticated Irony in Theodor Fontane's *Frau Jenny Treibel*	*113*
Six	Orality, Aggression, and Epistemology in Walker Percy's *The Second Coming*	*147*
	Conclusion	*179*
	Notes	*183*
	Index	*203*

Acknowledgments

I would like to thank Rainer Nägele and Richard Macksey for the generous help and exemplarity they have provided. Special thanks also go to Michael Fried for his attentive reading of each chapter and to Josué Harari, Jerry Christensen, and Dominick LaCapra for their valuable suggestions. I am grateful to Anne Whitmore for her careful assistance in preparing the book for publication and to Eric Halpern for his lucid editorial suggestions. I am grateful as well to Sydney Lévy, Laurence Rickles, Malina Stefanovska, and Charles Sherry for their help in proofreading the manuscript.

I am indebted to the Camargo Foundation and the Humanities Center of the Johns Hopkins University for the support they gave during the initial research and writing of the book.

An earlier version of chapter 6 was published in the *Arizona Quarterly,* volume 45, number 2, summer 1989.

Introduction

A tradition of interpretation at least as old as Aristotle's *Poetics* defines the concept of mimesis in terms of its grammatical object: mimesis is always mimesis of something. Such an understanding of the concept presupposes the priority, in both the temporal and evaluative senses of the word, of a model or an original. Aristotle's literary treatise provides strong support for this notion of mimesis. One of the many passages that emphasize the importance of the object of mimetic representation can be found in *Poetics* 25, where Aristotle states, "The poet being an imitator just like the painter or other maker of likenesses, he must necessarily in all instances represent things in one or other of three aspects, either as they were or are, or as they are said or thought to be or to have been, or as they ought to be."[1]

After its translation into Latin (in 1498) and Italian (in 1549), the *Poetics* gained widespread influence, and post-Aristotelian definitions of mimesis continued to be oriented around the mimetic object.[2] The distinction that developed during the Renaissance between mimesis, or the copying of nature, and *imitatio*, or the copying of classical authors, is exemplary in this respect. *Imitatio* rather than mimesis predominated until the eighteenth century, when the notion of the artistic genius as the creator of original imitations of nature led to a devaluation of the practice of copying the classics.[3] Goethe's statement that the artist must *"an die Natur halten, sie studieren, sie nachbilden"* [stay close to nature, study it, copy it] both reflects this new focus and indicates how theories of mimesis continued to be founded upon the assumption that the work of art was the representation of a discernible object whose existence was independent of that representation. The verb Goethe uses contains the preposition *nach,* which means after and indicates how the work of art follows its model in time and space.[4]

Theories of the novel, particularly the realist novel, have customarily installed that genre within the tradition of mimesis that I have briefly outlined above. While the amount of literature that has accumulated on the subject of mimesis and the novel makes it impossible to survey the field in any comprehensive way, I would like to enter the discussion by focusing on a particular point that I believe Georg Lukács's *Die Theorie des Romans: Ein geschichtsphilosophischer Versuch über die Formen der grossen Epik* (1916) persuasively develops. Lukács challenges the literary historical practice of defining mimesis in terms of its object. He does this by arguing that mimetic literature was the product of a historically specific social organization. Following Hegel, Lukács identifies Homeric Greece as the era that embodied such an organization and enabled the individual to be part of a unified social totality.[5] Within this totality, "ideology and production were in harmony; the products of culture could organically develop out of the soil of social being."[6] Lukács is claiming that mimetic literature is possible only when the individual entertains an integrated, nonalienated relationship with society.

The assumption that Homeric Greece afforded the social and historical conditions under which mimetic literature could flourish has numerous implications for the status of post-Hellenic literature and for the way we read such literature. For, while the conditions necessary for mimetic art may have passed, it is still the case that there are literary works that seem to represent a recognizable extraliterary space, in other words, that seem to be mimetic; those critical analyses that focus on the referents of representation lend support to this supposition. If we are to accept Lukács's claim about the historical impossibility of mimetic art in the post-Hellenic world, then such "realist" works, and their interpretations, pose a special challenge to Lukácsian literary analysis. They raise the question of how we are to read post-Hellenic texts without anachronistically assuming that they persist in mimetically reflecting an objective social totality. In addressing this issue, I focus specifically on the genre that Lukács identifies as the successor to the Homerian epic—the novel, which, according to Lukács, exhibits both continuities and discontinuities with its predecessor.

Lukács argues that since the decline of Greece, the individual and society no longer comprise a homogeneous totality. However, the concept of totality survives in Lukács's analysis of the historical shift from epic to novel. It undergoes a displacement, no longer referring to the relationship between the individual and society but to aesthetic form. Lukács sees the novel as a formal totality that structurally resembles the social totality of Homeric Greece. But, whereas he identifies the latter totality with objective reality, he views the formal totality of the novel as an effect of the subject who creates it. As the locus of subjectivity, the form of the novel manifests a complex interplay of totalizing and detotalizing impulses. For Lukács, then, the novel as a genre is a testimony both to the lost epic totality of the Greek world and to the productive creativity of the modern subject.

Lukács's understanding of novelistic subjectivity is noteworthy because it opposes an essentializing concept of the subject as self-identical and defined by reason.[7] Lukács develops such a concept by identifying a particular mode of irony, one associated with the writings of the German Romantics and Kierkegaard, as the structural principle of the novel. While he introduces these theories of irony exclusively in conjunction with his discussion of the novel, their implications are more far-reaching. Specifically, they suggest that all theoretical discourse, including discourse on the novel, is implicated in the process it claims to describe. The difficulty and elusiveness of Lukács's essay derive from the fact that its own structure bears witness to the self-implicating, self-subverting structure of Romantic irony. On the one hand, Lukács authoritatively claims to be purveying an objective history of literary forms. On the other hand, the history he narrates suggests that the vantage point requisite for the recording of such a totalizing history is precisely what is off limits to modern consciousness. I will argue that the apparent tension between the referential and rhetorical dimensions of Lukács's argument is indicative of the ironic structure of his text. Such a structure circumscribes the tenability of the historical statements Lukács makes about the genealogy of narrative structure. This does not mean that Lukács's essay invalidates its own assertions. Rather, its ironic structure bears them out, by staging the self-canceling nature of theoretical assertions. Put in terms of genre, Lukács's theory of the novel exemplarily gives way to its novelistic enactment.

While numerous studies of the novel have insisted upon the inextricability of the literary subject and the object it creates, my reading of *Die Theorie des Romans* is distinct in its identification of literary form as the locus of *ambivalent* subjectivity. One could see Erich Auerbach's *Mimesis* (1942) as a predecessor to my interpretation of *Die Theorie des Romans,* as it, too, addresses the issue of subjectivity in the novel.[8] I argue that Lukács views the loss of an objective social totality as coextensive with the birth of the modern subject and hence as a positive development. For Auerbach, by contrast, the loss of an objective social totality engenders the birth of modernism with its "ruthlessly subjectivistic perspectives." He regards the presence of the aesthetic subject in the form of the novel not only as disruptive but also as "a symptom of the confusion and helplessness . . . and decline" of the world.⁹ We could say that Auerbach's literary-historical schema isolates and sequences the totalizing and detotalizing tendencies of mimesis, tendencies that, according to Lukács, are by definition simultaneously present in the novel, if in differing degrees.

My reading of *Die Theorie des Romans* is speculative insofar as it attempts to bring to the fore issues that to some extent remain implicit in this work. Neither Lukács nor his critics have formulated these issues systematically. Since Lukács is primarily interested in the aesthetics of the novel, his analysis of subjectivity is subordinated to issues of literary form and referentiality. Nevertheless, the distinction he draws between the epic and the novel rests upon the changing role of the subject. I will attempt to articulate explicitly the concept of subjectivity with which he operates. In order to do this, I devote the second chapter of my study to an analysis of Freud's *Totem und Tabu* (1913), in which Freud examines the function of mimesis and of formal totality in the process of identity-constitution. My analysis juxtaposes the role of totality in the respective theories of Lukács and Freud, both of whom are interested in the consequences of the loss of a putative totality for the subject. Given the orientation of psychoanalysis, its vocabulary and concepts lend themselves to the articulation of questions of intra- and intersubjectivity. In this respect, Freud's study reads as an efficacious translation of Lukács's *geschistsphilosophische* discourse, one that clarifies and elaborates the questions concerning subjectivity raised in *Die Theorie des Romans*.

With the aid of Freud's mapping of the relationship between mimesis and identity-constitution, I derive from Lukács's study a working definition of the role of mimesis in the novel. The braiding together of the writings of these two theorists will, I believe, enhance understanding of the influence of Lukács's early writings on the Frankfurt School. Lukács, Adorno, and Benjamin commonly revive one sense of the Aristotelian concept of mimesis that was repressed in the dominant discourse on the novel, namely, the understanding of mimesis as what has been called an "enactive" mode.¹⁰ According to John D. Lyons and Stephen G. Nichols, Jr.,

> the other view of mimesis does not emphasize the independent existence of the object represented, but rather focuses on the gesture of the person or subject who undertakes to displace our attention from the world of pre-existent objects to the work itself. This kind of mimesis [is] more akin to performance than to representation as traditionally understood.¹¹

Benjamin and Adorno share with Lukács an understanding of mimesis that does not assume the presence of a representable object.[12] Mihai Spariosu characterizes Adorno's view thus:

> Mimesis as an adapting and correlating behavior does not presuppose a clear line of demarcation between subject and object or inner and outer, the two poles between which mimesis mediates, because it is understood as "an attitude *(Stellung)*" towards reality prior to the fixed opposition of subject and object.[13]

My readings of *Die Theorie des Romans* and *Totem und Tabu* explore how the "adapting and correlating behavior" of the mimetically oriented subject actively engages issues of intra- and intersubjective demarcation. Specifically, I develop from these texts a notion of projection as a process of demarcation that is at work in the mimetic "attitude."

In the chapters that follow my initial theoretical presentations, I give readings of four novels, in order to demonstrate the efficacy of Lukács's theory of novel form. A simple consideration guided my selection of novels: with the exception of *Jane Eyre,* each of them has been regarded canonically as realist and thus as an unmediated mimetic reflection of its extraliterary context. Ironically, it was Lukács who helped to promote this view of Balzac and Fontane through his late essays on those authors. Even though Brontë's work is customarily seen in its relation to the Gothic tradition, I argue that it reveals how the conventions of Gothic literature are extreme examples of tendencies germane to the genre of the novel as a whole.

Percy's *The Second Coming* postdates the classic age of American realism, but critics have nevertheless stressed its conformity to traditional realist precepts. Consequently, they have regarded it not only as a mimetic representation of modern social and existential issues but even as an attempt to provide solutions for real, extratextual problems. I argue that in this contemporary work, as in the other novels I analyze, an ostensible commitment to a strongly mimetic form of representation based on the priority of the object coexists with, indeed throws into relief, a coextensive circumscription of the mimetic impulse. In Percy's novel this circumscription takes the form of a self-reflexive, if elliptical and by no means linear, supplementary narrative about the role of representation in the constitution of subjectivity.

This supplementary narrative challenges the putative split between subject and object that underwrites the notion of mimesis as the representation of a discrete and perceptible object. It also criticizes the monolithic concept of subjectivity operative in the traditional realist aesthetic. I consider the implications of such a metanarrative in the context of issues that are either raised by the novelists in their theoretical writings or alluded to in the novels themselves. These include Balzac's intention to create a literary cosmos or *totalité,* Brontë's exploration of the relationship between death and authorship, Fontane's commitment to a poetics of *Verklärung,* and Percy's analysis of the role of metaphor in the process of identity-constitution.

By way of Freud, I have attempted to develop Lukács's structural analysis of novel form and also to demonstrate its continuing relevance both to textual interpretation and to theories of realism. By analyzing works from different cultures and periods, I suggest that historical divisions of linear periodization often fail to account for structural patterns common to texts of one genre. I do not mean to imply that the novels relate to their various contexts in a uniform or programmatic manner. On the contrary, it could no doubt be shown how each of the novels responds to its contextual determinants in historically specific ways and how the modes of mimesis deployed in each manifest degrees of historical variation that also reflect contextual constraints. These are important considerations that I believe should be pursued but that lie beyond the scope of my present analysis. It is my hope, however, that this study will provide the theoretical framework essential to the further elaboration of these problems.

One

Mimesis and Subjectivity in Lukács's *Die Theorie des Romans*

The Concept of Totality

Die Theorie des Romans opens with the rhetorically extravagant image, often cited by critics, of what Lukács calls integrated civilizations, in which soul and world are commensurate with each other:

> Selig sind die Zeiten, für die der Sternenhimmel die Landkarte der gangbaren und zu gehenden Wege ist und deren Wege das Licht der Sterne erhellt. Alles ist neu für sie und dennoch vertraut, abenteuerlich und dennoch Besitz. Die Welt ist weit und doch wie das eigene Haus, denn das Feuer, das in der Seele brennt, ist von derselben Wesensart wie die Sterne; sie scheiden sich scharf, die Welt und das Ich, das Licht und das Feuer, und werden doch niemals einander für immer fremd; denn Feuer ist die Seele eines jeden Lichts und in Licht kleidet sich ein jedes Feuer.

> Happy are those ages when the starry sky is the map of all possible paths—ages whose paths are illuminated by the light of the stars. Everything in such ages is new and yet familiar, full of adventure and yet their own. The world is wide and yet it is like a home, for the fire that burns in the soul is of the same essential nature as the stars; the world and the self, the light and the fire, are sharply distinct, yet they never become permanent strangers to one another, for fire is the soul of all light and all fire clothes itself in light.[1]

According to Lukács, one historically specific form of literary representation suits this harmonious, integrated world, namely, mimesis. The possibility of pure imitation, or mimesis, depends upon what Lukács terms a particular transcendental topography of the mind that is associated with Greek epic literature and characterized by a receptive relation of subject to object and of writer to world. The object presents itself to the subject as immanently meaningful. In the economy of this mental topography, *"Wissen ist nur ein Aufheben trübender Schleier, Schaffen ein Abzeichnen sichtbar-ewiger Wesenheiten"* (*TR* 24) ["knowledge is only the raising of a veil, creation only the copying of visible and eternal essences," 32]. The relationship between knowing and being is captured here in the image of an unveiling whose rhetorical efficacy is two-fold. First, the role of the seeker of meaning is spectatorial. Lukács describes the mental attitude of the seeker as passively visionary. His search entails no action or production beyond the gentle motion of the lifting of a veil. Second, the image of the veil invokes a rhetorical tradition that privileges the veil or cloak as the metaphor of figural language. This rhetorical tradition conceives of figural language as the mimetic representation of a pre-existent object. Augustine, for example, writes of metaphorical language, "In order that manifest truths should not become tiring, they have been covered with a veil, while remaining unchanged."[2] According to Augustine's description of the veil, the sign mediates, but does not alter, its referent.

It is precisely this mimetic relation of sign to referent that disappears, according to Lukács, in the literature reflecting the modern mentality or transcendental topography. Mimesis, which requires the immanence of meaning in life—the identity of image and significance—assumes the pre-existence of a representable totality. The novel narrates the loss of this antecedent totality. Lukács writes, *"Wir haben die Produktivität des Geistes erfunden: darum haben die Urbilder für uns ihre gegenständliche Selbstverständlichkeit unwiederbringlich verloren und unser Denken geht einen unendlichen Weg der niemals voll geleisteten Annäherung"* (*TR* 25) ["We have invented the productivity of the spirit: that is why the primaeval images have irrevocably lost their objective self-evidence for us, and our thinking follows the endless path of an approximation that is never fully accomplished," 33–34]. Just as thought follows the endless path of approximation, so, too, does art relinquish its mimetic claim. Art is no longer a copy of the world, but instead, an *"erschaffene Totalität"* (*TR* 29) ["created totality," 37].

Critics agree that the concept of totality operates as the central point of reference in Lukács's analysis of the novel, but they dispute its precise meaning. They usually assume that the reflection of the Greek world in the Homeric epic is for Lukács the embodiment of the concept of totality, one that contrasts with the modern world and thereby comments on it as well. Depending on whether they take that commentary as a positive or a negative reflection on the present, critics view the modern equivalent of the epic—the novel, and more specifically Lukács's conception of that genre—as either the unfortunate reflection of the postlapsarian present or the messianic harbinger of an impending utopia.[3]

J. M. Bernstein has emphasized the strategic role of totality in Lukács's analysis. Totality, according to Bernstein, figures "whatever it is which is lost" or lacking in modern (Kantian or Cartesian) notions of subjectivity.[4] While Bernstein recognizes that the image of the Greeks must be understood within the framework of Lukács's hermeneutic inquiry into the status of the modern novelistic subject, instead of following this line of thought to an effective conclusion, he soon lapses into an empirical opposition between past and present. He does this when he suggests that Lukács's use of such a dichotomy enables him to think about our own fragmented period. Bernstein thereby tacitly replaces the question of the problematically constituted modern subject with that of the objectively knowable modern period. He writes, "Lukács's point is not about a past unity which is forever lost to us, but about a present of separation which needs to be seen *as* fragmented in order to be understood correctly."[5]

While Bernstein is right in analyzing the image of the past in terms of what it reveals about some aspect of the present, he does not consider the grounds upon which Lukács constructs the opposition between past and present. By inquiring into what it is that totality figures in the novel, that is, by concentrating on the "real source" of the figure of totality, Bernstein avoids addressing the problem of the novel's form: "It is, then, because there are *no models* produced and validated outside of literature that literary forms are (become) 'visionary.' . . . It is the autonomy and not the created character of literary forms which makes them problematic."[6]

Bernstein attributes the disappearance of nonliterary models for the novel to the loss of community. Thus, according to him, the problem lies in the world "outside" of form. In pointing to an extraliterary cause, Bernstein implicitly assumes that the world upon which literature is modeled is accessible through direct experience, that is, without the mediation of form. His diagnosis of the problem of autonomy is striking because it glosses over the fact that, as he himself acknowledges, "Lukács is not altogether clear about the causes and therefore the nature of this autonomy."[7] Rather than investigating the ambiguity in Lukács's concept of autonomy, Bernstein replicates an interpretative practice that in another context he criticizes. He "hypostatis[es] ... the incomprehensible into an origin [and] thus subtly inverts the problem," thereby demonstrating what he calls a "reified understanding of understanding."[8]

Bernstein's assertion that the "causes" and "nature" of the novel's autonomy remain unclear in Lukács's argument is based upon the tacit assumption that Lukács is narrating a straightforward, empirical history of literary forms. Such an assumption prevents Bernstein from pursuing the implications of an earlier claim of his, namely, that "what controlled Lukács's use of the past is not a utopian philosophy of history, but a methodology."[9] I agree with Bernstein that the image of Greece is methodologically significant. Unlike him, however, I develop this idea by analyzing the issue of autonomy within the context of Lukács's comparative methodology. I begin by posing the following question: What rhetorical and strategic function does Greece have in Lukács's comparison of the epic with the novel? Since Lukács invokes the notion of autonomy as a contrast to the nonautonomous nature of the novel's predecessor, the epic, we can assess the ambiguity surrounding the notion of autonomy only by looking more carefully at the terms in which Lukács establishes what the novel has "lost" (to use Bernstein's term) with respect to the epic. To do this, we first have to appreciate the significance of the Greek epic in Lukács's essay.

A Question of Genre

What is the status of Greece in Lukács's argument? Insofar as Greece is synonymous with the concept of totality in Lukács's genealogy of narrative forms, its historical significance—specifically, the relation of the Hellenic epic to Hellenic society—cannot be separated from its significance as an ideal origin and point of departure for Lukács's analysis of the novel. To inquire into the status of Greece, then, is already to question the assumption that Greece is simply an empirical referent or the objective ground upon which Lukács constructs his analysis of literary form.

The peculiar tone of *Die Theorie des Romans* contributes to the reader's sense that the text is not simply a documentary history of literary forms grounded in empirical fact. For, in spite of its attempt to provide a classification of literary genres, the essay itself resists simple genre classification: although it calls itself a theory, it is organized as a historical chronicle and presented in the universalizing tone of myth. As Paul de Man observes,

One is particularly put off by the strange point of view that prevails throughout the essay: the book is written from the point of view of a mind that claims to have reached such an advanced degree of generality that it can speak, as it were, for the novelistic consciousness; it is the Novel itself that tells us the history of its own development, very much as, in Hegel's *Phenomenology,* it is the Spirit who narrates its own voyage. With this crucial difference, however, that since Hegel's Spirit has reached a full understanding of its own being, it can claim unchallengeable authority, a point which Lukács's novelistic consciousness, by its own avowal, is never allowed to reach. Being caught in its own contingency, and being indeed an expression of this contingency, it remains a mere phenomenon without regulative power.[10]

De Man's statement expresses the tension between the universality of Lukács's theoretical claims and the exposition of his theory, in which he argues that modernity does not have access to a universal epistemological overview. More specifically, inasmuch as Lukács narrates the historical evolution of the genre of the novel, he relies upon a linear temporality that, as the allusion to the *Phenomenology* indicates, implicitly attests to his having reached an absolute overview that would be immune to the "corrupting principle" of time (*TR* 122–23) [109]. But by the same token, Lukács speaks "novelistically" about the novel form and thereby destabilizes his referential claims. His own attempt to explain the novel's origins in terms of a real history of events is thus rendered problematic, as historical contextuality itself becomes inscribed into the realm of the novelesque.

It could plausibly be argued that the tensions in Lukács's work cancel out the objectivity of its claims. Rather than deepening our understanding of the genre of the novel, or even of specific novels, Lukács bombards us, and the works to which he refers, with an elaborate metaphysical vocabulary. Such a practice points primarily to Lukács's imposing will to power and to his desire to homogenize the diversity of writers of the novel—from Balzac to Tolstoy and from Goethe to Flaubert. Indeed, in his preface Lukács himself points to the limits of many of his readings; and if he thinks that certain of his analyses still merit consideration, the later, arguably superior work of other critics would seem to call even this claim into question. For example, while Lukács believes his interpretation of Flaubert's *L'Education sentimentale* could be "objectively justified" as a clairvoyant anticipation of a *"neue Funktion der Zeit im Roman—auf Grundlage der Bergsonschen 'durée'"* (*TR* 8) ["new function of time in the novel, based on the Bergsonian concept of *'durée,'"* 14], it could be argued that Proust's reading of the Flaubertian text (not to mention the work of succeeding readers of Flaubert) far exceeds Lukács's.

As valid as the foregoing criticism of *Die Theorie des Romans* may be, certain other considerations suggest that Lukács's study should perhaps be evaluated on other terms. Unlike Hegel, Lukács never states explicitly that he is narrating the objective history of a concept. His tone may suggest as much, but in fact, he expressly contests such a possibility when he writes, *"Es soll und kann hier keine Geschichtsphilosophie über die Verwandlung im Aufbau der transzendentalen Orte gegeben werden"* (*TR* 29) ["To propose a philosophy of history relating to the transformation of the structure of the transcendental *loci* is not our intention here, nor would it be possible," 37]. In another work Lukács indicates that references to Greece do not necessarily designate an empirical, historical reality but rather testify to a particular *exigency:*

> Tatsachen sind immer da und immer ist alles in ihnen enthalten, doch jedes Zeitalter bedarf anderer Griechen, eines anderen Mittelalters und einer anderen Renaissance. Jede Zeit wird sich die ihr notwendige schaffen und nur die unmittelbar aufeinander Folgenden glauben, die Träume der Väter seien Lügen gewesen, die man mit den eigenen neuen "Wahrheiten" bekämpfen müsse.

> Facts are always there and everything is always contained in facts, but every epoch needs its own Greece, its own Middle Ages and its own Renaissance. Every age creates the age it needs, and only the next generation believes that its fathers' dreams were lies which must be fought with its own new "truths."[11]

By relating historiography to the fulfillment of certain needs, Lukács implicitly suggests that historical reflection is never objective. History is not simply the reconstructed narrative of a collective (and collected) subject but rather a constructed narrative that arises for a certain purpose. These issues become important when we consider that the autonomy of the novel depends upon the contrast Lukács claims exists between it and its epic predecessor. Like every history, the one Lukács constructs is in response to a certain exigency. The objectivity of his historical narrative is thus called into question by the fact that it may be fulfilling certain unspoken needs.

In order to discover the exigency behind Lukács's narrative and the manner in which it informs the image of Greece, we will now consider Lukács's metatextual discussions of the genre of his own work, the essay; for in these discussions, Lukács explicitly elaborates the relationship between the rhetorical structure of the essay and the constitutive exigency standing behind it.

In his early collection of essays, *Die Seele und die Formen,* as well as in his preface to *Die Theorie des Romans,* Lukács makes it apparent that he conceives of the essay as a literary genre (*SF* 24) [13]. In his preface to *Die Theorie des Romans* he states that he took as his model the storytelling format of Boccaccio's *Decameron*. In Lukács's first version, a group of young people retreated from the current *Kriegspsychose* [war psychosis] to converse about questions of self- and mutual understanding (*TR* 5) [12]. These dialogues led into a discussion of the *"Ausblick auf eine Dostojewskijsche Welt"* (*TR* 6) ["outlook on a Dostoevskian world," 12]. He dropped this plan and instead Dostoevsky became the remote horizon delimiting the purview of his essay. Nevertheless, the initial proposal for the book's structure reveals Lukács's intention to present his thought in a literary form. This is not surprising, given his awareness of the question of form not only as topically relevant to his study but also as an issue that all writers, including essayists, must consider when presenting their material.

In a letter written to Paul Ernst while he was composing the first draft of *Die Theorie des Romans,* Lukács expressed the difficulties of finding an *"episch-essayistischen Stil"* ["epic-essayistic style"], which, he says, is necessary *"wenn man bereit sein muss und die (unglückliche) Anlage hat, alles auf die letzten Wurzeln zurückzuführen"* [when one must be prepared and is (unfortunately) predisposed to tracing everything back to its deepest roots].[12] Lukács links his own essayistic style to that of the epic writer's (he considers the novelist an epic writer) and aligns himself with the protagonists of the novel, whom he calls *die Suchende[n]* [searchers] (*TR* 51) [60, trans. modified]. The terms in which he describes his work emphasize that the essay writer, like the novel protagonist, engages in a search. He states that the value of his work *"besteht in meiner Selbsterkenntnis, dem zu-mir-Gelangen; was mir zu leisten gestaltet ist, das* bin *ich; wissen kann ich das nicht, nur es suchen, doch ich: ich bin eben das Suchen"* [consists in my self-recognition, in my coming to myself; what I am able to accomplish is what I *am;* I cannot know what I am, I can only search for it; but I: I am the search][13]

Not only the value of the essay, but also its form, bears a strong resemblance to that of the novel, which is structured as a journey towards self-knowledge.

> Der Prozess, als welcher die innere Form des Romans begriffen wurde, ist die Wanderung des problematischen Individuums zu sich selbst, der Weg von der trüben Befangenheit in der einfach daseienden, in sich heterogenen, für das Individuum sinnlosen Wirklichkeit zur klaren Selbsterkenntnis. (*TR* 70)
>
> The inner form of the novel has been understood as the process of the problematic individual's journeying towards himself, the road from dull captivity within a merely present reality—a reality that is heterogeneous in itself and meaningless to the individual—towards clear self-recognition. [80]

In both the essay and the novel, then, the modern subject attempts to arrive at self-consciousness. According to Lukács, this attempt at clear self-recognition is never completely successful and yet it can never be given up. In fact, Lukács identifies the endless striving for self-consciousness with the structural principle of both the essay and the novel.

Totality and Identity

The concept of totality plays a crucial role in Lukács's conception of the genres of the essay and novel; it is a means for constructing self-consciousness. Insofar as ancient Greece and the epic embody totality, we can begin to get a sense of their performative and strategic functions in Lukács's theory: they participate in the process of identity-constitution, which Lukács presents in theoretical terms. After inquiring into the precise role of totality in the construction of self-consciousness, we will be in a position to consider the contrast between the Greek epic and its autonomous counterpart, the novel, within the logic of the essay as it rhetorically enacts its theory of novelistic identity-constitution.

Lukács's discussion of the method through which the essayist constitutes his identity underscores the role of formal totality. This method

> erschafft sowohl das Urteilende wie das Geurteilte, sie umkreist eine ganze Welt, um ein einmal Daseiendes in eben seiner Einmaligkeit ins Ewige hinaufzuheben. Der Essay ist ein Gericht, doch nicht das Urteil ist das Wesentliche und Wertentscheidende an ihm (wie im System) sondern der Prozess des Richtens. (*SF* 31)
>
> creates both that which judges and that which is judged, it encircles a whole world, in order to raise to eternity, in all its uniqueness, something that was once there. The essay is a judgement, but the essential, the value-determining thing about it is not the

verdict (as is the case with the system) but the process of judging. [18, trans. modified]

The above statement suggests that the essay engages in a process of differentiation. It creates both the subject and the object of judgment by forming the object into a whole, into *"eine ganze Welt."* Given its form as a totality, the object can never specularly reflect the objectifying subject: the static, closed nature of the encircled form arrests the dynamic process associated with subjectivity. The paradox inherent in the notion of creating "something that was once there" captures this predicament of form in temporal terms. In making permanent the unique moment of that which was, *"ein einmal Daseiendes,"* the uniqueness and unrepeatability of the momentary being are lost. That is why Lukács places greater value on the process of judging than on the product or verdict of judgment.

According to Lukács, the judgment of the essayist signifies a longing that is intrinsically valuable. This longing *"nach Wert und Form, nach Mass und Ordnung und Ziel hat nicht bloss ein Ende, das zu erreichen ist, wodurch sie selbst dann aufgehoben und eine anmassende Tautologie wird"* (SF 30) ["for value and form, for measure and order . . . does not simply lead to an end that must be reached so that it may be cancelled out and become a presumptuous tautology," 17]. Though the essayist heralds the eternally impending approach of a normative basis for value, whose arrival would create a specular identity between subject and object, he is ambivalent about the realization of such a basis. Its establishment would cancel out the vital formation process that is so closely associated with subjectivity and so evident in the subject's ability to exceed the closed circle of definition. Hence Lukács's insistence upon the essayist's independent value in relation to this *"Wertbestimmer"* ["value definer"] (SF 29) [16]. The essayist both derives his legitimacy from the impending arrival of the other, that is, from the potential for identity between subject and object, and yet exists in his own right.

> Es scheint sehr fraglich, ob ein solcher, nur auf sich gestellt, unabhängig also von dem Schicksal seiner Verkündigung, einen Wert und ein Gelten beanspruchen darf. . . . So scheint der Essay als ein notwendiges Mittel zum letzten Ziel gerechtfertigt zu sein, als die vorletzte Stufe in dieser Hierarchie. Dies aber ist nur der Wert seiner Leistung, die Tatsache seiner Existenz hat noch einen anderen, selbständigeren Wert. Denn jene Sehnsucht wäre im gefundenen System der Werte erfüllt und also aufge-

> hoben, sie aber ist nicht bloss etwas, das einer Erfüllung harrt, sondern eine seelische Tatsache von eigenem Wert und Dasein: eine ursprüngliche und tiefe Stellungnahme zum Ganzen des Lebens, eine letzte, nicht mehr aufzuhebende Kategorie der Erlebnismöglichkeiten. Sie bedarf also nicht bloss einer Erfüllung, die sie ja aufheben würde, sondern auch einer Gestaltung, die sie — ihre eigenste und nunmehr unteilbare Wesenheit — zum ewigen Werte erlöst und errettet. Diese Gestaltung bringt der Essay. (*SF* 29–30)

> It seems highly questionable whether, left entirely to himself — i.e., independent from the fate of that other of whom he is the herald — he could lay claim to any value or validity. . . . Thus the essay seems justified as a necessary means to the ultimate end, the penultimate step in this hierarchy. This, however, is only the value of what it *does;* the fact of what it *is* has yet another, more independent value. For in the system of values yet to be found, the longing we spoke of would be satisfied and therefore abolished; but this longing is more than something just waiting for fulfillment, it is a fact of the soul with a value and existence of its own: an original and deep-rooted attitude towards the whole of life, a final irreducible category of possibilities of experience. Therefore it needs not only to be satisfied (and thus abolished) but also to be given form, which will redeem and release its most essential and now indivisible substance into eternal value. This giving of form is what the essay achieves. [16–17, trans. modified]

This passage presents a kind of précis of Lukács's understanding of the *modus operandi* of the essayist: through his assumption of a position (his *Stellungnahme*), the essayist attempts to come to himself, create himself, and realize his relation to the other. And, as the essayist creates that which is judged in the act of becoming judge, the positioning of the self is a simultaneous creation of the other — or, better, the creation of the possibility of recognizing the other. The assumption or seizing of a position, moreover, is responsible for the perception of the other as a totality, as *"[das] Ganz[e] des Lebens"* ["the whole of life"]. This created totality, which remains off limits to the creating self, bespeaks an alterity engendered through an act of delimitation that is both divisive and liberating in its effects. Divisive in the sense that it gives rise to a longing or desire, *Sehnsucht,* and hence suggests the inadequacy or incompleteness of the positioned self; and liberating in that the longing testifies to a certain vitality and dynamism, what Lukács calls *Erlebnismöglichkeiten* [possibilities of experience].

The original attitude towards the "whole of life" is a positioning towards a form whose alterity is a miscognition, a *méconnaissance,* in the sense in which Jacques Lacan uses the term: the other functions as the ideal unity that is alienating "by virtue of its capacity to render extraneous."[14] The giving of form alienates the self, which is more properly a positioning *[Stellungnahme]* than a discrete entity, in the very act of its creation. The self achieves this positioning through an act of *méconnaissance:* while the totalized form of the other becomes the basis for self-recognition (for *me-connaissance*), the self always remains non-identical to the external form it perceives as a totality and with which it attempts to identify.

According to Lukács, the essayist exists as the precursor of an objective source of meaning whose truth cannot be proven but only asserted.

> Nur durch die richtende Kraft der geschauten Idee rettet er sich aus dem Relativen und Wesenlosen—wer gibt ihm aber dieses Recht zum Gericht? Es wäre beinahe richtig zu sagen: er nimmt es sich; aus sich heraus erschafft er seine richtenden Werte. Aber nichts ist vom Richtigen durch tiefere Abgründe getrennt als sein Beinahe, diese schielende Kategorie eines genügsamen und selbstgefälligen Erkennens. Denn tatsächlich werden im Essayisten seine Maße des Richtens erschaffen, doch er ist es nicht, der sie zum Leben und zur Tat erweckt: es ist der grosse Wertbestimmer der Ästhetik, der immer Kommende, der noch nie Angelangte, der einzig zum Richten Berufene, der sie ihm eingibt. (*SF* 28–29)

> [The essayist] is delivered from the relative, the inessential, by the force of the judgement of the idea he has glimpsed; but who gives him the right to judge? It would be almost true to say that he seizes that right, that he creates his judgement-values from within himself. But nothing is separated from true judgement by a deeper abyss than its approximation, the squint-eyed category of complacent and self-satisfied knowledge. The criteria of the essayist's judgements are indeed created within him, but it is not he who awakens them to life and action: the one who whispers them into his ear is the great value-definer of aesthetics, the one who is always coming, the one never having arrived, the only one who has been called to judge. [16, trans. modified.]

In claiming that the criteria for the essayist's judgments are "almost" created within himself, Lukács avoids placing the subject in a position of absolute authority. At the same time, he lends authority to the very process in which this subject is inscribed. Indeed, the authority of the "one" is the authority of pure action; the one who never arrives is "always coming" and never in a static condition of "having arrived." To restrict the subject to the role of orchestrator in a process of its own design would be to confuse it with its "squint-eyed" approximation, the myopic overtones of whose image suggest the limits of knowledge based upon cognitive identification. Such putative knowledge would derive from a fixation of the ideal unity of the *méconnaissance* and would fail to take into account the process of form-giving [*Gestaltung*] of which that unity is only one stage.

Lukács intimates the intersubjective nature of this process through his invocation of the image of aural transmission: the voice of a potentiality, of one on the brink of appearing, who whispers into the ear of the essayist. The whispering voice is, more precisely, the image of a non-image, of a dynamic process, inasmuch as the penetration of the voice into the "body" of the essayist via the ear con-fuses, both spatially and temporally, the division of cognizing subject and cognized object. Like the subject created through *méconnaissance,* the essayist depends upon a oneness that is never quite identical to itself and never simply localizable either inside or outside.

Lukács's discussion of totality as a construction that facilitates the creation of the self enables us to recognize the performative force behind the image of Greek epic literature. Greece functions as an ideal fiction in Lukács's genealogy of narrative forms whose "truth" value resides in the process of delimitation, of which it is the effect. The fictitious nature of the image of the epic as an organic totality bears witness to the novelistic quality of the essay as a genre. For, according to Lukács, the novel, too, participates in the self's delimitation, through the creation of a totality that it identifies as an objective other. Lukács writes, *"Der Roman sucht gestaltend die verborgene Totalität des Lebens aufzudecken und aufzubauen"* (*TR* 51) ["The novel seeks, by giving form, to uncover and construct a totality of life," 60]. Thus, the novel both identifies something from without, that is, uncovers it, but in so doing constructs that which it finds outside of itself. The sustaining tension between these simultaneous processes of discovery and construction is the founding principle of the novel. It indicates the way in which the subjects of both the essay and the novel endeavor to constitute themselves, engaged, as they are, in a *"formende, Gestalt und Grenze gebietende Tat"* (*TR* 42) ["form-giving, structuring, delimiting act," 51].

Irony

Above I have posed the question of the historical significance of Greece within the framework of Lukács's understanding of identity as the effect of a process of demarcation that creates the other in a holistic form. I have traced the origin of such form to the theory of the subject implicit in Lukács's conceptualization of the essay as a genre. In so doing, however, I have focused on the initial, constructive moment of a process that is in fact two-fold. Lukács suggests that the novelistic subject desires to approximate the totality that remains off limits to it—hence its nostalgia for the lost epic totality of Greece. At the same time, Lukács maintains that the novelistic subject is aware that its nostalgia depends upon its misapprehension of the other as an autonomous, preexisting entity rather than as an effect of the process of intersubjective demarcation. Lukács names the expression of such awareness irony.

It was not until *Die Theorie des Romans* that Lukács presented a complete theory of irony.[15] Indeed, his discussion of irony comprises the most important theoretical contribution of his essay. At the same time, because the discussion combines an abstract metaphysical vocabulary with moments of heightened lyricism, it is also the most elusive part of the text. I attribute this to the fact that the essay actually enacts the theoretical principles it expounds, in compliance with Lukács's understanding of irony as a structural phenomenon characteristic of both the essay and the novel. The following analysis of Lukács's understanding of irony has a double significance for my study: it presents the terms through which we will be able to trace the movement of *Die Theorie des Romans*—an essay that not only presents a theory of irony but also performatively ironizes its own theory—and it constitutes the basis for my subsequent analysis of the ironic structure of four novels.

In *Die Theorie des Romans,* Lukács claims that irony defines the novel's structural principle. By pointing to the subject's status as a construct, irony undoes or detotalizes the holistic form the subject creates. Through structural irony the novel asserts its productive independence from all normative and transcendental determinations. Yet the novelist implicitly refers through irony to the absence of God, for which he substitutes his own creative productivity. In some sense, then, he remains determined by the transcendental structure of an absent origin. Lukács compares this negative determination to that of the mystic who aspires to the experience of a godhead beyond all formal concepts of a God but who still remains tied to that concept insofar as it functions as his point of departure:

> So ist in der vollendet geleisteten Form der Dichter frei Gott gegenüber, denn in ihr und nur in ihr wird Gott selbst zum Gestaltungssubstrat. . . . diese Subsumierung Gottes unter den technischen Begriff der Materialechtheit der einzelnen Formen zeigt das doppelte Antlitz des künstlerischen Schliessens und seine Einordnung in die Reihe der metaphysisch bedeutsamen Werke auf. (*TR* 80–81)

> When the form is perfectly achieved, the writer is free in relation to God because in such a form, and only in it, God himself becomes the substratum of form-giving. . . . such subsuming of God under the technical concept of the "material authenticity" of a form reveals the double face of an artistic creation and shows its true place in the order of metaphysically significant works. [91–92]

Lukács's understanding of irony conforms with the broadest general definition of the concept in its dual structure—the ironic statement says one thing and means another. The crucial twist in Lukács's notion of irony concerns the location of the ironic split, which Lukács contends is inherent in the very process of articulation. The rupture of meaning occurs within the process of signification, where meaning is always other than what is said and is rendered other through the act of saying. Like a tracer dye injected into the body of the text, irony has no distinct identity of its own, no definition. Its purpose is to highlight the process of identifying and defining.

In his revision of romantic irony, Lukács links the deformation, even the death, of the subject to cognitive structures. Knowledge of the self actually kills it: *"Das Sollen tötet das Leben, und jeder Begriff drückt ein Sollen des Gegenstandes aus: darum kann das Denken niemals zu einer wirklichen Definition des Lebens kommen"* (*TR* 39) ["The 'should-be' kills life, and every concept expresses a 'should-be' of its object; that is why thought can never arrive at a real definition of life," 48]. Lukács links the ironic form of the novel to conceptualization as such:

> Ironie bedeutet, als formelles Konstituens der Romanform, eine innere Spaltung des normativ dichterischen Subjekts in eine Subjektivität als Innerlichkeit, die fremden Machtkomplexen gegenübersteht und der fremden Welt die Inhalte ihrer Sehnsucht aufzuprägen bestrebt ist, und in eine Subjektivität, die die Abstraktheit und mithin die Beschränktheit der einander fremden Subjekts- und Objektswelten durchschaut, diese in ihren, als

> Notwendigkeiten und Bedingungen ihrer Existenz begriffenen, Grenzen versteht und durch dieses Durchschauen die Zweiheit der Welt zwar bestehen lässt, aber zugleich in der wechselseitigen Bedingtheit der einander wesensfremden Elemente eine einheitliche Welt erblickt und gestaltet. Diese Einheit ist jedoch eine rein formale; die Fremdheit und die Feindlichkeit der innerlichen und der äusserlichen Welten ist nicht aufgehoben, sondern nur als notwendig erkannt. (*TR* 64)

> As a formal constituent of the novel form this [irony] signifies an interior division of the normatively creative subject into a subjectivity as interiority, which opposes power complexes that are alien to it and which strives to imprint the contents of its longing upon the alien world, and a subjectivity which sees through the abstract and, therefore, limited nature of the mutually alien worlds of subject and object, understands these worlds by seeing their limitations as necessary conditions of their existence and, by thus seeing through them, allows the duality of the world to subsist. At the same time the creative subjectivity glimpses a unified world in the mutual relativity of elements essentially alien to one another, and gives form to this world. Yet this glimpsed unified world is nevertheless purely formal; the antagonistic nature of the inner and outer worlds is not abolished but only recognized as necessary. [74–75, trans. modified]

The splitting of the subject creates, on the one hand, a defensive interiority that attempts to oppose power complexes by impressing its desire upon the world and, on the other hand, a transcendental subject that sees beyond the split between subject and world. Recognizing the necessary antagonism between the interior and exterior worlds does not reify a historically specific relation between subject and object; rather it expresses, in the sense of outwardly projecting, the relation of the subject to itself. The split between interiority and exteriority is *"als notwendig erkannt"* [recognized as necessary], because it is inherent in cognition that the subject appears as other than itself. Just as the novel both uncovers and constructs a totality, so, too, does cognition both reveal and produce: the act of cognition creates what it observes. Hence Lukács's description of the subject as *"schauende und schaffende"* ["observing and creating"] (*TR* 65) [75, trans. modified].

According to Lukács, through irony the writing subject breaks through the abstractness of the mutually exclusive worlds of subject and object.

Diese Ironie ist die Selbstkorrektur der Brüchigkeit: die inadäquaten Beziehungen können sich zu einem phantastischen und wohlgeordneten Reigen von Missverständnissen und Vorbeigehen aneinander verwandeln, wo alles von vielen Seiten gesehen wird: als Isoliertes und Verbundenes, als Träger des Wertes und als Nichtigkeit, als abstrakte Absonderung und als konkretestes Eigenleben, als Verkümmern und als Blühen, als Leidenmachen und als Leiden. (*TR* 65)

The irony of the novel is the self-correction of fragility: inadequate relations can transform themselves into a fanciful yet well-ordered round of misunderstandings and cross-purposes, within which everything is seen as many-sided, within which things appear as isolated and yet connected, as full of value and yet totally devoid of it, as abstract fragments and as concrete autonomous life, as flowering and as decaying, as the infliction of suffering and as suffering itself. [75, trans. modified]

The ironic world of the novel embodies the principle of non-identity: things appear both as themselves and as their opposite. Judging from the context in which the passage above occurs, *"Selbstkorrektur der Brüchigkeit"* [self-correction of fragility] would seem to refer to an instability associated with subjectivity. The phrase comprises the third element in the series *Selbsterkenntnis, Selbstaufhebung, Selbstkorrektur* [self-recognition, self-abolition, self-correction] and follows the passage in which irony is associated with the abolition of subjectivity, which I read as the ambivalent process of recognition and annihilation that emphasizes the fragility of identity.[16]

Drawing upon a tradition that achieves one of its richest articulations in the works of Goethe, Lukács characterizes novelistic irony as daemonic:

Die vertriebenen und die noch nicht zur Herrschaft gelangten Götter werden Dämonen: ihre Macht ist wirksam und lebendig, aber sie durchdringt die Welt nicht mehr oder noch nicht: die Welt hat einen Sinneszusammenhang und eine Kausalverknüpftheit erhalten, die der lebendig wirkenden Kraft des zum Dämon gewordenen Gottes unverständlich ist und aus deren Augenpunkt gesehen sein Treiben als reine Sinnlosigkeit erscheint. Die Kraft seiner Wirksamkeit bleibt aber unaufgehoben, weil sie unauffhebbar [*sic*] ist, weil das Sein des neuen Gottes von dem Vergehen des alten getragen ist; und aus diesem Grund besitzt der eine—in der Sphäre des einzig wesentlichen, des metaphysischen Seins—dieselbe Valenz von Wirklichkeit wie der andere. (*TR* 75–76)

Fallen gods, and gods whose kingdom is not yet, become demons; their power is effective and alive, but it no longer penetrates the world, or does not yet do so: the world has a coherence of meaning, a causality, which is incomprehensible to the vital, effective force of a god-become-demon; from the demon's viewpoint, the affairs of such a world appear purely senseless. The demon's power remains effective because it cannot be overthrown; the passing of the old god supports the being of the new; and for this reason the one possesses the same valency of reality (in the sphere of the only essential being, which is metaphysical being) as the other. [86–87]

The demon dwells in the moment between *"nicht mehr"* ["no longer"] and *"noch nicht"* ["not yet"]. It exists only as the exceeding of the past and hence cannot be confined to a present moment that could be overcome. Lukács describes the demon not as a being but as a becoming: *"Götter werden Dämonen"* ["Gods become demons"]. The demon becomes through its *"wirksam[e] und lebendig[e]"* ["effective and alive"] power. Its lack of fixity is the very condition of its effectiveness, while signs of its presence are legible in the breakdown of sense. Cognitive categories such as *"Sinneszusammenhang"* ["coherence of meaning"] and *"Kausalverknüpftheit"* ["causality"] appear, from the viewpoint of the demon, as *"Sinnlosigkeit"* ["senseless(ness)"]. Lukács captures the vitality of the negative powers of the demonic in a quotation from *Dichtung und Wahrheit* in which Goethe defines the daemonic as the negation of definition:

"Es war nicht göttlich," sagte Goethe vom Dämonischen, "denn es schien unvernünftig; nicht menschlich, denn es hatte keinen Verstand; nicht teuflisch, denn es war wohltätig; nicht englisch, denn es liess oft Schadenfreude merken. Es glich dem Zufall, denn es bewies keine Folge; es ähnelte der Vorsehung, denn es deutete auf Zusammenhang. Alles was uns begrenzt, schien für dasselbe durchdringbar; es schien mit den notwendigen Elementen unseres Daseins willkürlich zu schalten; es zog die Zeit zusammen und dehnte den Raum aus. Nur im Unmöglichen schien es sich zu gefallen, und das Mögliche mit Verachtung von sich zu stossen." (*TR* 76)[17]

"It was not divine," Goethe wrote about the daemonic, "for it seemed irrational; it was not human, for it had no reason; not devilish, for it was beneficent; not angelic, for it often allowed room for malice. It resembled the accidental, for it was without consequence; it looked like providence, for it hinted at hidden connections. Everything that restricts us seemed permeable by it; it seemed to arrange at will the necessary elements of our existence; it contracted time, it expanded space. It seemed at ease only in the impossible, and it thrust the possible from itself with contempt." [87]

Goethe defines the daemonic negatively, describing what it is not. The passage quoted above is preceded in *Dichtung und Wahrheit* by a remark that emphasizes the resistance the daemonic poses to conceptualization in general: the daemonic *"unter keinen Begriff, noch viel weniger unter ein Wort gefasst werden könnte"* [could not be grasped through a concept or even less through a word].[18]

Lukács's text both describes the daemonic as a process of defiguration and rhetorically registers its effects. Consider the following passage in which the daemonic is presented as a force that unmasks and negates second nature:[19]

> Dann enthüllt sich plötzlich das Gottverlassene der Welt als Substanzlosigkeit, als irrationale Mischung von Dichtigkeit und Durchdringbarkeit: was früher als das Festeste erschien, zerfällt wie vertrockneter Lehm bei der ersten Berührung des vom Dämon Besessenen und eine leere Durchsichtigkeit, hinter der lockende Landschaften sichtbar waren, wird auf einmal zur Glaswand, an der man sich vergeblich und verständnislos—wie die Biene am Fenster—abquält, ohne durchbrechen zu können, ohne selbst zur Erkenntnis gelangen zu können, dass es hier keinen Weg gibt. (*TR* 79)

> Then, suddenly, the God-forsakenness of the world reveals itself as a lack of substance, as an irrational mixture of density and permeability. What previously seemed to be very solid crumbles like dry clay at the first contact with a man possessed by a demon, and the empty transparence behind which attractive landscapes were previously to be seen is suddenly transformed into a glass wall against which men beat in vain, like bees against a window, incapable of breaking through, incapable of understanding that the way is barred. [90]

The shift from a nonpossessed to a possessed form of intuition presents an allegory of the difference between mimetic and nonmimetic forms of representation. In the first, mimetic topos, the relation between the medium of representation and the object represented is that of proximity bordering on identity, separated by an all but invisible divide, a *"leere Durchsichtigkeit"* ["empty transparence"]. In the second, nonmimetic topos, the empty transparence becomes an impermeable wall barring access to the object. Corresponding to this shift is a switch in the forms of the two paradigms: in the first, the object predominates and is, not surprisingly, an embodiment of first or naive nature: the *"lockende Landschaft"* ["attractive landscape"]. With the erecting of the glass wall, the focus switches to the activity of the subject, which is depicted in the image of the duped bees vainly beating against the closed window. (One might even see the unenlightened bees as figures of unenlightened human subjects engaged in an impossible search for the signified behind the letter.) Moreover, a curious displacement occurs when first nature, the landscape barred by the window, returns, as it were, through the back door in the image of the bees. The bees thus function as a trace, metonymically recalling the naive landscape and thereby placing the contrasting metaphors of landscape and bees under the common sign of nonmimetic representation, which in this case means representation that is sentimental or self-reflexive as opposed to naive.

Lukács comments on the relation between the notion of estrangement and the sentimental when he writes:

> Die Fremdheit der Natur, der ersten Natur gegenüber, das moderne sentimentalische Naturgefühl ist nur die Projektion des Erlebnisses, dass die selbstgeschaffene Umwelt für den Menschen kein Vaterhaus mehr ist, sondern ein Kerker. . . . Die erste Natur . . . ist nichts als die geschichtsphilosophische Objektivation der Entfremdung zwischen dem Menschen und seinen Gebilden. (*TR* 55)

> Estrangement from nature (the first nature), the modern sentimental attitude to nature, is only a projection of man's experience of his self-made environment as a prison instead of as a parental home. . . . The first nature . . . is nothing other than the historico-philosophical objectivation of man's alienation from his own constructs. [64]

The process of projection, itself sentimental, posits certain ideas, such as that of a harmonious, accessible nature (for example, the attractive landscape of the passage discussed earlier), and then represses consciousness of the origins of these ideas in subjective desire. Through such repression ideas become ideals: *"Durch das als Unerreichbar—*

und — im empirischen Sinn — als Unwirklich-Setzen der Ideen, durch ihre Verwandlung in Ideale, ist die unmittelbare, problemlose Organik der Individualität zerrissen" (*TR* 68) ["The positing of ideas as unrealisable and, in the empirical sense, as unreal, i.e. their transformation into ideals, destroys the immediate problem-free organic nature of the individual," 78]. Irony calls to mind the subjective origin of ideas, their *"subjektiv-psychologischen Bedingtheit"* ["subjective-psychological conditionality"] (*TR* 81) [92, trans. modified].

Lukács's formulation of the contribution of the German Romantics to the concept of novelistic irony retains the Goethean notion that irony is a movement that disembodies or undermines identity. Lukács writes, *"Die Selbsterkenntnis und damit die Selbstaufhebung der Subjektivität wurde von den ersten Theoretikern des Romans, den Ästhetikern der Frühromantik, Ironie genannt"* (*TR* 64) ["The self-recognition and, with it, self-abolition of subjectivity was called irony by the first theoreticians of the novel, the aesthetic philosophers of early Romanticism," 74]. According to Friedrich Schlegel, in a self-reflexive text, an apparently mimetic representation is supplemented by a representation of the act of representation, which in turn becomes an object of reflection, in an infinite progression of mirroring. This process of *"schöne Selbstbespiegelung"* [beautiful self-mirroring] combines poetic reflection with a transcendental reflection on the grounds of the possibility of the poetic.[20] According to Schlegel, the endless multiplication of the mirrors of self-reflection perpetually defers the possibility of closure: *"Die romantische Dichtart ist noch im Werden, ja das ist ihr eigentliches Wesen, dass sie ewig nur werden, nie vollendet sein kann"* [Romantic poetry is still in a state of becoming, yes, that is its essential being, that it can always only become, that it can never be completed].[21]

Lukács adopts the Schlegelian notion of the openness of the work of art in his own conception of the novel. The novel strives for totality, but in representing this totality as the object of a search, it abolishes the immanence of the totality, the organic interrelation of its parts.

> Es ist auf einer qualitativ völlig neuen Grundlage wieder ein Standpunkt des Lebens erreicht, der der unauflösbaren Verschlungenheit von der relativen Selbstständigkeit der Teile und ihrer Gebundenheit an das Ganze. Nur, dass die Teile, trotz dieser Bindung, niemals die Härte ihres abstrakten Auf-sich-Gestelltseins verlieren können und ihre Beziehung zur Totalität eine zwar dem Organischen möglichst angenäherte, aber doch immer wieder aufgehobene begriffliche Beziehung ist und keine echtgeborene Organik. (*TR* 65)

Thus a new perspective of life is reached on an entirely new basis—that of the indissoluble connection between the relative independence of the parts and their attachment to the whole. But the parts, despite this attachment, can never lose their inexorable, abstract self-dependence: and their relationship to the totality, although it approximates as closely as possible to an organic one, is nevertheless not a true-born organic relationship but a conceptual one which is abolished again and again. [75–76]

This process of sublation, which is *"immer wieder"* ["again and again"] performed, reflects the nonhierarchical nature of irony. The closure of the novel's form, though analogous to the organic form of the epic, differs from the epic in that it is constantly abolished through irony. Representation is ironized, and the act of ironizing itself becomes the new object of irony. In the process of ironizing its representation, the subject undergoes the same ironization as its initial object. Self-reflection thus objectifies the subject in a process that is anything but stabilizing. Lukács contrasts this notion of the irony of the novel with a form of irony that establishes a *"kalte und abstrakte Überlegenheit, die die objektive Form zur subjektiven, zur Satire und die Totalität zum Aspekt verengen würde"* (*TR* 65) ["cold and abstract superiority which narrows down the objective form to a subjective one and reduces the totality to a mere aspect of itself," 75].

Novelistic irony refrains from incorporating the object as a mere aspect of itself; it thereby preserves intersubjective difference. At the same time, irony reveals that intersubjective difference originates within the subject. Even when projected outward, it remains the expression of an unbreachable self-difference. Lukács describes the split within the subject as an abyss: an *"unermessliche[r] Abgrund [liegt . . .] im Subjekt selbst"* (*TR* 28) ["an unfathomable chasm . . . lies within the subject himself," 37]. Thus, while irony reveals the nonobjectivity of the novelistic representation, it also reveals the non-unity of the ironic, creating subject. That is, both the subject and its creation are ironized: *"Ironie zwingt das schauende und schaffende Subjekt, seine Welterkenntnis auf sich selbst anzuwenden, sich selbst, geradeso wie seine Geschöpfe, als freies Objekt der freien Ironie zu nehmen"* (*TR* 65) ["In the novel the subject, as observer and creator, is compelled by irony to apply its recognition of the world to itself and to treat itself, like its own creatures, as a free object of free irony, 75].

Irony is an *intrasubjective* movement that expresses the relation between the simultaneous processes of self-transcendence and self-annihilation. The following line from Novalis, which Lukács cites, captures the infinite movement of irony: *"begonnen ist der Weg, vollendet die Reise"* (*TR* 63) ["The voyage is completed: the way begins," 73]. The subject is always on the search for itself. In each moment of homecoming it is confronted with yet another path that must be followed, another departure that must be made. The reversibility of the two clauses in the citation collapses the distinction between beginning and end: every beginning is its own completion and every completion, a beginning.[22]

Lukács does not associate the dizzying open dialectic of irony with a historically specific concept of subjectivity. If he had done so, we could diagnose the condition of the modern subject as an aberration in the history of the subject. We could point to a prior epoch of subjective harmony whose disappearance could be regarded as temporary. But Lukács makes it impossible to see the modern subject as anomalous. Although he defines the modern novel against the Greek epic, he also insists that Greek epic literature is a presubjective genre (a consideration that will be significant when we consider the autonomy of the novel). The epic is defined by *"grosse Subjektslosigkeit* [sic] *und Totalität"* ["great subjectlessness and totality"] (*TR* 49) [58, trans. modified]. Moreover, the world of the epic is timeless. Time is *"stillstehend und auf einen Blick zu übersehen"* (*TR* 108) ["static and can be taken in at a single glance," 122]. The subject of the modern epic (that is, of the novel) thus does not represent one form of subjectivity but subjectivity as such. For Lukács, the beginning of time and of subjectivity are identical, and irony reveals the violence inherent in every attempt to arrest time by imposing static form.

Thus, we see that: 1) Irony reveals that the split between subject and object is an effect of the logic of identity informing cognitive structures. 2) Irony is a structural principle of detotalization or daemonic defiguration. 3) Irony circumscribes mimesis. Whereas mimesis presupposes the objectivity of its referent, irony, by contrast, reveals the origins of intersubjective difference in intrasubjective non-identity that is projected outwards. In subverting the novel's claim to mimetic objectivity, irony simultaneously asserts the subjectivity of the novelistic creator. If this dual process of subversion and assertion represents, as Lukács says it does, the objective truth of the novel, it also represents the key to Lukács's essay on the novel, which is itself structured according to such a principle of irony.

The Return to Greece

We have seen how both the essay and the novel participate in a process of identity-constitution through the construction, and deconstruction, of an image of totality. Lukács's analysis of irony as a process of daemonaic detotalization enables us to appreciate the status of Greece in his essay on the novel. Given that the image of the whole helps to create the self, the concept of totality, which in *Die Theorie des Romans* is embodied in the Greek world, must also participate in a process of identity-constitution, one that specifically articulates itself as a mythico-historical narrative.

Lukács understands the function of time in the essayist's search for self-consciousness in a very precise way. In commenting on the temporal relation of Schopenhauer's *Parerga* to *The World as Will and Idea* he writes, *"Es ist kein bloss zeitlicher Unterschied, ob sie vor oder nach dem System stehen: diese zeitlich-historische Differenz ist nur ein Symbol der Trennung ihrer Arten"* (*SF* 30) ["Whether they occurred before or after the system is not simply a matter of a time sequence; the time-historical difference is only a symbol of the difference between their two methods," 17, trans. modified]. The historical distance between essayist and the world created through judgment bespeaks a difference not in time but in approach. It symbolizes two inseparable tendencies that become isolated through their representation. In *Die Theorie des Romans,* the historical distance between the Greek epic and the modern novel registers a similar difference, I would suggest—one not of time but of method or kind *[Art]*. As such, the image of the Greek world has a rhetorical and strategic function in Lukács's narrative of developing self-consciousness. The Greek other is not unrelated to the novelistic self; it is a *nachträglich* or belated effect of the process of positioning *[Stellungnahme]*, an image whose totality can only be approximated.

If the Greek world was a hypostatization of one moment in an ongoing process of identity-constitution, so, too, is the mimetic literature that characterizes it a kind of hypostatization—of one aspect of representation. The historicity of the categories of mimetic/nonmimetic literature, or nonautonomous/autonomous literature, is a temporalization of tendencies that coexist within the novel. Given that the autonomy of the novel is thus a critical fiction, any attempt to assess its relative value by comparing it to the nonautonomy of the epic lapses into a naively empiricist reading of Lukács's essay.

In *Die Theorie des Romans,* Lukács asserts that there was no ancient Greek counterpart of subjectivity as we understand it; he refers to the essential subjectlessness of the Greek epic and describes the novel as the *"Form der gereiften Männlichkeit im Gegensatz zur normativen Kindlichkeit der Epopöe"* (*TR* 61) ["art form of virile maturity, in contrast to the normative childlikeness of the epic," 71]. Given that the mimetic art of Greece is subjectless, the significance of the following statement about epic subjectivity must reside elsewhere than on the literal level of its meaning: Lukács writes that epic subjectivity *"wird lyrisch und nur die bloss hinnehmende, die sich in Demut zum reinen Aufnahmeorgan der Welt verwandelnde vermag der Gnade: der Offenbarung des Ganzen, teilhaftig zu werden"* (*TR* 44–45) ["becomes lyrical, but, exceptionally, the subjectivity which simply accepts, which humbly transforms itself into a purely receptive organ of the world can partake of the grace of having the whole revealed to it," 53]. Since, strictly speaking, there is no epic subjectivity that could submit itself to transformation, the notion of transformation must be understood as a temporalization of the difference in methods. The pure receptivity of the epic subject who imitates the totality of the Greek world is thus as mythical as the narratives it produces; in the economy of Lukács's theory of identity-constitution this epic subject functions as an initial "moment" in a process that encompasses both it and the stage that succeeds it.

The idea of a prior mimetic moment when subject and object were one, that is, when the whole of the world was an adequate structure in which the subject could recognize itself, is a projection of the subject's desire for a nonaliened relationship with its constructs. Lukács's lyrical nostalgia for the past notwithstanding, he identifies the attempt to replicate a condition when there existed positive models that could be copied with an aggressive desire to destroy: *"Jede Auferstehung des Griechentums ist nunmehr eine mehr oder weniger bewusste Hypostasis der Ästhetik zur alleinigen Metaphysik; ein Vergewaltigen und ein Vernichtenwollen der Wesenheit von allem, was ausserhalb des Bereichs der Kunst liegt"* (*TR* 30) ["Henceforth, any resurrection of the Greek world is a more or less conscious hypostasy of aesthetics into metaphysics—a violence done to the essence of everything that lies outside the sphere of art, and a desire to destroy it," 38].

If we consider the historical narrative Lukács constructs, in which the Greek world functions as the irretrievable, negative origin and archetype of the novel, we can detect traces of the process of projection that generates this narrative. He writes, *"Der Roman ist die Epopöe eines Zeitalters, für das die extensive Totalität des Lebens nicht mehr sinnfällig gegeben ist, für das die Lebensimmanenz des Sinnes zum Problem geworden ist, und das dennoch die Gesinnung zur Totalität hat"* (*TR* 47) ["The novel is the epic of an age in which the extensive totality of life is no longer directly given, in which the immanence of meaning in life has become a problem, yet which still thinks in terms of totality," 56]. This definition of the novel proceeds by developing a contrast between a prior version and the present version of one genre, the epic. The given historical reality of the novel emerges as a falling away from an originary fullness and self-presence. The identity of the novel, as the modern successor to the epic, is narrated in terms of a paradoxical legacy of discontinuity: the novel belongs to the epic genre inasmuch as it negatively retains, *in memoriam,* the image of a prior, meaning-filled world, yet itself differs from this image.

In retrospectively charting the consecutive displacement of the transcendental locus or origin of meaning, the narrative in question actually stages the movements of a thought defined by an origin it can only approximate; *"Gesinnung zur Totalität"* ["(thinking) in terms of totality"] *is* that narrative movement of positing and temporal distantiation—from the posited origin as well as from the act of positing—that establishes the uniqueness of the novel. As such, the mark of *Gesinnung* remains legible in the origin from which it has supposedly fallen off—in the *sinnfällig* [direct] givenness of the epic world as well as in the *Lebensimmanenz des Sinnes* [immanence of meaning in life]. *Sinnfällig—Sinnes—Gesinnung* constitutes a single figure of continuity which modern consciousness imposes upon the discontinuity between epic past and novelistic present. Indeed, the movement of *Sinn* [meaning] parallels the three phases or moments that *Die Theorie des Romans* designates as the history of its becoming: 1) the manifest, *sinnfällig* presence of transcendent meaning in life is characteristic of the epic. 2) *Sinn* then retreats into the transcendent realm of essence. This retreat is the subject of Greek tragedy, the genre of an age in which the immanence of meaning has become a problem in life—*Sinn* is now distant, having withdrawn from the empirical world but not yet disappeared completely from view. 3) *Sinn* finally vanishes, as in the world of the novel, and leaves its trace in the structural topography, the *Gesinnung,* of modern consciousness. The original meaning of *Gesinnung,* "desire," suggests that the circle completes itself: it is as if the desire of modernity provides the originary push that makes transcendent sense fall, makes *Sinn fäll—ig* and thus immanent.

If we look closely at the image of Greece, we see, as well, that it bears within itself the traces of its production by a modern subjectivity.

It thereby poses a problem for any interpretation of Lukács's thought that conceives of the relation between the Greek world and its epic representation as specular in nature. Lukács characterizes the Greek age as literally answering the questions posed by successive ages and shaped by their demands:

> Die Frage, als deren gestaltende Antwort das Epos entsteht, ist: Wie kann das Leben wesenhaft werden? Und das Unnahbare und Unerreichbare Homers—und strenggenommen sind nur seine Gedichte Epen—stammt daher, dass er die Antwort gefunden hat, bevor der Gang des Geistes in der Geschichte die Frage laut werden liess. (*TR* 22)
>
> The question which engenders the formal answers of the epic is: how can life become essence? And if no one has ever equalled Homer, nor even approached him—for, strictly speaking, his works alone are epics—it is because he found the answer before the progress of the human mind through history had allowed the question to be asked. [30]

Homer's answers reveal questions that not he, but the ages that follow him, ask. He is significant because he attests to the difference between his world and our own. Lukács continues:

> Wenn man will, so kann man hier dem Geheimnis des Griechentums entgegengehen: seiner vor uns aus undenkbaren Vollendung und seiner unüberbrückbaren Fremdheit zu uns: der Grieche kennt nur Antworten, aber keine Fragen, nur Lösungen (wenn auch rätselvolle), aber keine Rätsel, nur Formen, aber kein Chaos. (*TR* 22–23)
>
> This line of thought can, if we wish, take us some way towards understanding the secret of the Greek world: its perfection, which is unthinkable for us, and the unbridgeable gulf that separates us from it. The Greek knew only answers but no questions, only solutions (even if enigmatic ones) but no riddles, only forms but no chaos. [30–31]

Unlike his critics, Lukács refrains from evaluating this difference between worlds and the corresponding aesthetic changes either positively or negatively. He describes the shift as a paradoxical increase through negation: "*Unsere Welt ist unendlich gross geworden und in jedem Winkel reicher an Geschenken und Gefahren als die griechische, aber dieser Reichtum hebt den tragenden und positiven Sinn ihres Lebens auf: die Totalität"* (*TR* 26) ["Our world has become infinitely large and each of its corners is richer in gifts and dangers than the world of the Greeks, but such wealth cancels out the positive meaning—the totality—upon which their life was based," 34]. The canceling out of the positive meaning signals a shift from a passive to an active position. Whereas epic subjectivity was a purely receptive organ of the world, novelistic subjectivity is an autonomous producer of literature, a *"schaffende[s] Subjekt"* (*TR* 65) [creating subject]. The process of becoming a subject staged in *Die Theorie des Romans* enables us to recognize that the conditions—symbolized by the Greek world—under which mimesis is possible must always be exceeded. The Greek world, in other words, embodies a tendency in the self that alone does not suffice to create the subject. That is why its closed totality is represented as surpassed and why Lukács cautions against its resurrection.

Finally, in *Die Theorie des Romans,* the form and performative force of the image of Greece, which is that of a closed totality, functions precisely as does the fetish in Freud's analysis of that topic. In his well-known short essay on it, Freud states that the fetish acts as a surrogate for a putatively lost (maternal) totality and a phantasmatic object of desire.[23] As such, the fetish testifies both to the passing of the male child's belief that the mother possesses a phallus and to his refusal to accept the fact that the mother does not possess the phallus. While this dialectic of denial and insistence reveals nothing about the body of the mother, it does reveal how the child produces his image of the mother through narcissistic projections. The efficacy of the fetish derives from the force of its denegation. The child does not recognize the originary force of the projection that causes the mother to be perceived as either whole or fragmentary. That is, the fetishistic view of the mother does not take into account the fact that the identities of the self and the other are effects of representation.

In Lukács's essay, the golden age of the Greek epic functions as a kind of fetishistic totalized other. The tone of Lukács's text, which at times verges on the rhapsodic (such as when it sketches the picture of the golden age of narration—"Happy are those ages when the starry sky is the map of all possible ages . . . "), indicates the ambivalent status of the fetishistic fiction of Greece: Lukács speaks with great investment about an age that would seem to have objectively existed and that on an explicit level he treats as an empirical reality. Yet, my analysis of Lukács's own argument about the possibility of nonautonomous mimesis in the post-Hellenic world suggests that the Greek epic must function in Lukács's argument as a critical fiction, one that can only be read as an expression of Lukács's own ambivalent desire.

While the significance of the epic in *Die Theorie des Romans* is similar to that of the fetish, there are also crucial differences between the two. The fetishist cannot recognize the illusory nature of either his totalized identity or the identity of the (fragmented) other. He does not acknowledge that the fetish is a symptomatic effect of a process of (mis)representation that is produced through displacement and projection. Lukács's text, I have argued, operates with a theory of identity-constitution that, while not symmetrically self-reflexive, nevertheless lays bare the process of projection involved in creating an image of the other as a closed totality. Put slightly differently, in underscoring the importance of formal totality in the constitution of subjectivity, *Die Theorie des Romans* not only reveals how the fetish accounts for one moment of deception in the process of identity-constitution but also provides the basis for a theoretical assessment of its own *modus operandi*.

Two

Mimesis in a Two-way Mirror: Freud's *Totem und Tabu*

Freud's *Totem und Tabu* (1913) offers an interesting complement to Lukács's understanding of the role of mimesis in the constitution of subjectivity. While Freud explicitly addresses the relationship between the constitution of subjectivity and the circumscription of mimesis in his comparative study of obsessional neurosis and the taboo, the terms and emphasis of his analysis differ from those of Lukács's essay. Lukács articulates his argument in a literary and historical context while allegorically staging the function of aesthetic form in the creation of the subject. Freud, by contrast, explicitly inquires into the process of identity-constitution and discusses the shift in modes of representation—from mimetic to nonmimetic—within the context of that analysis. In underscoring the function of representation in the development of identity, Freud stresses the importance of the concept of unity, *Einheit,* in a way that parallels the significance Lukács accords the concept of totality. And yet Freud's text does not simply reiterate Lukács's argument. Rather, it reads like a translation of Lukács's literary-philosophical history of genres into a vocabulary more explicitly germane to questions of inter- and intrasubjectivity. Whereas Lukács identifies the world of the Homeric epic and the form of the novel with totality, Freud introduces the concept of *Einheit* in his complex discussion of the ego's identification with a totalizing image or representation.

My reading of *Die Theorie des Romans* emphasizes how its structure actually stages the theoretical precepts of the argument. I dwell upon the novelistic aspects of Lukács's theory in order to underscore a general point, namely, that Lukács's discussion of the dislocating effects of cognitive structures implies that narrative theories of subjectivity by definition participate in the processes they describe. My analysis of *Totem und Tabu* bears out this point and extends the foregoing analysis of *Die Theorie des Romans* in two ways. First, it articulates in psychoanalytic terms the implicit notion of the subject that is operative in Lukács's text. Second, it demonstrates how Freud's work rhetorically stages its own theoretical precepts—specifically the concept of projection—by subverting the oppositional structures that found its argument in the first place and by thus forcefully attesting to the efficacy of those very precepts.

Early in his analysis, Freud presents two modes of subject-object relation, one embodied by the taboo and the other by obsessional neurosis. Whereas the taboo is a *"soziale Bildung"* ["social structure"],[1] neuroses are *"asoziale Bildungen"* ["asocial structures"] (*TT* 91) [73]. According to Freud, in primitive societies it was expected that the violation of a taboo would be followed by punishment of the violator. This punishment would usually take the form of serious illness or death; but in instances when the act failed to be avenged spontaneously by fate, a collective feeling of outrage would arise among the savages, who felt threatened by the unavenged act and themselves administered the necessary punishment. The threat posed by the transgressor was not that he would repeat his violation but that his crime would awaken similar transgressive desires in the other members of the primitive society. Fear of the transgressor's contagion was fear of *Nachahmung* [mimesis]: *"Die Angst vor dem ansteckenden Beispiel, vor der Versuchung zur Nachahmung, also vor der Infektionsfähigkeit des Tabu ist hier im Spiele"* (*TT* 89) ["What is in question is fear of an infectious example, of the temptation to imitate—that is, of the contagious character of taboo," 71–72]. Within the logic of the taboo, the outcome of imitation was undisputably deadly for the imitator: he was deprived of *"die Frucht seines Wagnisses"* ["the fruit of his wager"] (*TT* 89) [72, trans. modified] by the collective, who inflicted upon him the punishment of death. This punishment, Freud relates, did not only oppose the violation; it repeated the violation and expressed, in a displaced form, the desire motivating the violation in the first place.

> Die Strafe gibt den Vollstreckern nicht selten Gelegenheit, unter der Rechtfertigung der Sühne dieselbe frevle Tat auch ihrerseits zu begehen. Es ist dies ja eine der Grundlagen der menschlichen Strafordnung, und sie hat, wie gewiss richtig, die Gleichartigkeit der verbotenen Regungen beim Verbrecher wie bei der rächenden Gesellschaft zur Voraussetzung.
> Die Psychoanalyse bestätigt hier, was die Frommen zu sagen pflegen, wir seien alle arge Sünder. (*TT* 89)

> The punishment will not infrequently give those who carry it out an opportunity of committing the same outrage under colour of

an act of expiation. This is indeed one of the foundations of the human penal system and it is based, no doubt correctly, on the assumption that the prohibited impulses are present alike in the criminal and in the avenging community.

In this, psycho-analysis is no more than confirming the habitual pronouncement of the pious: we are all miserable sinners. [72]

In primitive society, then, the temptation to imitate was socially detrimental, and the taboo protected the very foundation of the social order by requiring the collective renunciation of transgressive desires.

Whereas the primitive individual feared that the violation of a taboo would result in the violator's being punished, in obsessional neurosis the fear of retribution is displaced from the violator to another.

> Wenn der Kranke etwas ihm Verbotenes ausführen soll, so fürchtet er die Strafe nicht für sich, sondern für eine andere Person, die meist unbestimmt gelassen ist, aber durch die Analyse leicht als eine der ihm nächsten und von ihm geliebtesten Personen erkannt wird. Der Neurotiker verhält sich also hiebei wie altruistisch, der Primitive wie egoistisch. (*TT* 89)

> What the patient fears if he performs some forbidden action is that a punishment will fall not on himself but on someone else. This person's identity is as a rule left unstated, but can usually be shown without difficulty by analysis to be one of those closest and most dear to the patient. Here, then, the neurotic seems to be behaving altruistically and the primitive man egoistically. [71]

Freud traces the fear for the well-being of another back to an original fear, doubly displaced, for the well-being of the self:

> Der Vorgang ist einigermassen kompliziert, aber wir übersehen ihn vollständig. Zugrunde der Verbotbildung liegt regelmässig eine böse Regung—ein Todeswunsch—gegen eine geliebte Person. Diese wird durch ein Verbot verdrängt, das Verbot an eine gewisse Handlung geknüpft, welche etwa die feindselige gegen die geliebte Person durch Verschiebung vertritt, die Ausführung dieser Handlung mit der Todesstrafe bedroht. Aber der Prozess geht weiter, und der ursprüngliche Todeswunsch gegen den geliebten anderen ist dann durch die Todesangst um ihn ersetzt. (*TT* 90)

> The process is a little complicated, but we can follow it perfectly. At the root of the prohibition there is invariably a hostile impulse—a death wish—against a loved person. This impulse is

repressed by a prohibition and the prohibition is attached to some particular act, which, by displacement, represents perhaps a hostile act against the loved person. There is a threat of death if this act is performed. But the process goes further, and the original death wish against the other is replaced by a *fear* that he may die. [72, trans. modified]

The taboo and the neurosis thus both behave egoistically, with the crucial difference that the neurosis dissimulates its egoism; its brutality consists in its cloaking of its true attitude in a contrary appearance. Although Freud assures his readers that the complicated nature of the displacements will not obscure their significance, the terminological shift in the name of the object of aggression from *"eine geliebte Person"* ["a loved person"] to *"de[r] geliebte ander[e]"* ["the loved other"] incorporates an element of indeterminacy regarding the precise identity of that other, who is *"eine der ihm nächsten und von ihm beliebtesten Personen"* ["one of those closest and most dear to the patient"]. This indeterminacy acquires a certain *intrasubjective* resonance when we consider it in light of Freud's description of a stage of development that is recapitulated in obsessional neurosis.

In tracing the development of the libidinal trends in the individual, Freud notes that in his *Drei Abhandlungen zur Sexualtheorie* he had identified two basic stages of libidinal organization. In the first, the autoerotic stage, the subject does not yet choose an external erotic object; rather, the separate instinctual components of sexuality independently satisfy themselves in the subject's own body. This stage is then succeeded by one in which the subject unifies its sexual instincts and cathects an object outside itself. But in *Totem und Tabu* Freud adds to the schema an intermediate stage, which has the paradoxical status of being a kind of nonstage inserted into or split off from the first stage and characterized by temporal nonspecificity: it is a stage that is superseded and yet is never entirely abandoned. In this "narcissistic" phase, *"die Person verhält sich so, als wäre sie in sich selbst verliebt"* (*TT* 109) ["the subject behaves as though it were in love with itself," 89, trans. modified]. In other words, the subject is his own *geliebte Person*.

> In diesem Zwischenstadium, dessen Bedeutsamkeit sich der Forschung immer mehr aufdrängt, haben die vorher vereinzelten Sexualtriebe sich bereits zu einer Einheit zusammengesetzt und auch ein Objekt gefunden; dies Objekt ist aber kein äusseres, dem Individuum fremdes, sondern es ist das eigene, um diese Zeit konstituierte Ich. (*TT* 109)

At this intermediate stage, the importance of which is being made more and more evident by research, the hitherto isolated sexual instincts have already come together into a single whole and have also found an object. But this object is not an external one, extraneous to the subject, but it is his own ego, which has been constituted at about the same time. [88–89]

The narcissistic relation of the subject to itself is thus a splitting apart of the self that is intimately, if not determinately, related to the creation of the very unity that Freud associates with the organization of the social instincts. In discussing the socializing force of the taboo, Freud similarly emphasizes the notion of the fusion of the self into a whole. He writes that the social instincts of the taboo are derived *"durch Zusammentreten von egoistischen und erotischen Komponenten zu besonderen Einheiten"* (*TT* 90) ["from a combination of egoistic and erotic components into particular unities," 72, trans. modified]. He again calls attention to this process at the end of the chapter entitled *"Das Tabu und die Ambivalenz der Gefühlsregungen"* ["Taboo and Emotional Ambivalence"], when he notes that the social instincts originate *"aus der Vereinigung egoistischer und erotischer Anteile"* (*TT* 91) ["from the combination of egoistic and erotic elements," 73].

Returning now to Freud's description of the brutal egoism of the neurosis, we can detect a crucial difference between it and the egoism of the social instincts. The socializing force of the taboo derives from the fact that it is a combination of distinct elements or substantial parts, *Anteile,* of both an egoistic and an erotic nature, into a particular unity. The asocial neurosis, by contrast, is not characterized by the combination of parts into a unity but by an *"Einstellung eines brutalen Egoismus"* ["attitude of brutal egoism"] (*TT* 90) [72], which is less stable in character. This attitude, moreover, is literally a kind of losing of the ego, as *Einstellung* also means abandonment or calling off. Freud invokes the image of the scar to denote the resolution of ambivalence that facilitates the creation of the ego. He writes: *"Wo früher der befriedigte Hass und die schmerzhafte Zärtlichkeit miteinander gerungen haben, da erhebt sich heute wie eine Narbenbildung die Pietät und fordert das: De mortuis nil nisi bene"* (*TT* 83) ["Where, in earlier times, satisfied hatred and pained affection fought each other, we now find that a kind of scar has been formed in the shape of piety, which declares 'de mortuis nil nisi bonum,'" 66]. We can thus compare the difference in stability between the social, egoistic uniting of elements and the asocial, egoistic attitude as the difference between a scar and a wound. That is, the neurosis, which still exhibits atavistic vestiges, reproduces the "wound" of emotional ambivalence and egoistic instability reminiscent of that earlier narcissistic stage that Freud suspects is never completely overcome.

It is through projection that the ego builds up the "scar tissue." Projection also helps to construct the image of the external world:

> Die Projektion der unbewussten Feindseligkeit beim Tabu der Toten auf die Dämonen ist nur ein einzelnes Beispiel aus einer Reihe von Vorgängen, denen der grösste Einfluss auf die Gestaltung des primitiven Seelenlebens zugesprochen werden muss. In dem betrachteten Falle dient die Projektion der Erledigung eines Gefühlskonfliktes; sie findet die nämliche Verwendung in einer grossen Anzahl von psychischen Situationen, die zur Neurose führen. Aber die Projektion ist nicht für die Abwehr geschaffen, sie kommt auch zustande, wo es keine Konflikte gibt. Die Projektion innerer Wahrnehmungen nach aussen ist ein primitiver Mechanismus, dem z.B. auch unsere Sinneswahrnehmungen unterliegen, der also an der Gestaltung unserer Aussenwelt normalerweise den grössten Anteil hat. Unter noch nicht genügend festgestellten Bedingungen werden innere Wahrnehmungen auch von Gefühls- und Denkvorgängen wie die Sinneswahrnehmungen nach aussen projiziert, zur Ausgestaltung der Aussenwelt verwendet, während sie der Innenwelt verbleiben sollten. (*TT* 80–81)

> The projection of unconscious hostility on to demons in the case of the taboo upon the dead is only a single instance of a number of processes to which the greatest influence must be attributed in the shaping of the primitive mind. In the case we have been dealing with, projection served the purpose of dealing with an emotional conflict; and it is employed in the same way in a large number of psychical situations that lead to neuroses. But projection was not created for the purpose of defence; it also occurs where there is no conflict. The projection outwards of internal perceptions is a primitive mechanism, to which, for instance, our sense perceptions are subject, and which therefore normally plays a very large part in determining the form taken by our external world. Under conditions whose nature has not yet been sufficiently established, internal perceptions of emotional and intellective processes can be projected outwards in the same way as sense perceptions; they are thus employed for building up the external world, though they should by rights remain part of the *internal* world. [64]

Freud later adds, *"Der einen Annahme dürfen wir uns aber getrauen, dass diese Neigung, seelische Vorgänge nach aussen zu projizieren, dort eine Verstärkung erfährt, wo die Projektion den Vorteil einer psychischen Erleichterung mit sich bringt"* (*TT* 113) ["It is, however, safe to assume that that tendency (to project mental processes towards the outside) will be intensified when it promises to bring with it the advantage of mental relief," 92]. It could be said that the *Vorteil* of projection creates the *Anteile* of the social instincts: this relief is one of im-parting to the subject an organization that is based upon both the splitting of ambivalence and the assigning of the created emotions to asymmetric psychical positions. The conditions "whose nature has not yet been sufficently established," I would speculate, might be explained as a relationship between the two effects of projection that Freud's description presents as independent phenomena: the building up of the subject occurs through the act of endowing the world with a form. That is, externalization and self-differentiation are part of the same process.

Freud emphasizes the importance of translating the objective constructs of projection back into their subjective unconscious origins: *"Vergessen wir auch nicht daran, dass es vom Stadium der Systembildung an zweierlei Ableitungen für jeden vom Bewusstsein beurteilten Akt gibt, die systematische und die reale, aber unbewusste"* (*TT* 82) ["We must not forget that, at and after the stage at which systems are constructed, two sets of reasons can be assigned for every psychical event that is consciously judged—one set belonging to the system and the other set real but unconscious," 65]. It is precisely the unconscious subjective origin of the system of his projections that the obsessional neurotic does not recognize when he identifies the other as the possible object of aggression. With this in mind it is necessary to consider the nature of Freud's distinction between the "healthy" egoism of the taboo and the brutal egoism behind the altruistic fear. Are the two really opposites, the former being an asocial construction and the latter a social construction? Or might they, as well, be poles in a system, in Freud's theory of the difference between taboo and the neurosis, and as such, in need of a certain translation back into *"innere Wahrnehmungen"* ["internal perceptions"]?

The taboo, it will be remembered, facilitates the creation of the social instincts through the combination, *Zusammentreten,* of egoistic and erotic elements into particular unities. While the creation of these unities occurs through the splitting of ambivalence, that is, through projection, it is possible, indeed necessary, to recognize the origin of the newly isolated tendencies in the subject. The obsessional neurosis, by contrast, is not composed of predominantly social instincts: "*Somit ist das Überwiegen der sexuellen Triebanteile gegen die sozialen das für die Neurose charakteristische Moment*" (*TT* 90) ["The fact which is characteristic of the neurosis is the preponderance of the sexual over the social instinctual elements," 73]. These sexual instincts, furthermore, do not facilitate the consolidation of the self into a whole. Freud writes, "*Das Sexualbedürfnis ist eben nicht imstande, die Menschen in ähnlicher Weise wie die Anforderungen der Selbsterhaltung zu einigen*" (*TT* 91) ["The sexual need is not capable of uniting men in the same way as are the demands of self-preservation," 74, trans. modified]. This statement can be read two ways: first, as meaning that the sexual need is not capable of uniting men into social bodies for the common purpose of self-preservation; and second, that the sexual need of the individual does not work towards his preservation. That is, sexual needs do not consolidate the self but work towards its splintering and conversely work against the demands of self-preservation.[2] This intrasubjective reading becomes that much more plausible when we consider that the immediately preceding sentence in Freud's text also pertains to an intrasubjective phenomenon: "*Bei der Triebanalyse der Neurosen erfährt man, dass in ihnen die Triebkräfte sexueller Herkunft den bestimmenden Einfluss ausüben*" (*TT* 91) ["If we analyze the instincts at work in the neuroses, we find that the determining influence in them is exercised by instinctual forces of sexual origin," 73–74].

The brutal egoism of the obsessional neurosis consists, paradoxically, in its lack of a stable ego and in its inability to recognize the self in the projected object. Freud links the inability to recognize the role of the subject in the formation of a picture of the world to a form of unselfconscious imitative representation, that is, to a representation in which the conscious self does not recognize itself.

> Wenn Spiel und imitative Darstellung dem Kinde und dem Primitiven genügen, so ist dies nicht ein Zeichen von Bescheidenheit in unserem Sinne oder von Resignation infolge Erkenntnis ihrer realen Ohnmacht, sondern die wohl verständliche Folge der überwiegenden Wertung ihres Wunsches, des von ihm abhängigen Willens und der von ihm eingeschlagenen Wege. (*TT* 104)

> If children and primitive men find play and imitative representation enough for them, this is not a sign of their being unassuming in our sense or of their resignedly accepting their actual impotence. It is the easily understandable result of the paramount vir-

tue they ascribe to their wishes, of the will that is associated with those wishes and of the methods by which those wishes operate. [84]

Children and primitive men attach extreme importance to their wishes, to the extent that they find sufficient satisfaction in their private hallucinations. The fulfillment of wishes through play is an asocial phenomenon not because it deprives society of the subject's predisposition towards collective activity but because the will to power drives the child and the primitive man. This will to power Freud understands in the *"allgemeinere [Bedeutung] des Angreifens, der Bemächtigung, des Geltendmachens der eigenen Person"* (*TT* 90) ["general sense of attacking, of getting control, and of asserting oneself," 73].[3] The methods in the service of that will entail a violence that is apparent in their description: *eingeschlagen* means smashed or knocked out. Freud indicates the specific nature of this violence:

> Es besteht also jetzt eine allgemeine Überschätzung der seelischen Vorgänge, das heisst eine Einstellung zur Welt, welche uns nach unseren Einsichten in die Beziehung von Realität und Denken als solche Überschätzung des letzteren erscheinen muss. Die Dinge treten gegen deren Vorstellungen zurück. (*TT* 105)

> A general over-valuation has thus come about of all mental processes — that is, an attitude towards the world, which, according to our knowledge of the relation between reality and thought, must appear to us as an over-valuation of the latter. Things become less important than their representations. [85, trans. modified]

Representation imposes itself over its object in a way that obfuscates the difference between object and imposing desire. The ban on imitation enforced by primitive society is thus a ban on a particular relation of domination inextricably linked to the logic of imitation. The desire to be like the other, to imitate him, entails a desire to do away with the other and is identical to the brutal egoism of the neurosis disguised by the appearance of altruistic nobility. This egoism is brutal because it does not recognize its own desires in the desires of the other — as, by contrast, the taboo prohibition does. Since, however, the "thing" portrayed in imitative representation is a tendency within the self, the relief afforded by projection arises at the expense of a splitting of the self into an aggressive opposition between self as subject and self as object, which is aggressive precisely because it is not recognized as the splitting of a self-difference.

The splitting of the self seems to contrast directly with the uniting of the self that facilitates the formation of the social instincts; whereas in projection things step back [*zurücktreten*] in face of their representations, it is through the *"Zusammentreten von egoistischen und erotischen Komponenten zu besonderen Einheiten"* (*TT* 91) ["stepping together of egoistic and erotic components into particular unities," 73, trans. modified] that the social instinct of the taboo arises. The brutality of obsessional neurotic egoism is that of a self-violence based upon a necessary expropriation of an aspect of the self, or, in other words, based upon a masochistic impulse to kill off part of the self in the process of neurotic identity-constitution. The neurotic fear for the wellbeing of "a loved one" can, according to this logic, be understood as the projection outward of the subject's fear for the preservation of his own self, which comes under siege as soon as the self is represented but not recognized in its representation. This might also explain the apparent paradox that serves as Freud's point of departure for his discussion of ambivalence, namely, as Samuel Weber notes, the fact that "the violation of the taboo-prohibition entails the expectation that the violator will be punished."[4] It could thus be speculated that the transgressor of the taboo is not discouraged by the consequences of his deed, because he is externalizing the self-destructive impulses characteristic of an egoism that is not yet a proper self but is only an attitude.

By understanding the brutal egoism of the subject in terms that emphasize the subjective origins of the object of aggression, rather than viewing the object of aggression as being unrelated to the subject, one can avoid assuming what is in fact the outcome of the neurotic process of projection, namely, the split between subject and object. The apparent neurotic altruism, I would argue, is in reality the reflection of a state of self-lessness. To understand it thus also avoids hypostatizing the same kind of oppositional splitting within an identity—that of the neurosis as being internally divided between an appearance (of altruism) and an essence (of egoism)—that characterizes the very workings of the neurosis. While the neurosis reflects the narcissistic relation of subject to itself, the subject cannot itself reflect upon this relation, because, strictly speaking, there is no stable self. This is also the reason, I believe, why Freud generally refers to the subject of his study as a condition—obsessional neurosis—and not an identity—the obsessive neurotic.

The inability to reflect upon the representational nature of the process of projection constitutes, I would argue, a kind of "neurotic," asocial form of representation, an *asoziale Bildung.* The link between projection and representation is, of course, indicated in Freud's description of both the obsessional neurosis and the taboo as *Bildungen:* in the concept of *Bildung* it is possible to read the coexistence of the notions of the linguistic image and of form, because *Bild,* in addition to signifying the concept of construction, also means metaphor and form.

To find an example of a process of representation that is not self-reflected we can look to Freud's presentation of the primal scene in his case history of the "Wolf Man," in which an asocial construction forms one component of a complex scene of representation. The material from the "Wolf Man" case is of interest inasmuch as it stages a scene in which representation and identity-constitution intertwine. Indeed, Freud notes that the question of the historical veracity of the scene is *"eigentlich nicht sehr wichtig"* ["not in reality a matter of very great importance"].[5] The temporal stages represented in the primal scene have a structural rather than historical pertinence.

Freud describes a scene in which a child of one and one-half years witnesses his parents having intercourse. He calls the reader's attention to a pre-Oedipal moment in which the child identifies with the place of the mother, who is the object of the father's desire. The child interprets his mother's facial expression as signifying her enjoyment of what he nevertheless perceives as an act of violence inflicted by the father; he *"musste erkennen, dass es sich um eine Befriedigung handle"* ["was obliged to recognize that what he was faced by was a process of gratification"].[6] Desire in the eyes of the child thus becomes linked to a notion of self-violence; it develops from a form of identification—desire to be in the position of another, the mother—that implicitly threatens the self with annihilation. Returning for a moment to the neurotic attitude of altruism, we can now understand more clearly why the neurosis might be representing itself accurately: the subject's fear for the well-being of the other, which is really the self, is a projected hypostatization of a moment of masochistic identification that in normal development is overcome and yet which persists. In Freud's description of the primal scene, both its overcoming and its persistence are illustrated: the "proof" of the child's hypothesis about the link between desire and self-annihilation is discovered when he observes the female genitals. By seeing the mother's genitals, the child becomes conscious of his difference from her. His awareness of this difference emerges through his first act of interpretation. He views his mother in a way that insures his self-preservation: he sees her as castrated; that is, he narcissistically construes her difference as a version, however inadequate, of himself. As Freud writes, the child *"entdeckte die Vagina und die biologische Bedeutung von männlich und weiblich. Er verstand jetzt, aktiv sei gleich männlich, passiv aber weiblich"* ["discovered the vagina and the biological significance of masculine and feminine. He understood now that active was the same as masculine, while passive was the same as feminine"].[7]

Freud, in his account of the child's experience, becomes involved in the same process of projective identification as does the child. He attributes to the child a self-conscious awareness of his own implication in a scene of interpretation that produces *Bedeutung* [significance]. In saying that the child understood [*verstand*] the meaning of a biological distinction, Freud seems to imply that the child is cognizant of his active role in constructing a (reductive) equivalence between masculinity and activity, femininity and passivity. And yet, the success of the child's identification with a masculine position depends upon his confusion of the performative and the cognitive. While the child plays the role of the interpreter of a representation that, through identification, he constructs, he views his construction as a given, as something that he uncovers, *entdeckt*.

In renouncing his identification with the maternal position, the child shifts from *"die passive Einstellung"* ["the passive position"], to defending against this passivity with the masculinity he creates from his threatened narcissism: *"Aus dem bedrohten Narzissmus schöpfte er die Männlichkeit, mit der er sich gegen die passive Einstellung zum Vater wehrte"* ["It was from his threatened narcissism that he derived the masculinity with which he defended himself against his passive attitude towards his father"].[8] As is the case with both the attitude of brutal egoism adopted by the obsessional neurosis and the mimetic relation of the epic subject to the world, the child's pregenital organization is a state of pre-identity, in which the ego is an attitude *[Einstellung]* before becoming, through projection, the more substantial scar. This scarring occurs by locating the wound in the place of the other: the child realizes that "particular unity" of the ego by externalizing his sense (or non-sense) of non-identity, that is, by displacing it onto the image of the fragmented other. Freud writes that *"jetzt sah er [das Kind] mit eigenen Augen die Wunde . . . und verstand, dass ihr Vorhandensein eine Bedingung des Verkehrs mit dem Vater war"* ["[the child] saw with his own eyes the wound . . . and understood that its presence was a necessary condition of intercourse with his father"]. Freud's representation of the primal scene also renders legible its own participation in the very projection it is describing. The positions of the theorist and the child converge in Freud's image of the ego as a scar. It is as if Freud appropriates this image from the child (for whom it has a real history, which Freud recounts).[9]

In his analysis of the primal scene, Freud reinscribes the superseded pregenital moment into the genital phase of libidinal organization: he discloses that the child interrupts his parents by screaming because he passed a stool and explains this act in light of the child's possession of *"einen unbewussten Begriff . . . , den des vom Körper abtrennbaren Kleinen"* ["an unconscious concept . . . of a little one that can become separated from one's body"] and which can be given up *"um die Gunst eines geliebten Anderen zu gewinnen"* ["in order to gain the favor of some other person whom he loves"].[10] This handing over of the feces, Freud states, *"wird seinerseits zum Vorbild der Kastration"* ["becomes the prototype of castration"].[11] As such, it reflects the persistence, even after its temporal succession, of that mode of pregenital identification that, it will be recalled, is the precondition for the child's identification with the place of the mother. It is important to note here that the mode of identification associated with the imitative desire to be in the place of the mother is never fully transcended; rather, although renounced, it returns in a displaced form.

Freud explicitly draws a parallel between works of art and the projections of primitive men, such as those underlying imitative magic: *"Den Projektionsschöpfungen der Primitiven stehen die Personifikationen nahe, durch welche der Dichter die in ihm ringenden entgegengesetzten Triebregungen als gesonderte Individuen aus sich herausstellt"* (*TT* 82n) ["The projected creations of primitive men resemble the personifications constructed by creative writers; for the latter externalize in the form of separate individuals the opposing instinctual impulses struggling within them," 65n]. Though Freud points to the similarity between the projections of primitive men and works of art, his language figures the crucial difference, as spatial distance, between them; while they stand close to each other *"nahestehen,"* there is no indication that they are contiguous. This is worth noting, because associations based upon contiguity, *"vorgestellte Kontiguität"* ["imagined contiguity"], are precisely the underlying assumptions of primitive magic (*TT* 102) [83].

Freud writes that behind imitative magic is the desire to achieve mastery over men, animals, and objects. In a footnote, he speculates, *"Das biblische Verbot, sich ein Bild von irgendetwas Lebendem zu machen, entstammte wohl keiner prinzipiellen Ablehnung der bil-*

denden Kunst, sondern sollte der von der hebräischen Religion verpönten Magie ein Werkzeug entziehen" (*TT* 99) ["It seems probable that the biblical prohibition against making an image of any living thing originated not from any objection to the plastic arts, but from a desire to deprive magic (which was abominated by the Hebrew religion) of one of its tools," 80]. The renunciation of magic is an attempt to circumvent the implicit will to domination motivating the construction of images and effigies.

Given Freud's suggestion that the work of art resembles, but is not identical to, the projections of primitive men, we could say that the work's distinguishing attribute is, like the renunciation of magic, its refusal of the will to domination behind the mimetic impulse. This is another way of describing the movement of detotalization that Lukács defines as structural irony. Freud and Lukács do not suggest that the work of art can bypass its inaugural, constative point of departure, its grounding in the assumption of a mimetic relation between representation and its object; but they do encourage us to formulate a distinction between the two. Perhaps we could identify the difference between the work of art on the one hand and the projections of the primitive individual and secondary identifications of the child on the other, in the circumscription by art of the will to dominate. The work of art both relies on the mimetic drive and exposes the origin of representations, including those that claim to be objective, in the will to power subtending projection.

The structure of Freud's own text attests to its status as an aesthetic composition rather than a primitive projection or secondary identification. It reveals its origins in projection in a number of ways. We saw how the opposition between the taboo and the obsessional neurosis depended upon the projection outward of an intrasubjective process of self-violence into an intersubjective allegory of brutal altruism. We also traced how Freud projected his own self-conscious role of interpreter onto the child in the primal scene. We can find a third, particularly pointed example of the effects of projection in the following passage, in which Freud attempts to offer a unified theoretical account of projection. His description of the process of self-differentiation—the creation of unconscious and conscious processes—actually displaces the subject of his theory.

> Was wir so, ganz ähnlich wie der Primitive, in die äussere Realität projizieren, kann kaum etwas anderes sein als die Erkenntnis eines Zustandes, in dem ein Ding den Sinnen und dem Bewusst-

sein gegeben, *präsent* ist, neben welchem ein anderer besteht, in dem dasselbe *latent* ist, aber wiedererscheinen kann, also die Koexistenz von Wahrnehmen und Erinnern, oder, ins Allgemeine ausgedehnt, die Existenz *unbewusster* Seelenvorgänge neben den *bewussten.* (*TT* 115)

When we, no less than primitive man, project something into external reality, what is happening must surely be this: the recognition of a state in which something is directly given to the senses and to consciousness (that is, is *present* to them), and alongside it another, in which the same thing is *latent* but capable of reappearing. In short, the co-existence of perception and memory, or, putting it more generally, the existence of *unconscious* mental processes alongside the *conscious* ones. [93–94, trans. modified]

Freud begins with the claim that he is describing a phenomenon of recognition: in projection, two states are recognized as being of a subjective origin. This is particularly striking given the fact that in order for projection to bring with it the advantage of mental relief, it is precisely the subjective origins of the projections that must *not* be recognized. The asymmetry of unconscious and conscious psychical processes permanently bars the possibility that the self could become so transparently self-reflective. While Freud's statement seems to suggest the possibility of perfect self-cognition, the necessary separation engendered by projection is reflected in the asymmetry between the activity of a specifically designated subject—the "we" in "when we, no less than primitive man, project . . . "—and the ensuing description of a static condition no longer attributable to that "we." What results from this act of projection is a "recognition" ["*Erkenntnis*"], the identity of whose agent remains unspecified.

The subjective nature of the act of recognition recedes even further in Freud's restatement of the process in general terms: the recognition of two states becomes "the existence" of two processes, so that the emphasis shifts from an act of cognition, which is possible only from a position that is not itself implicated in its object, to a condition of actually *being* these states.[12] It must therefore be the theorists of projection, those with "intensified conscious perception," and not the projecting subject, whom Freud addresses in the above paragraph, as he does in the following statement:

Die primitiven Menschen [hatten] durch Projektion innerer Wahrnehmungen nach aussen ein Bild der Aussenwelt entwickelt, welches wir nun mit erstarkter Bewusstseinswahrnehmung in Psychologie zurückübersetzen müssen. (*TT* 81)

Owing to the projection outwards of internal perceptions, primitive men arrived at a picture of the external world which we, with our intensified conscious perception, have now to translate back into psychology. [64]

Freud's theoretical formulation of projection demonstrates how impossible it is to develop an objective theory, even one about the impossibility of objectivity. The concept of theory and the attribute of objectivity are mutually exclusive. And yet, subject as it is to the process it attempts to describe, *Totem und Tabu* proceeds according to the principle of structural irony that Lukács identifies as the defining principle of the essay and the novel. I would suggest that the persuasive force of both *Die Theorie des Romans* and *Totem und Tabu* can be measured by the extent to which both works, in the course of elaborating their theories of the constitution of subjectivity, actually *stage* the interplay between the assumption that mimesis is a viable mode of representation and the ironic subversion of this assumption.

Three

Dreadful Discovery in Balzac's *La Recherche de l'Absolu*

In Balzac's *La Recherche de l'Absolu* (1834), Balthazar Claës, a scientific genius, devotes his life to a search that causes not only the ruin of six family fortunes, but also the death of his angelic wife, Joséphine. From a position of intellectual and social eminence—as a young man he had studied with Lavoisier and his family was regarded with *"une sorte de respect religieux"* ["a sort of religious respect"]—he is eventually cast from society like a pariah:[1] *"Pour toute la société, Balthazar était un homme à interdire, un mauvais père, qui avait mangé six fortunes, des millions, et qui cherchait la pierre philosophale au Dix-Neuvième siècle"* (830) ["In the view of society as a whole, Balthazar was a man to be tabooed, a wicked father who had squandered six fortunes, millions, and who was seeking the philosopher's stone in the nineteenth century," 298].

Interpreters of *La Recherche* emphasize its conflictual structure. Albert Béguin, for example, organizes his reading around the opposition between *"un mythe de la famille"* and *"un mythe de la pensée."*[2] Madeleine Fargeaud, invoking a normative standard of mental health in order to diagnose Balthazar's behavior as a form of delirium, reads his *"cas"* as *"médicalement 'exemplaire.'"*[3] According to Josué Harari, the theme of the text is the incompatibility of knowledge and desire: "We meet here one of the most venerable themes in Western thought: that knowledge cannot acquire or have access to the truth except on the condition of liberating itself from desire, and especially from sexual desire."[4] In keeping with the exalted stakes of the novel, Balthazar is customarily regarded as the embodiment of demonic genius, and Joséphine, by contrast, as the ideal of angelic matrimonial devotion.[5] Physically, as well, these characters have been described as antithetical, Joséphine being *"une pauvre fille contrefaite et boiteuse,"* (676) ["a poor, deformed, lame girl," 36] and Balthazar *"un homme jeune et bien fait"* (676) ["a young and handsome man," 36]. All of these heuristic oppositions conform to what Peter Brooks has identified as the essential melodrama of the Balzacian text, which figures "our constant premise that life is truly inhabited by primal, intense, polarized forces — forces primal and intense because they are polarized — that can be made manifest."[6]

As is well known, the extraordinary architecture of *La Comédie humaine* relies upon dynamics of exchange and circulation, whereby characters intertextually appear and reappear from one work to the next, creating a self-enclosed literary universe. Within this intertextual economy, *La Recherche de l'Absolu* is an anomaly: Balthazar and Joséphine Claës are born in this particular text and die in the course of its unfolding. Since *La Recherche* thus appears to deviate from the tenets structuring *La Comédie*, it is tempting to adopt a conflictual intertextual framework similar to that invoked in specific analyses of the novel and thereby to oppose *La Recherche* to the other texts in *La Comédie*. Indeed, the setting of the novel seems to provide further justification for this framework: unlike any other novel in *La Comédie*, *La Recherche* takes place in Flanders. Even the text's evolution is curiously obscure. As Madeleine Fargeaud notes, "Its appearance, like its conception, like its destiny, falls under the sign of mystery. No prenatal life, no subterranean movement seems, at first glance, to have served as a prelude to the birth of *La Recherche de l'Absolu*."[7]

The apparent uniqueness of *La Recherche* in the Balzacian canon has seemed to engender in its readers a desire to domesticate the novel. To this end critics have undertaken extensive research into the novel's origins and sources in the fields of science, history, art, and architecture. In this connection, too, science has become the primary object of interpretation, presumably because it is more properly philosophical than the domestic themes that initially warranted the novel's inclusion in the *Scènes de la vie privée*.[8]

While the research done into the manifold contexts of the novel has contributed greatly to our understanding of its themes and references, the emphasis on context has also encouraged critics to overlook, if not actively exclude, certain of the novel's internal structural attributes. In addition, readers have become disinclined to consider that *La Recherche* may be related to *La Comédie* in subtle ways. Indeed, the exclusive emphasis on extraliterary referents appears problematic in light of five considerations which I will now address at length.

1. Science is undisputably of great thematic importance in the novel, but as Harari observes, "for every page on which science is a subject of discussion, we read twenty pages about inheritances and judicial

comings-of-age, wasted fortunes and their financial ramifications, notarized acts and contracts between father and children . . . the central themes—death of the mother, inadequacies of the father, struggle between daughter and father—remain sufficiently intact."[9] In order to privilege science over other motifs, it is necessary to overlook this complicated account of family politics in the text and thereby to assume that these sets of relations are both independent of and secondary to the scientific concerns. Moreover, although the story begins with a lengthy description of the house in which the principal scenes of the narrative take place, not only is Balthazar's laboratory omitted from the description, but with few exceptions, readers and characters are barred from even entering the laboratory, as if to suggest that our attention should be focused elsewhere.[10] At times our exclusion from the laboratory is violent, for example, when Joséphine attempts to enter the garret where her husband is working: *"Pour la première fois de sa vie, elle connut la colère de Balthazar; à peine avait-elle entrouvert la porte, qu'il fondit sur elle, la prit, la jeta rudement sur l'escalier, où elle faillit rouler du haut en bas"* (690) ["For the first time in her life, she knew Balthazar's wrath. She had hardly opened the door, when he rushed at her, seized her, and pushed her roughly back into the hall, where she nearly fell from top to bottom of the stairs," 60]. Joséphine's violent expulsion from Balthazar's workplace encapsulates the sense of frustration and rejection issuing from the reader's attempt to discover the nature of Balthazar's undertaking. If Joséphine's inquiry, *"Mais que cherchait-il"* ["But what was he seeking?"] (694) [65], succinctly formulates the interpreter's recurrent refrain, Balthazar's belief that *"Joséphine ne savait pas!"* ["Joséphine did not know!"] (691) [61] all too fittingly applies to us as readers of this text.

2. Even the seemingly straightforward fact that this novel is set in Flanders and hence is removed from the customary "French" context of Balzac's stories is complicated by other pertinent details: in the Flemish town of Douai, *"le ton, les modes, les façons de Paris . . . dominent"* (661) ["the tones, the styles, the manners of Paris are in the ascendant," 10–11]. And if Paris is present only as an "overtone," the precise location of the Claës house suggests that the French capital is literally of central significance: *"La maison où se sont passés les événements de cette histoire se trouve à peu près au milieu de la rue de Paris"* (661) ["The house in which the incidents of this tale occurred is situated almost in the middle of Rue de Paris," 11]. As if to underscore the French influence, over the door of the house hangs a statuette of Saint Geneviève, patron saint of Paris.

3. While Joséphine and Balthazar are antithetical in appearance, the repetitions in the detailed descriptions of their respective physiognomies and physiques make it difficult to locate the precise place of the difference between being *"bien fait"* [handsome] and *"contrefait"* [deformed]; their difference seems to be less one of essence than of organization: Joséphine's *"épaisse chevelure noire retombait en boucles sur les épaules"* (668) ["mass of thick, black hair fell in curls over her shoulders," 22], while Balthazar's *"abondante chevelure blonde, peu soignée, retombait sur ses épaules"* (671) ["abundant light hair, of which he took but little care, fell over his shoulders," 27]. Joséphine's forehead is *"très bombé"* ["very prominent"] (668) [22], and similarly Balthazar's *"large front offrait d'ailleurs les protubérances"* (671) ["broad forehead was marked by . . . protuberances," 27]. While the membrane between Joséphine's nostrils is *"si mince que sa transparence permettait à la lumière de la rougir fortement"* (668) ["so thin that its transparence permitted the light to redden it," 23], Balthazar seems to exhale fire: *"on eût dit qu'il jetait par ses narines la flamme qui dévorait son âme"* (671) ["you would have said that he breathed forth through his nostrils the flame that consumed his soul," 27–28]. Joséphine, who is *"bossue et boiteuse"* ["deformed and lame"] (668) [23], is not the only one whose gait reflects a deformity; Balthazar, as well, has the bearing of a cripple: *"Sa haute taille se voûtait légèrement, soit que ses travaux l'obligeassent à se courber, soit que l'épine dorsale se fût bombée sous le poids de sa tête"* (670–71) ["His tall figure was slightly bent, whether because the work in which he was engaged compelled him to stoop, or because the spinal column had curved under the weight of his head," 26].

4. On the level of plot we can also detect a strong structural pattern of repetition in difference. Joséphine's death is doubled by Balthazar's at the end of the novel. Both protagonists, moreover, are stricken with paralysis. In Balthazar's case, the affliction is explicit: *"Son corps décrépit ne soutint pas la réaction affreuse qu'il éprouva dans la haute région de ses sentiments, il tomba frappé d'une attaque de paralysie entre les bras de Lemulquinier"* (832) ["His decrepit body could not withstand the terrible reaction which he underwent in his sentiments, he fell, stricken with paralysis, into the arms of Lemulquinier," 302]. While it is never expressly stated that Joséphine is paralyzed, in a letter to Madame Hanska, Balzac indicates as much. He writes, Madame Claës *"se meurt: la paralysie gagne l'autre jambe"* [dies: paralysis overtakes the other leg].[11] Joséphine does not want to spend her final days in her bedroom, and so her bed is moved into the parlor: *"Les médecins*

avaient favorisé le voeu de son coeur en trouvant cette pièce plus aérée, plus gaie, et plus convenable à sa situation que sa chambre" (746) ["The doctors had approved her heartfelt wish, considering that room more airy, more cheerful, and more suitable for one in her condition than her bedroom," 153]. On his death bed, Balthazar literally assumes Joséphine's place: his bed is also set up in the parlor: *"Tous les matins, ses enfants se rendaient près de lui, restaient pendant la journée dans le parloir en dînant devant son lit, et ne sortaient qu'au moment où il s'endormait"* (834) [Every morning his children went to him, remained in the parlor throughout the day, dining by his bedside, and did not leave him until he went to sleep," 304]. A final parallel in the two deaths concerns the fact that both characters die uttering a single word. Joséphine cries out *"Marguerite"* while Balthazar screams *"Eureka,"* which the narrator glosses as *"J'ai trouvé."* As if to highlight the significance of the structure of repetition or doubling, the Claës house consists of one building that is visible from the street, and *"une seconde maison absolument semblable au bâtiment situé sur le devant de la rue, et qui, dans la Flandre, porte le nom de quartier de derrière"* (665) ["a second house exactly like the one on the street and known in Flanders by the name of *quartier de derrière*," 17].

5. In order to identify the novel as deviant with respect to the other texts in *La Comédie humaine,* it is necessary to assume that setting, character, motif, and theme are the chief identifying marks of the Balzacian oeuvre. In structural terms, though, the novel of course belongs to the cosmos of *La Comédie.* After all, Balzac did not position *La Recherche* outside of *La Comédie;* rather, it is one component of the *Études philosophiques.* It could even be argued here that the novel is doubly at home in *La Comédie,* having been successively subsumed by Balzac under two separate subdivisions: the text first appeared in 1834 in the *Scènes de la vie privée* of *La Comédie;* when, in 1845, the third edition of *La Comédie* was published, *La Recherche* had been moved into the *Études philosophiques* along with *La Peau de chagrin, Melmoth reconcilié, Le Chef-d'oeuvre inconnu,* and *Jésus-Christ en Flandre.* As such, readings of the novel must come to terms with both the continuities and the discontinuities between it and the totality of *La Comédie.*

In the broadest sense, we could say that a common structure of repetition loosely unites the five points we have just raised: the relationship of science to other thematic concerns found in both the novel and *La Comédie,* the setting of the story, the physical identities of Balthazar and Joséphine as based on a difference in the arrangement of descriptive elements, the repetitive movement of the plot, and the position of the novel in *La Comédie*. While such a structure of repetition does not negate difference—clearly Balthazar and Joséphine remain distinct characters, science *is* an important concern in the text, Flanders is *not* France—it nevertheless complicates the oppositions that do organize the text and its relation to other texts within the Balzacian universe. I contend that these repetitions are indicative of a supplementary if implicit structural irony that runs throughout the text. By means of this irony, the narrative voice distances itself from the logic of oppositional thinking, precisely because it is this logic that leads Balthazar to his death in his pursuit of the Absolute. In what follows I explore how the novel explores the relationship between oppositional thinking and narcissistic projection. While such thinking is depicted as violent in nature, it is also shown to be a constitutive moment in the process of identity-constitution that neither Balzac nor Balthazar can avoid.

The narrator in the novel never directly comments on the value of Balthazar's quest for the Absolute, but both Marguerite and her suitor, Emmanuel, the two survivors in the novel recognized for their prudence and clairvoyance, approve of Balthazar's endeavor. They claim that Balthazar's attempt to discover the Absolute is admirable and valuable, in spite of the fact that it eventually results in his total self-consumption—his death—not to mention the consumption of six family fortunes and the death of his wife. Emmanuel states, *"Malheureusement, ma chère Marguerite, s'il a tort comme chef de famille, il a raison scientifiquement; et une vingtaine d'hommes en Europe l'admireront, là où tous les autres le taxeront de folie"* (786) ["Unfortunately, my dear Marguerite, although as head of the family he is doing wrong, from a scientific standpoint he is doing right, and a score of men in Europe will admire him while everybody else calls him mad," 222]. Despite being the victim of her husband's endeavor, even Joséphine agrees with Emmanuel, although she has one reservation. She says, *"Il ne pourrait avoir tort que dans la forme, ses intentions seront toujours nobles"* (752) ["He could not do wrong except in form, his purpose will always be noble," 164, trans. modified]. Balthazar, then, is irreproachable from a scientific perspective, yet wrong in form. What could his formal failing possibly be? What does it mean to be wrong in form? And how might Balthazar's formal transgressions account for the novel's irony? We know that in the first fifteen years of his married life Balthazar displayed the utmost sensitivity to matters of form: *"Jamais son attachement ne quitta les formes de la passion"* (679) ["His attachment never laid aside the outward forms of passion," 41]. If we look at the scene in which Balthazar's scientific interests are first rekindled and in which he most extensively explains his project, we will find an indication of his decisive turn away from proper form.

During the overnight visit of a Polish officer, Monsieur Wierzchownia, Balthazar and his guest converse about science. Balthazar later recounts the discussion to Joséphine. The quoted conversation between the men, which is really more of a soliloquy than a dialogue, is composed of two parts. In the first section, Wierzchownia explains the principles of unitary chemistry, the purpose of which is *"dédui[re] l'existence de l'Absolu! Une substance commune à toutes les créations, modifiée par une force unique"* (717) ["(to deduce) the existence of the *Absolute!* A substance common to all created things, modified by a single force," 104]. Harari has convincingly shown that the principles of unitary chemistry do not begin to exhaust the scope of the problems Balthazar, following Wierzchownia's lead, seeks to solve. Not only does Balthazar want to reduce organic and inorganic matter to as few common substances as possible, he also wants to explain the principle of diversification. Harari writes,

> Posing the problem of the unity of nature and its capacity for diversification—in other words, wondering whether at the origin of all living things there is a single unique substance that diversifies itself, through time and history, to produce plants, animals, and sentient beings—is no longer a problem of chemistry, but one that rightfully belongs in the realm of biology.[12]

Harari then notes that, while the solution to the chemical problem resides in the domain of biology, the answer to the biological problem lies in yet another discipline: "The scientific hypothesis of the unity of matter and its diversification is subordinated to the philosophical hypothesis concerning the relationship between man and the act of creation."[13] Harari supports this claim by citing a passage from Balzac's *"Questions intéressantes pour les connaissances humaines"*:

> What would be the way to substitute for the words of Metaphysics a language of conventional and simple signs which might, *as in the exact sciences,* prevent errors from slipping in and which, by making it proceed from demonstrated propositions to propositions still to be resolved, from truth to truth, would give it the possibility of reaching the most unknown things and of tearing aside the last veil of nature?[14]

Although Harari does not state as much, this passage orchestrates yet another displacement: the question proper to metaphysics is none other than a semiotic question. At the root of philosophical speculation is the desire to substitute an accurate system of signs for the imprecise substitutions of the words of metaphysics, which do not simply represent but also distort, that is, they fail to "prevent errors from slipping in." In the *Préface des études de moeurs au XIXe siècle,* Balzac, referring to himself in the third person, writes that in order to prepare for the novel, *"Il a demandé à la chimie ce qu'elle avait fait, jusqu'où elle était allée; il en a appris la langue"* [He asked chemistry what it had done, where it was going; he learned its language].[15] Although Harari elides Balzac and Balthazar in his discussion of the philosophical underpinnings of scientific research, their aims are distinct: Balzac directs his research toward the acquisition of scientific knowledge through the acquisition of a scientific *language;* Balthazar's research, by contrast, is not semiotic but substantive in nature—he believes that the Absolute is a discrete object that can be identified and appropriated. The novel plays out the tension between these two conceptions of the Absolute as well as the fatal danger inherent in the confusion of one with the other.

Wierzchownia indicates that the Absolute is both substance and medium of articulation.

> "Une substance commune à toutes les créations, modifiée par une force unique, telle est la position nette et claire du problème offert par l'Absolu et qui m'a semblé *cherchable*. Là vous rencontrerez le mystérieux Ternaire, devant lequel s'est, de tout temps, agenouillée l'Humanité: la matière première, le moyen, le résultat. Vous trouverez ce terrible nombre Trois en toute chose humaine, il domine les religions, les sciences et les lois. . . . Vous êtes un élève de Lavoisier, vous êtes riche et maître de votre temps, je puis donc vous faire part de mes conjectures. Voici le but que mes expériences personnelles m'ont fait entrevoir. La MATIÈRE UNE doit être un principe commun aux trois gaz et au carbone. Le MOYEN doit être le principe commun à l'électricité négative et à l'électricité positive. Marchez à la découverte des preuves qui établiront ces deux vérités, vous aurez la raison suprême de tous les effets de la nature. Oh! monsieur, quand on porte là," dit-il en se frappant le front, "le dernier mot de la création, en pressentant l'Absolu, est-ce vivre que d'être entraîné dans le mouvement de ce ramas d'hommes qui se ruent à l'heure fixe les uns sur les autres sans savoir ce qu'ils font." (717)

"A substance common to all created things, modified by a single force, such is the precise and clear position of the problem presented by the Absolute, a problem which seemed to me *seekable*. There you will find the mysterious Ternary, before which mankind has knelt in all ages: original matter, the cause, the result. You will find the terrible number Three in everything human, it dominates religions, sciences, laws. . . . You are a pupil of Lavoisier, you are rich and master of your time, so that I can properly confide to you my conjectures. This is the result to which my own private experiments have caused me to look forward. The ONE SUBSTANCE must be a principle common to the three gases and carbon. The MEDIUM must be the principle common to positive electricity and negative electricity. Proceed to the discovery of the proofs which will establish these two truths, and you will possess the supreme secret of all the results produced by nature. Oh monsieur," he said, striking his forehead, "when one carries *here* the last word of creation, feeling a conviction of the existence of the *Absolute,* can one call it living to be carried hither and thither in the rush of this multitude of men, who push and jostle one another at fixed times of the day without knowing what they are doing?" [104, trans. modified]

The Absolute consists of *"deux verités"* ["two truths"]: it is a material "substance," as Balthazar would have it, and a dynamic "medium," as Balzac would agree. But since every articulation *of* the Absolute, which is known as *"le dernier mot de la création"* ["the last word of creation"], must speak through the word, that is, through itself, it cannot reach a position outside itself from which to become the detached object of articulation.

As Wierzchownia states, the Absolute offers a *"position;"* its meaning, therefore, derives from its differential relation to other elements. It is *cherchable,* seekable, but since there is no single point where meaning accumulates, the Absolute is at best an endpoint orienting the search: *"Le mystérieux Ternaire dont on s'occupe depuis un temps immémorial, ne se trouvera point dans les analyses actuelles qui manquent de direction vers un point fixe"* (716) ["The mysterious Ternary, which has occupied men's minds from time immemorial, will not be found in analyses conducted according to present methods, which lack direction toward a fixed point," 102]. In this sentence *point* signifies both a stable self-identity, *un point fixe,* and the displacement or negation of meaning, *ne se trouvera point.* The use of the word *point* to signify two contradictory things underscores the manner in which the meaning of the Absolute, or absolute meaning, is distributed across points and hence can never be arrested at any one, self-identical position on the signifying chain.

Wierzchownia's descriptions of the Absolute continually play upon the dual understanding of the Absolute as semiotic form and as substance. For example, he says the following about the Absolute, or "great Ternary": *"Tous les grands chercheurs de causes occultes avaient pour mot d'ordre le Trismégiste, qui veut dire le grand Ternaire"* (718) ["All the great seekers for hidden causes had for their shibboleth *Trismegistus,* which means the great Ternary," 105, trans. modified]. The shibboleth [*mot d'ordre*] of the seekers of hidden causes, which is literally a "word of order," implicitly bespeaks the linguistic nature of the Absolute, which is both signified by the great Ternary and literally motivated by a desire to speak—*veut dire*—it. The Absolute, we could say, is identical to the differential structure of language that subtends the opposition between subject and object. It both structurally enables identity, including its own, to be demarcated or named and yet "itself" defies the logic of identity.[16] Thus, to find the Absolute would be to experience the dissolution of identity that paradoxically defines it. No wonder, then, that the name of the affliction that renders it impossible to utter the Absolute as a discrete and stable object of discourse—*Trisme,* or lockjaw—is inscribed into its own signifier: *Trismegistus.*

While *"la matérialité la plus exquise est empreinte dans toutes les habitudes flamandes"* (659) ["the most exquisite materiality is imprinted upon all the Flemish habits," 7, trans. modified], Balthazar is oblivious to all materiality, including that of discourse. I, on the other hand, have based the above reading of Wierzchownia's soliloquy upon the "materiality" of his discourse, that is, on its differential or "absolute" structure. I have traced a problem inherent in the Absolute as Wierzchownia describes it, namely, the way in which it cannot be apprehended as a stable object of analysis. Insofar as the Absolute *is* language, it cannot be its own subject and object. But in order to find *this* meaning in Wierzchownia's words, I have assumed that meaning coalesces in one place, in the material signifiers of Wierzchownia's discourse, and to do so I have had to interrupt the chain in which these signifiers are situated. If I have turned a dynamic process into a product, collapsed sign into referent, the text will allow for no such *coup.* A crucial piece of information disclosed by Balthazar at the beginning of his discussion with Wierzchownia subverts the reliability of the signifiers themselves: Balthazar prefaces his account by remarking, *"Il me dit confidentiellement et à voix basse de solennelles paroles dont, aujourd'hui, le sens général est seul resté dans ma mémoire"* (715) ["He talked with me in an undertone, confidentially and in solemn words, of which the general sense only has remained in my memory," 10, trans. modified]. Since Balthazar is an unreliable reporter—he cannot remember the precise words of his interlocutor—it is impossible to know whether I have analyzed Wierzchownia's comments or an inaccurate version of them. The truth of my own reading, based as it is upon words of questionable reliability, must itself remain undecidable.

Strangely enough, despite Balthazar's avowed memory lapse, the narrative he relates is still structured like a quoted dialogue; the use of this format suggests that there is no way around the structure of discourse as the place of meaning. This place, however, is paradoxically no place at all, but rather, as the meaning of the quoted text has suggested, a series of displacements. To the extent that the narrative retains the form of direct quotation and even compels Balthazar to do the same, it appears implicitly to diverge from and even rebuke Balthazar's inattention to language. I would suggest that Joséphine's criticism of Balthazar, that he is wrong in form, implies that Balthazar does not recognize that identity is not a question of essence but of form, of differentiation through form. Balthazar mistakes Wierzchownia's description of the Absolute for an object that can be found rather than understanding it as the linguistic grounds upon which subject and object are delimited.

Wierzchownia literally embodies the notion that identity is a linguistic effect. His power derives from the fact that his soul embodies discourse: Joséphine recalls Wierzchownia thus: *"Je me suis souvent impatientée de ce que ma mémoire me fit si souvent revoir ses deux yeux semblables à deux langues de feu"* (714) ["I have often lost patience with myself because my memory so often brings before me those two eyes of his, like tongues of flame," 99]. Given that Wierzchownia's identity is linguistic—the eyes reveal his essence as language—it is not surprising that the source of Balthazar's inspiration lies in a self that is not stable. Wierzchownia states:

> Mon corps va, vient, agit, se trouve au milieu du fer, des canons, des hommes, traverse l'Europe au gré d'une puissance à laquelle j'obéis en la méprisant. Mon âme n'a nulle conscience de ces actes, elle reste fixe, plongée dans une idée, engourdie par cette idée, la recherche de l'Absolu. (717)

> My body goes and comes, acts, finds itself in the midst of guns and troops and fire, travels from one end of Europe to the other

at the dictates of a power which I obey while I despise it. My mind is unconscious of my acts, it remains absorbed by one fixed idea, benumbed by that idea, the Search for the Absolute. [104–5]

As Wierzchownia acknowledges, he is subject to the effects of a destabilizing force as he searches for the Absolute: his body and mind function independently. In Balthazar's case, the precise connection between the absence of a unified self and the quest for a discrete object becomes unmistakable: he attempts to consolidate his identity through his quest for the Absolute. He sees himself as literally selfless: *"Il n'y rien de personnel . . . en moi"* (781) ["There is nothing personal in me," 215, trans. modified], he states, and he consistently employs the rhetoric of self-constitution when commenting on his scientific progress. In his moments of rapture, he conveys his desire to find an exclusive and executive self, a *"seul moi,"* that would not share itself with the other; perched on the threshold of an experiment, he cries, *"Songe donc que si moi, moi le premier, si je trouve, si je trouve, si je trouve!"* (720) ["Just think if I, I the first, if I find — if I find — if I find!" 109, trans. modified]. When Balthazar returns from the exile imposed upon him by Marguerite, Lemulquinier, who had accompanied his master, enters the abandoned laboratory only to find that a diamond has been produced in their absence. Balthazar reacts angrily over the fact that he was not *"le premier"* to enter the laboratory: *"Le chimiste, qui avait tout oublié, jeta un regard sur le vieux Flamand, et ce regard ne pouvait se traduire que par ces mots: 'Tu es allé le premier au laboratoire!'"* (822) ["The chemist, who had forgotten everything, looked at the old Fleming, and that glance could be translated only by these words: '*You went to the laboratory first!*'" 286].

Balthazar's search leads at best to his exclusion and at worst to his destruction. At times Balthazar makes the self-consuming nature of his project explicit: *"Je me consume en efforts gigantesques"* ["I am consuming myself in superhuman efforts"], he says (781) [215]. Referring to himself in the third person he implores Joséphine, *"Sois indulgente pour un homme qui n'a jamais cessé de penser à toi, dont les travaux sont tout pleins de toi, de nous"* (700) ["Be indulgent to a man who has never ceased to think of you, whose labors are all filled with you, with us," 76]. His use of language here is symptomatic: he cannot seem to find the place of the first person pronoun in the signifying chain, because he sees identity as consisting of an unchanging essence rather than of a series of shifting linguistic positions.

Balthazar's search for the self takes the form of a search for a series of concrete but exchangeable objects that his "mania" alternately cathects. By considering two of the objects he pursues in addition to pursuing the Absolute, we can learn more about the role that his search for the Absolute plays in the formation of a stable identity. Early in the novel we learn that Balthazar inherited from his father a valuable collection of tulips. The significance of these flowers resides in their symbolic equivalence with Joséphine.

> La passion de Balthazar Claës pour sa femme . . . semblait, comme il le faisait observer lui-même, employer sa constance innée dans la culture du bonheur qui valait bien celle des tulipes vers laquelle il penchait dès son enfance, et le dispensait d'avoir sa manie comme chacun de ses ancêtres avait eu la sienne. (685)

> Balthazar Claes's passion for his wife . . . seemed, as he himself remarked, to employ its inborn constancy in cultivating happiness, which was quite as well worth while as the cultivation of tulips, toward which he had been inclined from his childhood, and relieved him from the necessity of having his mania, as each of his ancestors had had. [50]

The name Balthazar gives to a particular hybrid of his tulips establishes a further connection between Joséphine and the flower. Balthazar has arranged the tulips in pots in the garden. At the apex of one of these arrangements *"s'élevait une tulipe Gueule-de-dragon que Balthazar possédait seul. Cette fleur [était] nommée* tulipa Claësiana" (710) ["was a *gueule-de-dragon* tulip of which Balthazar owned the only specimens. It was called *Tulipa Claësiana*," 91]. The editor of the novel remarks that according to the editorial gloss in the *Dictionnaire classique d'histoire naturelle* published in 1830, this tulip is also referred to as a *tulipe flamande*. The name of the tulip is a variation on the "Tulipa clusiana," which means *"tulipe de l'Ecluse"* (632). Since Joséphine is the dominant Flemish female Claës, or *Claësiana*, the French "Claësiana" flower is a symbol of Joséphine. As such, Emmanuel's reaction to the flowers reveals something about his reaction to Joséphine as well. He says:

> Mademoiselle, c'est de belles fleurs, mais pour les aimer, il faut sans doute en avoir le goût, savoir en apprécier les beautés. Ces fleurs m'éblouissent. L'habitude du travail . . . me fait sans doute préférer ce qui est doux à la vue. . . . Peut-être est-ce pour cela que je préfère une pâquerette sur laquelle tout le monde passe. (743-44)

They are beautiful flowers, mademoiselle, but in order to love them, one must have the taste for them, must be able to appreciate their beauties. They dazzle me. The habit of work . . . doubtless leads me to prefer those which are softer to the eye. . . . Perhaps that is why I prefer a field-daisy over which everybody walks. [148–49]

The tulips are visually harsh, even blinding—*éblouissantes*—and eminently inaccessible, in contrast to the daisies over which everyone walks. The name of the flower matches this optic aggressiveness: *gueule-de-dragon* literally means "mouth of a dragon."

The connection between Joséphine and the tulips is strengthened by the fact that the tulips reappear in a scene in which they are metonymically linked to Joséphine and to the notion of an enclosure [*écluse*]. Although it is August (when tulips do not normally bloom), in Joséphine's bedroom, *"la fastueuse gaieté d'une femme triomphante éclatait dans les splendides couleurs des tulipes qui s'élevaient du long cou de gros vases en porcelaine chinoise"* (712) ["the ostentatious gaiety of a victorious woman burst forth in the gorgeous colors of the tulips which protruded from the long necks of corpulent Chinese vases," 96]. The following comment further underscores the bedroom's associative relation to the *écluse: "Longtemps avant que les moeurs anglaises n'eussent consacré la chambre d'une femme comme un lieu sacré, celle d'une Flamande était impénétrable"* (711–12) ["Long before English customs had consecrated a woman's bedroom as a holy place, the bedroom of a Flemish woman was impenetrable," 96].

The aggressiveness associated with the appearance and perception of the tulips reappears in the scenes of seduction between Balthazar and Joséphine. Joséphine is determined to woo Balthazar back from her rival, science; in order to exert her powers, she mobilizes the symbolic language of her body.

"Allons, tais-toi," dit-elle, "tu me ferais mourir de douleur. Oui, je ne supporterais pas, cher, de voir ma rivale jusques dans les transports de ton amour."

"Mais, ma chère vie, je ne pense qu'à toi, mes travaux sont la gloire de ma famille, tu es au fond de toutes mes espérances."

"Voyons, regarde-moi?"

Cette scène l'avait rendue belle comme une jeune femme, et de toute sa personne, son mari ne voyait que sa tête, au-dessus d'un nuage de mousselines et de dentelles.

"Oui, j'ai eu bien tort de te délaisser pour la Science. Maintenant, quand je retomberai dans mes préoccupations, eh bien, ma Pépita, tu m'y arracheras, je le veux."

Elle baissa les yeux et laissa prendre sa main, sa plus grande beauté, une main à la fois puissante et délicate.

"Mais, je veux plus encore," dit-elle.

"Tu es si délicieusement belle que tu peux tout obtenir."

"Je veux briser ton laboratoire et enchaîner ta Science," dit-elle en jetant du feu par les yeux.

"Hé bien, au diable la Chimie."

"Ce moment efface toutes mes douleurs," reprit-elle. "Maintenant, fais-moi souffrir si tu veux."

En entendant ce mot, les larmes gagnèrent Balthazar. (723)

"Hush! Hush! you will break my heart," she said. "No dear, I cannot endure to see my rival even in the transports of your love."

"But, my dear life, I am thinking only of you, my labors are the glory of my family, you are at the bottom of all my hopes."

"Look at me!"

That scene had made her as beautiful as a young woman, and of her whole person her husband saw naught but her face above a cloud of lace and muslin.

"Yes, I did very wrong to abandon you for science. Now, when I relapse into one of my fits of preoccupation, do you rouse me from it my Pépita; I want you to do it."

She lowered her eyes and let him take her hand, her greatest beauty, a hand at once strong and delicate.

"But I want something more," she said.

"You are so deliciously lovely that you can obtain everything."

"I want to destroy your laboratory and chain up your science," she said, her eyes flashing fire.

"Very well, to the devil with chemistry!"

"This moment wipes out all my sorrow," she rejoined. "Now make me suffer if you choose."

At those words, Balthazar could not restrain his tears. [114–15]

In this extraordinary scene, Balthazar's gaze is focused upon Joséphine's head, which is floating as if severed from her body. Joséphine's powers of attraction are converted first into her wish to destroy Balthazar's laboratory and then into her wish to suffer. As we will see, this dialectic of ambivalent desire, of alternate domination and subordination, plays itself out throughout the novel and reaches its final term in Joséphine's and Balthazar's respective deaths.

Joséphine's ability to transfix Balthazar is even more pronounced in the following passage:

> Parée de sa belle chevelure noire parfaitement lisse et qui retombait de chaque côté de son front comme deux ailes de corbeau, Mme Claës enveloppée d'un peignoir qui lui montait jusqu'au cou et que garnissait une longue pèlerine où bouillonnait la dentelle alla tirer la portière en tapisserie qui ne laissait parvenir aucun bruit du dehors. . . . Balthazar, un moment abîmé dans la contemplation de cette tête olivâtre qui se détachait sur ce fond gris en attirant et satisfaisant le regard, se leva pour prendre sa femme et la porta sur le canapé. C'était bien ce qu'elle voulait. (713)

> With her beautiful black hair, perfectly smooth, falling on each side of her face like the wings of a raven, Madame Claes, enveloped in a *peignoir* which extended to the neck and over which was a long pelerine flounced with lace, drew the tapestry portière, which excluded all sounds from without. . . . Balthazar, who had lost himself a moment in contemplation of that dark face which stood out against the gray background, attracting and satisfying the eye, rose, took his wife in his arms, and carried her to the couch. That was just what she wanted. [97–98]

The fascination Joséphine holds for Balthazar derives from the sight of her head, which, emerging from her *peignoir*, recalls another more explicitly unsettling story about a female head. I am referring to Freud's interpretation of the Medusa myth. Like the bedroom scene, the myth concerns the acting out of ambivalent desire. According to Freud, the male viewer, catching sight of the female genitals, becomes conscious of his own identity by perceiving sexual difference as a threat to the self. The story of Medusa thus aligns the constitution of male identity with the positioning of the self before an image of the other the self has constructed. If the scenario is to be effective, the male subject must repress knowledge of the subjective act of representation through which the other is perceived as different. Confronted with the threatening view of the other, the self arises, coming into the fullness of its feeling of identity by stiffening before the static representation of the other. In my earlier discussion of the primal scene in Freud's case history of the "Wolf Man," I noted that Freud identified the moment of the (male) ego's scarring, of its inception, with the displacement of an image of fragmentation onto the other. In renouncing his identification with the maternal position, the child understands sexual difference in metaphoric terms of totality and fragmentation (since the "wound" is the necessary and threatening precondition for intercourse with the father, its discovery leads the child to renounce his desire). This renunciation is only effective if the child represses consciousness of the function of representation, of its constitutive role in establishing difference (self/ other, masculine/feminine) in terms of a narcissistic image of wholeness and fragmentation. What the child sees he assumes exists in objective reality. The interpretative act through which he makes such an assumption, which entails the projection of his own vulnerability into a scene that must appear violent in comparison to his essential passivity, is repressed from the narrative he constructs for himself.

The belligerence of the Medusa, who turns men to stone, is particularly pertinent to the terms in which Joséphine expresses her own sexuality; above all she does not want to abdicate her *"puissance de femme"* ["power of woman"] (698) [74, trans. modified]. The aggressive connotations of this statement are echoed in the drive to dominate that motivates her comment to Balthazar, *"Moi seule, monsieur, dois être la source de vos plaisirs"* (714) ["I alone, monsieur, should be the source of all your pleasures," 99]. The image that captivates thus also captures the other: *"Ses yeux d'Espagnole fascinaient quand elle s'apercevait que Balthazar la trouvait belle en négligé"* (677) ["Her Spanish eyes were bewitchingly beautiful when she saw that Balthazar considered her lovely in négligé attire," 38]. A more precise translation of *fascinaient* would be "[they] beautifully bewitched," as Joséphine's own reaction to the reaction she inspires is in effect an action. Indeed, Joséphine's head displays the apotropaic qualities characteristic of the Medusa image: not only is it severed from her body, but its hair, arranged like the "wings of a raven" recalls the snakes on the Medusa head that reassure the viewer of the presence of the maternal phallus in the moment when its absence becomes identifiable.

Balthazar initially reacts to Joséphine by adopting the classical stance of the transfixed viewer *"abîmé dans la contemplation"* ["lost in contemplation"]. In light of the Medusa scenario, the phrase *"tu peux tout obtenir"* ["you can obtain everything"] acquires greater significance, since it is precisely the integrity of the self, *le tout* [wholeness], that is called into question when confronting the image of the castrating woman/mother, who possesses the power to obtain that *tout* from her male spectator. With the aggressivity of an identity threatened by the castrating power of the image, Balthazar, in another scene, mobilizes his energy in order to incorporate that "delicious" image before it obtains the *tout* of which it is desirous:

Il prit aussitôt Mme Claës dans ses bras, ouvrit la porte qui donnait sur la petite antichambre, et franchit si rapidement le vieil escalier de bois que la robe de sa femme ayant accroché une gueule des tarasques qui formaient les balustres, il en resta un lé entier arraché à grand bruit. Il donna, pour l'ouvrir, un coup de pied à la porte du vestibule commun à leurs appartements; mais il trouva la chambre de sa femme fermée. (699)

He at once took Madame Claes in his arms, opened the door leading into the small anteroom, and ascended the old wooden staircase so swiftly that his wife's dress, having caught on the jaw of one of the monsters which formed the balusters, a whole breadth was torn out with a great noise, and remained behind. He opened the door of the vestibule common to their apartments with a kick; but he found his wife's room locked. [75]

Balthazar's assistant discovers the damage caused by this scene. He tells Balthazar, *"Monsieur en emportant madame . . . a déchiré la robe, ce n'est qu'un méchant bout d'étoffe; mais il a brisé la mâchoire de cette figure, et je ne sais pas qui pourra la remettre. Voilà notre escalier déshonoré, cette rampe était si belle!"* (702) ["When Monsieur carried madame upstairs . . . he tore her dress; it is only a paltry bit of cloth, but it broke the jaw of that figure and I don't know who can mend it. So there's our staircase dishonored, that baluster was so fine!" 80, trans. modified]. Lemulquinier's assessment of the damage done to the staircase in terms of a feminine code of honor—it is a beautiful baluster that becomes *déshonoré*[17]—coupled with the sexually overdetermined structural configuration of the anteroom, steps, and vestibule and the aggressive motions of climbing and kicking lend this sequence a highly symbolic charge.[18] It is as if this moment of allegorical defloration reverses the distribution of authority between the powerful, Medusa-like Joséphine and the captive Balthazar. This reversal is further suggested by the breaking of the jaw of the decorative monster, whose patently oral focus suggests its emblematic relation to the images of incorporation associated with Joséphine (such as the *gueule-de-dragon*).

Lemulquinier's comments also reveal how the violence of Balthazar's desire for Joséphine is in fact the product of his desire to uncover the Absolute. While surveying the damaged staircase, Lemulquinier makes the connection between the scene of seduction and the quest for the Absolute: *"'Qu'arrive-t-il donc,' se dit Mulquinier, 'pour que ce ne soit pas un désastre? mon maître aurait-il trouvé l'absolu?'"* (702)

["'What the deuce has happened,' said Mulquinier to himself, 'that's no harm? Can it be that my master has found the *Absolute?*'" 80].

We have already noted that Joséphine relies upon her power to transfix Balthazar's gaze: *"Regarde-moi,"* she commands. The emphasis upon the visual perception as the locus of (violent) seduction is reinforced in the description of Joséphine's bedroom, which is decorated like a sanctuary and designed to guard the trophies of battle. The room is designed to muffle sound and thereby help to capture Balthazar's eye: *"les rideaux soigneusement tirés trahissaient un désir de solitude, une intention jalouse de garder les moindres sons de la parole, et d'enfermer là les regards de l'époux reconquis"* (712–13) ["the curtains, carefully drawn, betrayed a desire for solitude, a jealous purpose to keep to herself the slightest sound of the voice, and to confine within those walls the glances of her reconquered husband," 97].

The image of wholeness determines Joséphine's sense of identity, or rather, lack of it. She attempts to internalize the totalizing form of Balthazar's narcissistic representation of her. In so doing, she implicates herself in an intra- and intersubjective struggle for power that mirrors the double ambivalence characteristic of Balthazar's desire. The intersubjective aggressivity we have already tracked in Joséphine's relation to Balthazar is further legible in the oxymoronic description of her hand as *"à la fois puissante et délicate"* ["at once strong and delicate"] (723) [114], a phrase that captures the ambivalence of a beauty implicated in this intersubjective struggle for power. From the standpoint of intrasubjectivity, the appropriation of an image of the self organized around the poles of totality and fragmentation makes it necessary for Joséphine to banish whatever cannot be assimilated to those terms. This self-exclusion, or more precisely, the exclusion of all that does not conform to the totality of the image, explains why Joséphine's language and actions betray strong, if not explicit, intimations of her masochism. For example, after securing Balthazar's promise that he will abandon chemistry, she says, *"Maintentant, fais-moi souffrir si tu veux"* (723) ["Now, make me suffer if you choose," 115].

Joséphine does not recognize her own subjugation to forms of representation. Even her experience with books reinforces her masochism. Virtually illiterate, she is initiated into the domain of representation through a collection of works that espouse the very practice of self-denial in which she excels.

> Par une bizarrerie assez explicable chez une fille d'origine espagnole, Mme Claës était ignorante. Elle savait lire et écrire; mais

> jusqu'à l'âge de vingt ans, époque à laquelle ses parents la tirèrent du couvent, elle n'avait lu que des ouvrages ascétiques. (681)

> By an anomaly readily explained in a young woman of Spanish origin, Madame Claes was uneducated. She knew how to read and write, but, up to the age of twenty, when her parents took her from the convent, she had read none but ascetic works. [44]

If knowing how to read literature entails recognizing the difference between forms of fiction and the self, clearly Joséphine is a naive reader: she takes the ascetic works she reads as a model for her life; she relates to literature mimetically.

As a literal reader, Joséphine attempts to approximate the holistic form of the image; and yet, since the connection between the image and Joséphine's self is arbitrary, an intersubjective other must visually certify the connection. This explains why Joséphine's life depends upon a principle *"visiblement . . . en dehors d'elle"* ["visibly outside of her person"] (680) [43, trans. modified].[19] In order for the visual spectacle to appear convincing, Joséphine must masochistically repress whatever aspects of her self resist totalization. But try as she may to expel alterity from her self-representations, the resulting tableaux formally incorporate traces of self-division, as in the case of the seductive images of her severed head. The masochism of self-decapitation is a compensatory outgrowth of the symbolic death she must undergo in expelling alterity. Her death drive expresses itself more generally in her *"projets de suicide causés par un mot et dissipés par une intonation de voix"* (676) ["thoughts of suicide aroused by a word and dissipated by an inflection of the voice," 36].

The nickname Balthazar gives to Joséphine formalizes her identity as the circulating signifier of desire. *Pépita,* the diminutive of *Joséphine,* is a variation of *pépite,* which means nugget of gold. Her name therefore embodies the substance that has the dual status of being "one commodity among others . . . and at the same time *primus inter pares,* since it stands over all other commodities as that which represents their value of exchange in general, and thus allows for their circulation."[20] In addition, *Pépita* in German means hound's tooth, a kind of pattern or fabric.[21] This is interesting in light of Balthazar's family history:

> Les Van Claës furent jadis une des plus célèbres familles d'artisans auxquels les Pays-Bas durent, dans plusieurs productions, une suprématie commerciale qu'ils ont gardée. Pendant longtemps les

Claës furent dans la ville de Gand, de père en fils, les chefs de la puissante confrérie des Tisserands. (661)

The Van Claes were formerly one of the most illustrious families of artisans to whom the Low Countries owed the commercial supremacy in several products, which they have always retained. For a long time, the Claes were, generation after generation, leaders of the powerful guild of weavers in the city of Ghent. [11, trans. modified]

Indeed, it is as if Joséphine is yet another fabric woven on the looms of patriarchal desire. Consequently, she is preoccupied with images of sartorial wholeness; seamless fabric is of great importance to her.

And so, despite the violent promise of penetration intimated by the ripping of Joséphine's dress on the devouring jaw of the ornamental monster, Balthazar is stopped from moving beyond the image of wholeness enveloping Joséphine. Upon reaching the staircase landing, *"il trouva la chambre de sa femme fermée. Il posa doucement Joséphine sur un fauteuil en se disant: 'Mon Dieu, où est la clé?'"* (699) ["he found his wife's room locked. He placed Joséphine gently on an armchair, saying to himself, 'Great Heaven! where is the key?'" 75, trans. modified]. Although he finds the key, Joséphine still remains inaccessible. She prevents the seduction from occuring by insisting on repairing her dress immediately and also by urging Balthazar to change into clothing that is not filled with *"tous ces trous"* ["all these holes"] (701) [78]. Balthazar's literal and symbolic failure to penetrate beyond the image of his wife is reiterated as he leaves her room and cannot pass through the connecting door: *"Balthazar voulut passer dans sa chambre par la porte de communication, mais il avait oublié qu'elle était fermée de son côté. Il sortit par l'antichambre"* (701) ["Balthazar attempted to go to his own room through the door connecting it with his wife's; but he had forgotten that it was locked on his side. He went out through the anteroom," 78]. It is noteworthy that the door is locked from within Balthazar's room, for this suggests the ambivalence of Balthazar's desire; his aggressive pursuit of Joséphine is the obverse of his avoidance of her. Were he to penetrate the image to the "castration" behind it, his own fear of fragmentation would be confirmed. As such, the frustration of his desire *is* its fulfillment. This explains why not only Joséphine, but also he, is preoccupied with clothing, which intimates the existence of a totality. After Balthazar leaves Joséphine's bedroom, he meets Marguerite, who has come to help her mother dress. He says, *"Bonjour, mon enfant, tu es bien jolie aujourd'hui dans cette robe de mousseline, et avec cette ceinture rose"* (701) ["Good afternoon, my child! you are very pretty to-day in your muslin dress and with that pink belt!" 78–79]. Sensitive to the desire her father's words express, Marguerite in turn advises her mother, *"Oh! Mettez donc une autre ceinture, celle-ci est trop fanée* (701) [Oh! do put on another belt, this one is too faded," 79].

The motif of clothing is immediately displaced into the garden: *"Quand Marguerite fut sortie, Mme Claës jeta un coup d'oeil à ses enfants par les fenêtres de sa chambre qui donnaient sur le jardin, et les vit occupés à regarder un de ces insectes à ailes vertes, luisantes et tachetées d'or, vulgairement appelés des couturières"* (702) ["When Marguerite had gone, Madame Claes glanced at the children through her window which looked on the garden and saw them intently watching one of the shiny, gold-spangled, green-winged insects vulgarly called 'darning needles,'" 79]. The description contains three encoded allusions to Joséphine: the sewing implement used to repair holes, the wings like the wings of her hair, and the gold color like the gold of her name. In this moment of *mise-en-abyme,* Joséphine plays the role of voyeur observing a scene of spectatorship. The constellation allegorizes the medusan moments in the texts, enabling Joséphine to confront a scenario of her own desire and thereby to observe herself as the totalizing image of the other's desire, commanding the gaze of the other(s). The timeliness of this spectatorial moment, coming as it does after Joséphine's near exposure, confirms the reassuring effects of such moments of visual perception.

Joséphine's physical deformities throw light upon her moral assessment by her confessor, the Abbé de Solis, who is also crippled. Indeed, the Abbé himself is a spectacle of lameness:

> Il marchait difficilement, car, de ses deux jambes menues, l'une se terminait par un pied horriblement déformé, contenu dans une espèce de sac de velours qui l'obligeait à se servir d'une béquille. . . . Son dos voûté, son corps desséché offraient le spectacle d'une nature souffrante et frêle. (738)

> He walked with difficulty, for one of his slender legs ended in a horribly deformed foot, which he wore in a sort of bag of velvet, and which compelled him to use a crutch. . . . His bent back, his withered body, presented the spectacle of a frail and discarded frame. [141]

The Abbé's indifference to the cloaking of his physical handicap contrasts with Joséphine's desire to hide her deformities. She attempts, literally and figuratively, to recover the loss of self entailed in appropriation of an image of wholeness. She therefore compensates for her perceived lack or wound by becoming adept in techniques of dissimulation: she *"parut vouloir dissimuler . . . ses défauts corporels en appuyant la main sur une chaise, pour se traîner avec grâce"* (713) ["seemed to try to disguise her bodily infirmities . . . by resting her hand on a chair in order to walk gracefully," 98]. Light becomes her enemy: *"Malheureuse au grand jour, elle aurait été ravissante s'il lui avait été permis de ne vivre qu'à la nuit"* (677) ["Unhappy in broad daylight, she would have been ravishing if it had been possible for her to live only at night," 38, trans. modified].

When she cannot cloak herself in darkness, she relies upon a sartorial strategy:

> Eclairée par le désir de plaire constamment à l'homme qu'elle aimait, elle savait se vêtir admirablement sans que son élégance fût disparate avec ses deux vices de conformation. Son corsage ne péchait d'ailleurs que par les épaules, l'une étant sensiblement plus grosse que l'autre. (673)

> Enlightened by the desire to be always attractive to the man she loved, she was able to dress in admirable taste, while at the same time her costume was never incongruous with her two vices of conformity. Indeed, she had no physical defect above her waist except that one of her shoulders was perceptibly larger than the other. [30–31, trans. modified]

Joséphine's desire to cloak her deformities accounts for the Abbé's remark that she was *"presque sans péché"* ["almost without sin"] (750) [160]. Her "slight sin" might be that she unreflectively conforms to the image of femininity proffered to her, despite, or perhaps because of, the sacrifices entailed. This would explain the moral overtones of the description of her handicap as *"deux vices de conformation"* ["two vices of conformity"].

As in his attachment to the *gueule-de-dragons* and to Joséphine, Balthazar, in his quest for the Absolute, is seeking to consolidate his identity. He does this by construing intersubjective difference in phallic terms. He locates the "wound" in Joséphine, while simultaneously denying its existence, in order to preserve an image of himself as whole. Conversely, Joséphine, who accepts the terms Balthazar imposes, acts out the masochism that comes into play when the wounding of the self becomes the necessary precondition for its identification with an image of totality.

In light of the significance of wounding and deformity in the narrative of identity-constitution in *La Recherche,* we cannot help but question the authorial decision to depict Joséphine as crippled. Is there a difference between the narcissistic representations of the (feminine) other as fragmented or lacking and Balzac's representation of Joséphine as deformed? The scene in which Joséphine is introduced into the text provides the first indication of what is at stake in Balzac's depiction of Joséphine.

> En 1812, vers les derniers jours du mois d'août, un dimanche, après vêpres, une femme était assise dans sa bergère devant une des fenêtres du jardin. Les rayons du soleil tombaient alors obliquement sur la maison, la prenaient en écharpe, traversaient le parloir, expiraient en reflets bizarres sur les boiseries qui tapissaient les murs du côté de la cour, et enveloppaient cette femme dans la zone pourpre projetée par le rideau de damas drapé le long de la fenêtre. Un peintre médiocre qui dans ce moment aurait copié cette femme, eût certes produit une oeuvre saillante avec une tête si pleine de douleur et de mélancolie. La pose du corps et celle des pieds jetés en avant accusaient l'abattement d'une personne qui perd la conscience de son être physique dans la concentration de ses forces absorbées par une pensée fixe; elle en suivait les rayonnements dans l'avenir, comme souvent, au bord de la mer, on regarde un rayon de soleil qui perce les nuées et trace à l'horizon quelque bande lumineuse. Les mains de cette femme, rejetées par les bras de la bergère, pendaient en dehors, et la tête, comme trop lourde, reposait sur le dossier. Une robe de percale blanche très ample empêchait de bien juger les proportions, et le corsage était dissimulé sous les plis d'une écharpe croisée sur la poitrine et négligemment nouée. Quand même la lumière n'aurait pas mis en relief son visage qu'elle semblait se complaire à produire préférablement au reste de sa personne, il eût été impossible de ne pas s'en occuper alors exclusivement. (667)

One Sunday after vespers, in the latter part of August, 1812, a woman was sitting in her easy-chair at one of the garden windows. The sun's rays fell obliquely on the house, shone slantwise across the parlor, expired in fantastic reflections on the wainscoting which covered the wall on the courtyard side, and enveloped the woman in the zone of purple projected by the damask curtain hanging at the window. A mediocre painter who had copied that woman at that moment, would certainly have produced a striking picture, with a face so overflowing with sorrow and melancholy. The attitude of the body, as well as the position of the feet, which were thrust forward, indicated the prostrated condition of one who loses consciousness of her physical being in the concentration of her powers due to their being absorbed by a fixed thought; she followed its gleams into the future, as frequently, on the seashore, we gaze at a sunbeam which pierces the clouds and makes a band of light along the horizon. Her hands were hanging listlessly over the arms of the chair, and her head, as if it were too heavy, rested against the back. A white percale dress, very simply made, prevented one from forming an accurate idea of her proportions, and her bust was disguised beneath folds of a scarf crossed over her breast and carelessly tied. So that, even if the light had not shone full upon her face, which she seemed to prefer to show rather than the rest of her person, it would have been impossible not to give one's attention exclusively to it. [21–22, trans. modified]

The final part of this description is in some sense the most significant, because it focuses upon the central point of attraction in this tableau, Joséphine's imposing, captivating face. The placement of her face above the folds of a scarf and the mention of her percale dress anticipate the other scenes in the novel in which her head is depicted as floating above a cloud of fabric and set against a dark background. If those other scenes of symbolic decapitation highlight visual perception, it is not surprising that the trope of pictorial representation unmistakably dominates this scene as well: neither language nor sound nor movement animates this tableau; the narrative organizes itself around the interplay of light and form and renders Joséphine anonymous, if not inanimate. Her face, body, feet, hands, and head are as immobile and disparate as the lifeless objects around her. The extent of her mental absorption is figured through the incorporation of her body by light and shadow. The parts of her body that do remain visible are fractured and intercalated with the chair on which she is sitting; her hands and head could almost be appendages to the chair's arms and back.

The lack of technical proficiency implicit in the reference to the *"peintre médiocre"* suggests that the affective presence of the model would make pictorial replication an easy, almost automatic task even for a painter of inferior calibre. The negative connotations of *"médiocre"* might suggest as well that only second-rate painters would undertake the project of painting this portrait. And yet, if this is the case, why does Balzac defer to the authority of the second-rate painter in this crucial introductory scene? Why does he need the painter's (hypothetical) rendering of Joséphine? Stated differently, why does he distance himself from his own verbal representation of Joséphine by placing it under the sign of (mediocre) painting? Balzac accomplishes several goals through this narrative displacement. To begin with, he avoids ontologizing the image of woman as fragmented, by representing it as clearly the effect of (inferior) representation. Second, while the opening description suggests a medusan scenario—Joséphine's absorption elicits a specular reaction from her hypothetical viewer, who cannot take his eyes off her head—this scenario is softened or domesticated through its painterly rendering. There is no real viewer, and even if there were, the erotic, intersubjective aggressiveness that will pervade the later scenes is displaced here into an act of artistic production. The third and perhaps most important advantage of mediating the initial description of Joséphine through the figure of the mediocre painter concerns the proximity and distance it enables Balzac to assume in relation to this tableau: he can use it to launch his own narrative and at the same time dissociate himself from it. The tableau is a (negative) point of departure for him, the product of an unsatisfying pictorial perspective whose inferiority is assigned to and thereby contained by the figure of the painter.

The medusan moment, we recall, derives from the tendency to project a subjective reaction onto the object and then to naturalize this reaction by attributing its origin to the object itself. As Bernard Vannier notes, this process of unreflected projection is, for Balzac, indigenous to a certain mode of realism.

> A la limite, le sentiment de l'artiste semble se confondre avec celui du modèle et le signe se réduire à son référent . . . l'Idéal serait un contact *immédiat* avec le référent. . . . il s'agit bien d'une rature de l'oeuvre elle-même, d'un effacement du *faire* pour reprendre un terme cher à Balzac. Seul compte le modèle, l'original de l'oeuvre. L'illusion réaliste dissimule la production elle-même, c'est-à-dire la mise en oeuvre d'un certain vraisemblable.[22]

> In the end, the feeling of the artist seems to become indistinguishable from that of the model, and the sign seems to be reduced to its referent . . . the ideal would be *unmediated* contact with the referent. . . . it really amounts to an erasure of the work itself, of an effacement of the *doing,* to use a favorite term of Balzac's. Only the model counts, the original. The realist illusion dissimu-

lates production itself, which is to say the creation of a certain verisimilitude.

As the portrait of Joséphine reveals, this *"illusion réaliste"* is not without its sexual-political dimension; the violent effects of this illusion are manifest in the fragmentation of Joséphine's body and the medusan role in which she is cast. Balzac alludes to the relation between writing, woman, and violence when he observes, *"La femme et le papier sont deux choses blanches qui souffrent tout"* [Woman and paper are two white things that suffer everything].[23] By aligning Joséphine's introduction into the text with an unsatisfying—*médiocre*—pictorial perspective, Balzac distances himself from the realist tableau and sets up a model that his own narrative will use as a point of departure. He thereby gestures toward a concept of literary realism that is not synonymous with the visual or mimetic and implicitly suggests that representation is always informed by the desire and position of the viewer; every image bears the imprint of its painter. We can characterize the shift from mimesis to another mode of representation in terms of the objects being represented: mimesis aspires to a rendering of the object as it (ideally) exists, apart from the viewing subject, whereas the latter mode incorporates into the representation of the object the aspect of subjective perception. The mimetic mode would not register this subjective presence but rather attempt to dissimulate it.

The painterly moment in *La Recherche* belongs to a more extensive, if elliptical, meditation on pictorial representation running through the text. The motif of painting is first introduced shortly after the novel begins.

> Enfin, il est rare que la peinture des lieux où la vie s'écoule ne rappelle à chacun ou ses voeux trahis ou ses espérances en fleur. La comparasion entre un présent qui trompe les vouloirs secrets et l'avenir qui peut les réaliser est une source inépuisable de mélancolie ou de satisfactions douces. Aussi est-il presque impossible de ne pas être pris d'une espèce d'attendrissement à la peinture de la vie flamande, quand les accessoires en sont bien rendus. . . . Quelque prix que l'homme passionné puisse attacher aux tumultes des sentiments, il ne voit jamais sans émotion les images de cette nature sociale où les battements du coeur sont si bien réglés que les gens superficiels l'accusent de froideur. (658)

> Moreover, it seldom happens that a description of places where men have passed their lives does not remind each one who reads it either of his broken vows or his budding hopes. The comparison between a present which disappoints one's secret wishes and a future which may gratify them is an inexhaustible source of melancholy or of placid satisfaction. So it is that it is almost impossible to avoid a sort of emotion in the presence of a painting of Flemish life when its accessories are faithfully depicted. . . . Whatever value the passionate man may attach to the turmoil of sentiments, he never witnesses without emotion the images of that social nature where the pulsations of the heart are so carefully regulated that superficial people reproach it with coldness. [6–7]

Whereas the description of the tableau symbolically rendered by the brush of the painter emphasized the model's emotions, the above description of the *peinture des lieux* stresses the reaction of the spectator: Flemish painting stimulates the desire of the viewer and causes him to reflect upon his own unsatisfied hopes. More important, the images of fulfillment offered to the viewer are not of an unchanging essence but of social, and hence mutable, nature—*"les images de cette nature sociale"* ["the images of that social nature"].

The idea that Flemish realism concerns itself with that which is changing, and thus implicitly temporal, is even more explicit in the following passage:

> Ce pays, si nativement terne et dépourvu de poésie, se composa une vie originale et des moeurs caractéristiques, sans paraître entaché de servilité. L'Art y dépouilla toute idéalité pour reproduire uniquement la Forme. Aussi ne demandez à cette patrie de la poésie plastique ni la verve de la comédie, ni l'action dramatique, ni les jets hardis de l'épopée ou de l'ode, ni le génie musical; mais elle est fertile en découvertes, en discussions doctorales qui veulent le temps et la lampe. Tout y est frappé au coin de la jouissance temporelle. L'homme y voit exclusivement ce qui est, sa pensée se courbe si scrupuleusement à servir les besoins de la vie qu'en aucune oeuvre elle ne s'est élancée au-delà du monde réel. . . . rien donc ne se façonne à demi, ni les maisons, ni les meubles, ni la digue, ni la culture, ni la révolte. (660)

> That country, naturally so dull and devoid of poesy, shaped for itself an original mode of life and characteristic manners, without seeming to incur the reproach of servility. Art stripped off all

idealism to reproduce form alone. Do not look to that country, therefore, for poetry in plaster, nor for vigorous comedy, nor for dramatic action, nor for the bold flights of the epic or the ode, nor for musical genius; but it is fertile in discoveries, in learned discussions which require both time and the midnight oil. Everything there bears the stamp of temporal enjoyment. Men see exclusively what *is,* their mind adapts its attitude so scrupulously to promote the necessities of life, that it has never overstepped the limits of the real world in any work. . . . nothing is done by halves, neither their houses nor their furniture, nor their dikes nor their farming, nor their revolutions. [9–10]

The passage addresses the question of Flemish originality in the context of aesthetic production. The originality of the country consists in its ability to reproduce form. A distinct oddness concerning the concept of aesthetic form begins to emerge here when we consider it in relation to the *idéalité* ["idealism"] against which it defines itself. Given that the kinds of art mentioned characteristically retain a sense of dynamism, motion, and vitality associated with movement, it would seem to follow that Flemish art, by contrast, would be identified with permanence and stasis. And yet, Flemish aesthetic form also bears the imprint of a temporality, a *"jouissance temporelle"* ["temporal enjoyment"]. What is distinct about this latter temporality, however, is its implication in a concept of subjective pleasure. The indissolubility of Flemish aesthetic form and a certain subjective influence is reinforced in the above passage by the mention of a second factor, namely, *"les besoins de la vie"* ["the necessities of life"]. These subjective determinations of Flemish art are particularly striking, because they are not opposed to objective art forms but rather commensurate to them: Flemish art focuses upon *"le monde réel"* ["the real world"], upon *"ce qui est"* ["what *is*"]. This is, in short, a realist aesthetic that insists upon the determinant presence of subjectivity in aesthetic forms. Considering that, in the novel, visual perception is the locus of desire and the medium of identity-constitution, it is no accident that the act of seeing—*"l'homme y voit"*—marks the intersection of pleasure, need, and objectivity. Nor is it surprising that the reference point of totalization, so dominant in visual representation, is also present in the final sentence of the passage, although dissimulated by the sentence's negative syntax: *"rien donc ne se façonne à demi, ni les maisons, ni les meubles, ni la digue, ni la culture, ni la révolte"* ["nothing is done by halves, neither their houses nor their furniture, nor their dikes nor their farming, nor their revolutions"].

If the Flemish pictorial realists represent the subjective determinations of images of the real, then Balzacian realism, in representing the constitutive role of representation, does the same. For Balzac, painting is not opposed to writing; the visual and the verbal are not antithetical modes of expression assigned to different projects. Balzac, too, creates a *"peinture des lieux"* ["description of places"] and justifies the need for his literary *"préparations didactiques"* ["didactic preparations"] (a phrase whose pedagogic connotations recall the *"discussions doctorales"* ["learned discussions"] of painting) by referring to the effects of Flemish painting upon the viewer.[24] In addition, the allusion to Flemish art as requiring *"le temps et la lampe"* ["time and the midnight oil"] recalls the literary practices of Balzac himself as embodied by Dante in *Les Proscrits: "En rentrant au logis, l'étranger s'enferma dans sa chambre, alluma sa lampe inspiratrice et se confia au terrible démon du travail, en demandant des mots au silence, des idées à la nuit"* ["On returning to the house, the stranger locked himself into his room, lighted his inspiring lamp, and abandoned himself to the demon of work, calling upon the silence for words, upon the night for ideas"].[25]

The difference between the work of the mediocre painter and the exemplary Flemish painter carries over into Balzac's text and is legible in the implicit distinction the narrator/author establishes between a conception of identity as essence and a conception of identity as a form or image contingent upon the viewer's structural position. The following passage exemplifies this difference:

> Dans la position particulière où se trouvait Mme Claës, toute femme aurait voulu rassembler autour d'elle les choses les plus élégantes; mais elle l'avait fait avec un goût exquis, sachant quelle influence l'aspect de ce qui nous entoure exerce sur les sentiments. Chez une jolie créature c'eût été du luxe, chez elle c'etait une nécessité. Elle avait compris la portée de ces mots: "On se fait jolie femme!" (712)

> In the peculiar position which Madame Claes occupied, any woman would have striven to collect around her the daintiest objects; but she had done it with exquisite taste, knowing what influence the aspect of our surroundings exerts upon the feelings. In a pretty creature, it would have been luxuriousness; in her case, it was a necessity. She realized the full meaning of the words: "A woman makes herself pretty!" [96]

In the bedroom are the makings, in the truest sense, of a woman. Although Joséphine believes that she must hide herself under a cloak of womanly amenities, the above passage reveals that "womanhood" is a *"position particulière"* ["peculiar position"] — gleaned from the maxim, *"on se fait jolie femme"* ["a woman makes herself pretty"]. Adopting the trappings of woman is thus an act of sexual and grammatical positioning whereby the *"on"* [one], through interpretation, becomes a gendered subject.

The difference, then, between the narrator's understanding of the process of identity-constitution and Joséphine and Balthazar's understanding of it is that the narrator recognizes the representational nature of identity, while Balthazar and Joséphine do not. At the same time, the text reveals that such recognition is possible in fiction alone, for both Balthazar and Joséphine die when they discover that identity is not a question of stable essence but an effect of positioning.

Balthazar's death is the culmination of an illness that is itself brought on by a specific incident. Old and decrepit at the end of his life, Balthazar has again abandoned himself to his pursuit of the Absolute and, in his daughter's absence, liquidated part of the fortune she had reamassed. On a morning walk he and Lemulquinier are passed by a group of school children who stop to deride them:

> "Tiens, vois-tu celui-là dont la tête est comme un genou?"
> "Oui."
> "Eh bien, il est savant de naissance."
> "Papa dit qu'il fait de l'or," dit un autre.
> "Par où? C'est-y par là ou par ici?" ajouta un troisième en montrant d'un geste goguenard cette partie d'eux-mêmes que les écoliers se montrent si souvent en signe de mépris. . . .
> "A la chienlit!" crièrent les enfants. (831–32)

> "I say, do you see that one with a head just like a knee?"
> "Yes."
> "Well, he's a scholar by birth."
> "Papa says he makes gold," said another.
> "Where? There or here?" added a third, indicating slyly that part of his body to which school boys so often point in token of contempt. . . .
> "Listen to the jack-pudding!" cried the children. [300–301]

The children proceed to provoke the men, covering them with mud and eliciting a peculiar phenomenon: *"Balthazar, dont les facultés avaient été jusqu'alors conservées par la chasteté naturelle aux savants chez qui la préoccupation d'une découverte anéantit les passions, devina, par un phénomène d'intussusception, le secret de cette scène"* (832) ["Balthazar, whose faculties had been preserved thus far by the purity natural to great scientists, who are so engrossed by their preoccupation that their passions are deadened, divined, by the phenomenon of intussusception, the secret significance of that scene," 302]. We learn that the precise significance of the scene lies in the children's discovery of Balthazar's terrible secret: Balthazar *"se débattait moins contre la mort que contre l'effroi de voir ses enfants pénétrant le secret de sa misère"* (833) ["[was] struggling not so much against death as against the horror of having his children discover the secret of his misery," 302, trans. modified].

The children's actions and reactions both point to and spell out Balthazar's secret. The analogy the first child draws between Balthazar's head and knee derives its derogatory force from the confusion or collapse of difference it orchestrates between two parts of the body, metonymically, between body and mind. The gesture of the third child replicates this confusion in a sexual register and thereby further specifies it. By pointing to *là* [there] and *ici* [here] while inquiring into the site of the production of gold, the child in effect rehearses the juvenile, "cloacal" theory of sexual reproduction according to which feces, gold or money, and children, as well as the acts through which they are produced, are symbolically interchangeable. In the novel, this associative chain is reinforced by the throwing of the mud, the properties of which contribute to the scatological overtones of the scenario, and by the children's final exclamation, *"à la chienlit."* The editorial gloss on this expression indicates that it is a cry uttered during carnival by children as they run down the streets with their masks (1694). The gloss omits the earliest and literal meaning of *chienlit*, namely, one who *chie au lit* [defecates in bed].[26] According to the cloacal theory of reproduction, babies and feces are detachable parts of the body that can be used like money (or gold) as gifts. Freud identifies this childhood theory with the pregenital phase of sexual organization that precedes the ego's investment in an image of the body as a whole.[27] By symbolically recapitulating a stage prior to the resolution of the Oedipus complex, the children's actions reveal that Balthazar's horrible secret concerns his lack of sexual determination, that is, of genital sexuality.

And yet, as Balthazar's following reaction suggests, the absence of genital sexuality is more precisely a *loss* of sexual identity: *"Son corps décrépit ne soutint pas la réaction affreuse qu'il éprouva dans la haute région de ses sentiments, il tomba frappé d'une attaque de paralysie entre les bras de Lemulquinier"* (832) ["His decrepit body could not withstand the terrible reaction which he underwent in his sentiments, he fell, stricken with paralysis, into the arms of Lemulquinier," 302]. Though for the most part the paralysis subsides, it remains in the instrument of articulation: *"Quand la paralysie eut cessé par degrés, elle resta sur la langue qu'elle avait spécialement affectée"* (833) ["After it had gradually left the other parts of his body, it continued to affect his tongue, which it had attacked with especial severity," 303]. The anxiety that the discovery generates is manifest in Balthazar's paralysis, which is reminiscent of the apotropaic stiffening that befalls the spectator who is confronted with the Medusa. Moreover, the suspension of Balthazar's powers of speech suggests that he has regressed to a condition analogous to that which precedes the decline of the Oedipus complex, that is, before symbolic representation (understood here as linguistic articulation) organizes sexuality around the narcissistic poles of (genital) totality or fragmentation. Balthazar's swoon into Lemulquinier's arms, as if in a comatose embrace, reinforces repeated allusions to the men's homoeroticism and contributes further to the sense of Balthazar's destabilized sexuality.

Balthazar's death recapitulates the question of his sexual instability in terms of the constitutive representational underpinnings of identity.

> Le vieillard se livrait à des mouvements d'une force incroyable pour secouer les liens de la paralysie; il désirait parler et remuait la langue sans pouvoir former de sons; ses yeux flamboyants projetaient des pensées; ses traits contractés exprimaient des douleurs inouïes; ses doigts s'agitaient désespérément, il suait à grosses gouttes. . . . Emmanuel . . . s'empressa de décacheter le journal pour voir si cette lecture ferait diversion aux crises intérieures qui travaillaient Balthazar. En dépliant la feuille, il vit ces mots, *découverte de l'absolu*, qui le frappèrent vivement, et il lut à Marguerite un article où il était parlé d'un procès relatif à la vente qu'un célèbre mathématicien polonais avait faite de l'Absolu. Quoique Emmanuel lût tout bas l'annonce du fait à Marguerite qui le pria de passer l'article, Balthazar avait entendu.
>
> Tout à coup le moribond se dressa sur ses deux poings, jeta sur ses enfants effrayés un regard qui les atteignit tous comme un éclair . . . il leva une main crispée par la rage et cria d'une voix éclatante le fameux mot d'Archimède: EUREKA! *(j'ai trouvé).* Il retomba sur son lit en rendant le son lourd d'un corps inerte, il mourut en poussant un gémissement affreux, et ses yeux con-

vulsés exprimèrent jusqu'au moment où le médecin les ferma le regret de n'avoir pu léguer à la Science le mot d'une énigme dont le voile s'était tardivement déchiré sous les doigts décharnés de la Mort. (834–35)

The old man struggled with incredible strength to shake off the bonds of paralysis; he tried to speak, and moved his tongue, but could make no sound; his flaming eyes shot forth thoughts; his distorted features expressed the most intense agony; his fingers moved convulsively; the sweat stood in beads on his forehead. . . . Emmanuel . . . made haste to open the newspaper, to see if by reading he could not relieve the internal agony by which Balthazar was afflicted. As he unfolded the paper, he saw the words: *Discovery of the Absolute,* which startled him, and he read to Marguerite an article concerning a lawsuit relative to the sale of the Absolute, by a celebrated Polish mathematician. Though Emmanuel read the heading in a low voice to Marguerite, who requested him to omit the article, Balthazar overheard.

Suddenly the dying man raised himself on his hands, cast upon his terrified children a glance that blinded them like a flash of lightning . . . he raised one hand, clenched in fury, and cried in a voice of thunder the famous word of Archimedes: EUREKA!—*I have found!*—He fell back upon his bed with the dull thud of a lifeless body; he died uttering a ghastly groan, and his distorted eyes expressed, up to the moment that the physician closed them, his regret that he had not been able to bequeath to science the word of an enigma from which the veil was torn away too late by the fleshless fingers of death. [305–6, trans. modified]

The scene described above represents not one but two discoveries. The first Absolute, a commodity that is under litigious dispute, provides a jarring contrast to the second Absolute. The ambiguity of the verb *entendre,* which means both to overhear and to understand, encourages us to relate the two discoveries causally. It is as if Balthazar's sublime discovery is set in motion by the news of the first travesty of discovery. While consistent with the aura of tragedy that has surrounded his story, this reading is complicated by one narrative detail. We learn that Balthazar cannot hear well: *"Si les yeux de Balthazar avaient conservé cette lucidité sublime . . . le sens de l'ouïe s'était affaibli chez lui"* (830) ["Although Balthazar's eyes had retained that sublime lucidity . . . his sense of hearing was weakened," 299]. Given this impairment, the question arises as to whether Balthazar could have heard Emmanuel when he softly read aloud the headline. If we assume that Balthazar did not hear, then his discovery cannot be understood as the sublime counterpart to the more prosaic discovery reported in the newspaper.

What, then, does happen at the end of Balthazar's life? If we read *"Balthazar avait entendu"* as "Balthazar had *understood,"* rather than "heard," we can speculate in a different direction. Perhaps Balthazar has come to understand something, and it is this understanding that kills him. For it was only by *misunderstanding* Wierzchownia's description of the Absolute as linguistic process that he could proceed with his search for a discrete and stable object. Now, Balthazar finally discovers the linguistic nature of the Absolute: it is *"le mot d'une énigme"* ["the word of an enigma"]. Given my reading of his search as the quest for a stable subjectivity, we could conclude that when Balthazar discovers the Absolute, he realizes that his own self is not an essence but an unstable effect of the dispersive, differential structure of language, which is precisely what Wierzchownia had been telling him.

And yet, Balthazar never indicates that he has actually found something. The narrator parenthetically glosses Balthazar's *"Eureka"* as *"j'ai trouvé,"* thereby retaining the logic of the search with its assumption that one always finds an object. But Balthazar himself never reveals what, if anything, his search has uncovered. Nor does he ever directly state that he has discovered *"le mot d'une énigme"* ["the word of an enigma"]. This is the narrator's interpretation of Balthazar's facial expression. All we can conclude with any certainty, then, is that the narrator understands Balthazar's death as being causally related to his discovery of the Absolute. The language of the interpretation even strengthens the uncertainty surrounding the significance of Balthazar's death in the moment that it attempts to assign it meaning. The narrator describes the act of revelation as fleshless fingers of death tearing aside a veil to disclose the Absolute. This image reintroduces associations that strain against a reading of Balthazar's death as being coterminous with a discovery. Specifically, the image of the veil recalls the artful veiling that Joséphine practiced to stimulate, frustrate, and thereby perpetuate Balthazar's desire. Guarantor of an eclipsed presence, the veil as linguistic figure construes the discovered, or uncovered, Absolute as a version of the maternal phallus, which is itself yet another figure of projected narcissistic wholeness that reduces the other to a version of the same. The figure of the veil thereby reinscribes narcissistic associations of fetishism into the very scene that supposedly signifies Balthazar's newfound, if fatal, understanding of identity in nonessentializing terms.[28] All we can safely conclude from this final scene is that it testifies to the narrator's desire to see Balthazar's death as coinciding with the discovery of the Absolute.

Like Balthazar, Joséphine dies uttering a single word—*Marguerite,* the name of her daughter. This structural parallel suggests that her death engages similar issues of interpretation and narratorial desire. Marguerite's gloss on her own name provides the first indication of what is at stake in such an utterance: *"La perle est, dit-on, le fruit d'une maladie"* (788) ["The pearl, they say, is the result of a disease," 225]. Marguerite's remark is in response to Balthazar's comment that, according to Laurence Sterne, *"Margarita veut dire une perle"* (788) ["Margarita means a pearl," 225]. Whereas Balthazar intends to draw Marguerite's attention to one of his (and Balzac's) literary favorites, Marguerite chooses to emphasize the pathological nature of the pearl's, and by analogy her own, genealogy. Marguerite is the offspring of a disease. And while her parental lineage is, of course, dual, another meaning of "Marguerite," which Emmanuel provides, establishes the priority of the matrilineal connection: "Marguerite," he observes, is a name for the daisy. Emmanuel discloses the second meaning of Marguerite's name when he and Marguerite are in the Claës garden admiring Balthazar's collection of tulips. His comment, which is intended to emphasize the difference between tulips and daisies, simultaneously bespeaks the difference between Marguerite and her mother, of whom the tulips are symbolic.

> L'habitude du travail . . . me fait sans doute préférer ce qui est doux à la vue. . . . Peut-être est-ce pour cela que je préfère une pâquerette sur laquelle tout le monde passe. (743–44)

> The habit of work . . . doubtless leads me to prefer those which are softer to the eye. . . . Perhaps that is why I prefer a field-daisy over which everybody walks. [148–49]

The daisies are soft to the eye and accessible. They present a sharp contrast to the beautiful but blinding tulips. Such a contrast enables us to understand why Joséphine, on her deathbed, cries out the name of her daughter. The miraculousness of Marguerite's restorative powers—she fully reacquires the Claës family fortunes, pays all of her father's debts, refurbishes the rooms he had stripped, and even has an indirect role in finding spouses for her brother and sister—suggests that she is an ideal figure whose identity exists in sharp counterpoint to Joséphine's and whose name implicitly alludes to such an opposition.

In contrast to Joséphine, Marguerite cannot be confined to a stable role; at any given moment her identity depends upon the position she occupies with respect to others. This is exemplified in the criss-crossing of conventionally masculine and feminine attributes between Emmanuel and Marguerite. Whereas she, as head of the household, fills the roles of father and husband, Emmanuel has the charm characteristic of a *"vierge"* ["maiden"] (739) [142] and displays *"mouvements féminins"* ["feminine movements"] (740) [143]. The following passage provides a further indication of Marguerite's sexual mobility. It describes Marguerite's accession to a position of social responsibility as the acquisition of a sexual identity that is suggestively masculine: *"Enfin elle acheva son éducation virile, elle se préparait évidemment à exécuter le plan qu'elle méditait si son père succombait encore une fois dans son duel avec l'Inconnu (X)"* (794) ["At last, she finished her virile education, she was evidently preparing to execute the plan she had formed, in the event that her father succumbed once more in his duel with the Unknown (X)," 237, trans. modified]. The explicit masculinity of Marguerite's "virile" education calls attention to Marguerite's ability to transgress borders of gender. One might even argue that the reference to Balthazar's search for the Absolute as a duel with the *"Inconnu (X)"* in the context of a discussion of Marguerite establishes a connection between Marguerite and the Unknown. As such, the grapheme X could be read as marking a place of gender distinction that might equally be filled by the *e* of femininity or left blank to signify the masculine gender. Balthazar's search for the unknown would thus be the search for the definitive mark of sexual identity, which, precisely because it depends upon a differential grammar, can never be stabilized. This grammatical dependence also explains why the search for the Absolute is a ceaseless *recherche,* that is, a textual quest. The textuality of the quest is supported by the fact that Marguerite's fluid sexual identity corresponds to her command of the constitutive, though unstable, power of representation. Unlike her mother, who cannot comprehend how the happiness of a whole family can be destroyed by *"une seule phrase et par un seul mot"* (718) ["a single sentence, a single phrase," 106], Marguerite knows the power of the word: *"tout est dit"* ["everything is said"] (779) [212], she says, implying as well that the whole—*"tout"*—is linguistic.

We can now understand why Balthazar and Joséphine both die uttering a final word. These words bespeak an understanding of identity as pure movement. Marguerite's fluid identity depends upon her particular relation to the other and upon the shifting grammatical positions she assumes. In this respect she subverts the concept of identity that privileges stability and stasis. While the logic of the novel's symbolism suggests that Marguerite embodies an ideal of identity as contingent and relational, it is important to note that there is no indication that Joséphine recognizes this about Marguerite. Like Balthazar's cry, "Eureka," Joséphine's cry, "Marguerite" signifies a moment of revelation, not necessarily of revelation for Joséphine but for the reader, who acquires insight into the narrator's desire to see Joséphine's death as signifying her recognition of the ideal her daughter represents. We could even say that the text marks the impossibility of the characters' acquiring such epiphanic insight; to utter the Absolute, *"le mot d'une énigme,"* is both to have the last word and to be had by that word, to enunciate the enigma of the word and be dispersed by it.

While the double deaths that punctuate *La Recherche* lend it an aura of sublimity, the text also intimates the possibility that the reader is being duped, and it thereby satirically mitigates this sublimity. According to Fargeaud's documentation, a "merchant of the Absolute" sold cloth in the Passage Colbert, and in Balzac's courtyard, scrawled on the walls, could be read, "Factory of the Absolute."[29] The final scene of the novel incorporates these mundane embodiments of the Absolute when it suggests that the Absolute is an object that can be bought and sold. What are we to make of these two incongruent ways of identifying the Absolute? And why, if the text is in some sense satirizing the search for the Absolute, must there be two victims, two deaths, the doubleness of which indicates a certain excess, not only in the characters' obsessions but in the authorial agency that exacts such severe penalties for these obsessions? This excess becomes even more troubling (because less contained) when we note the obvious overlap in the names of protagonist and author: both Balthazar and Balzac begin with "Bal" and contain a "za" in their final syllable.

In this novel, the narrator/author seldom addresses his audience directly. The occasions on which he does thus carry a certain weight, because they afford the opportunity to separate the authorial voice from that of the protagonist, who in part bears his name. By analyzing the most elaborated authorial commentary in the text, we may perhaps gain insight into the nature of the overlap between author and protagonist, and also into the reason why Balzac both mocks Balthazar and violently, irreversibly expels him from *La Comédie.*

The novel opens with an authorial diatribe against a particular mode of reading. Balzac protests against those *"personnes ignorantes et voraces qui voudraient des émotions sans en subir les principes générateurs, la fleur sans la graine, l'enfant sans la gestation"* (657) ["ignorant and greedy persons . . . who seek emotion without undergoing its generative principles, the flower without the seed, the child without gestation," 5]. But unlike those critics who look to contexts, Balzac refers the reader to a site within the text for the story's source or seed. He locates the *"principe générateur"* ["generative principle"] in the history and *"reliques domestiques"* ["domestic relics"] of nations and individuals (657) [5]. These sites and structures are linked to *"les événements de la vie humaine"* ["the events of human life"] (657) [5] with the rigor of a logical argument: *"De part et d'autre, tout se déduit, tout s'enchaîne. La cause fait deviner un effet, comme chaque effet permet de remonter à une cause. Le savant ressuscite ainsi jusqu'aux verrues des vieux âges"* (658) ["In both directions everything can be logically deducted, everything forms a link in the chain. Causes foreshadow effects, just as each effect enables us to go back to its cause. Thus the scholar re-creates even the little excrescences of bygone ages," 5–6]. Whereas the desire of *voraces,* or hungry, readers bespeaks the interiorizing, aggressive urge to incorporate the other that characterizes the narcissistic and mimetic rendering of identity in terms of totality or fragmentation (we need only think of the image of the *délicieuse* Joséphine who, according to Balthazar, could *tout obtenir*), the scholarly totality, Balzac suggests, issues from a process of logical deduction that is much more controlled and patient. Through his painstaking knowledge, the scholar establishes a chain of connections, a dynamic and temporal totality of causes and effects. But, given the ironic emphasis throughout the novel upon the inextricability of created totalities and narcissism, we must question Balzac's claim that his narrative totality is radically distinct from the negative kind of totality he identifies with the desire of his readers. Is there not, after all, something narcissistic about construing the role of scholar—which is of course what Balthazar claims to be as well—as one of a lifesaver who resuscitates [*ressuscite*] dead traces?

To answer this question, we will take the narrator's cue and examine the architecture and domestic relics that initiate this story. It becomes immediately apparent that the country's history of political and economic subjugation is told as an allegory of identity-constitution. The past of Flanders is characterized by an ongoing series of

> vicissitudes politiques qui les ont successivement soumises aux Bourguignons, aux Espagnols, aux Français, et qui les ont fait fraterniser avec les Allemands et les Hollandais. De l'Espagne, elles ont gardé le luxe des écarlates, les satins brillants, les tapisseries

à effet vigoureux, les plumes, les mandolines, et les formes courtoises. De Venise, elles ont eu, en échange de leurs toiles et de leurs dentelles, cette verrerie fantastique où le vin reluit et semble meilleur. De l'Autriche, elles ont conservé cette pesante diplomatie qui, suivant un dicton populaire, fait trois pas dans un boisseau. Le commerce avec les Indes y a versé les inventions grotesques de la Chine, et les merveilles du Japon. Cependant, malgré leur patience à tout amasser, à ne rien rendre, à tout supporter, les Flandres ne pouvaient guère être considerées que comme le magasin général de l'Europe, jusqu'au moment où la découverte du tabac souda par la fumée les traits épars de leur physionomie nationale. (659–60)

political vicissitudes, which subjected it successively to the Burgundians, the Spaniards, and the French, and compelled its people to make common cause with the Germans and the Dutch. From their Spanish associations they retained the rich shades of scarlet, glossy satins, showy carpets, feathers, mandolins, and courteous manners. From Venice they received, in exchange for their linen and laces, the fanciful glassware wherein the wine sparkles and seems to taste better. From Austria they derived that ponderous diplomacy which, according to a popular saying, takes three steps in a bushel measure. Trade with the Indies caused an influx of the grotesque inventions of China and the marvels of Japan. And yet, despite its patience in retaining everything, in letting nothing go, in enduring everything, Flanders could hardly be looked upon except as the general store of Europe down to the period when the discovery of tobacco welded together with smoke the scattered features of the national physiognomy. [8–9, trans. modified]

The allegorical history of Flanders is, more accurately, an act of prosopopoeia, in the sense of a giving face, as Paul de Man defines it.[30] The processes of accumulation, retention, and endurance are described as the activities of a self, or, paradoxically, of a non-self, striving to unify itself, to acquire a totalized identity—*"tout amasser, rien rendre, tout supporter"* ["retaining everything, . . . letting nothing go, . . . enduring everything"]. But this drive to totalize only increases the country's facelessness; the identity of Flanders becomes synonymous with a metonymic space: it is known as the anonymous place of exchange, the *"magasin général"* ["general store"] of Europe. And while the narrator identifies the discovery of tobacco as the critical turning point in the country's development, this turning point is ironized: the national features of the country are welded together, but with smoke, that is, with a substance that signifies not composition but combustion and consumption. Thus, although the discovery of tobacco enables the country to find its own signifier of material wealth, that signifier also makes the Flemish physiognomy go up in pipe smoke, as it were, thereby perpetuating its history of internal division. The sentence that concludes the allegory underscores the interrelation of the "welding" of an identity and the fragmentation of the self: *"Dès lors, en dépit des morcellements de son territoire, le peuple flamand exista de par la pipe et la bière"* (660) ["Since then, notwithstanding the clipping of its territory, the Flemish people has existed through the pipe and beer," 9].

The allegorical history of Flanders reveals a conception of the *tout* as a pre-existent and pretextual given. While such a totality is an object that can be amassed, its accumulation results in the uncontrolled reduplication of a site of ceaseless exchange rather than in the ability to participate in the activities of exchange and importation themselves. And yet, these two forms of totality are not independent of one another. The constitution of the Flemish identity is finally based on the acquisition or importation of a series of objects from the outside world, and it is this process of internalization that creates the fragments, that is, enacts the *morcellement* [clipping] of its territory. Through this fragmentation, the self comes into existence and endures.

While Flanders is the ostensible referent in the above passage, we can detect certain allusions to the literary practices of Balzac himself. The metaphor of Flemish identity as soldered echoes the following comment by Balzac: *"Le génie de l'artiste consiste à choisir les circonstances naturelles qui deviennent les éléments du Vrai Littéraire, et, s'il ne les soude pas bien . . . eh! bien, l'oeuvre est manquée"* [The genius of the artist consists in choosing the natural circumstances that become the elements of literary Truth, and, if he does not weld them well . . . then the work is unsuccessful].[31] Like the process of Flemish identity-constitution, artistic creation entails the activity of soldering. We may suspect that it shares properties with the process of self-constitution allegorized in the description of Flanders quoted above. Balzac suggests as much when, writing to Madame Hanska of his progress, he refers to the text as *"un grand, beau, magnifique sujet"* [a great, fine, magnificent subject].[32] The grammatical indeterminacy of this *sujet* — it could be either a subject or object — leaves it open to a double reading. In either case, this *sujet* exercises a precarious effect upon its author: "La Recherche de l'Absolu *me tue. C'est un immense sujet"* ["*The Quest of the Absolute* is killing me. It is an immense subject"], he confides to Madame Hanska.[33]

Although the mechanics of Balthazar's research are never described, the physical sign of his labor is visible to all and a source of particular anguish to Joséphine:

> Par moments, se reprochant sa complaisance pour une passion dont le but était impossible et que M. de Solis condamnait, elle se levait, allait à la fenêtre de la cour intérieure, et regardait avec terreur la cheminée du laboratoire. S'il en échappait de la fumée, elle la contemplait avec désespoir, les idées les plus contraires agitaient son coeur et son esprit. Elle voyait s'enfuir en fumée la fortune de ses enfants; mais elle sauvait la vie de leur père. (731)

> At times, reproaching herself for her indulgence for a passion whose end was impossible of attainment and which Monsieur de Solis condemned, she would leave her chair, go to the window on the inner courtyard, and look up with terror at the laboratory chimney. If smoke were pouring from it, she would gaze at it in despair, her heart and mind stirred to the depths by the most contrary ideas. She saw her children's fortune flying away in smoke, but she was saving their father's life. [128]

Smoke, we recall, ironically cemented together the allegorical identity of Flanders, indicating the unification, however evanescent, of a disparate physiognomy. If the history of Flanders is, as the narrator indicates, the structural prefiguration of the narrative's events, then, in this passage as well, smoke metonymically signals the place where a project of identity-constitution is being undertaken, by both Balthazar and the authorial presence behind him.

In spite of Balzac's insistence to the contrary, the creation of a subject, with the attendant narcissism, is thus a project common to author and protagonist. Both Balzac and Balthazar are engaged in the pursuit of a totality. Balzac's literary project is to create *"un tout homogène, un ensemble complet"* [a homogeneous totality, a complete ensemble],[34] while Balthazar's *"mission"* is *"de tout voir, de tout savoir, de tout comprendre"* (727) ["to see everything, to know everything, to understand everything," 122]. The aesthetic totalities of both *La Comédie* and of each text belonging to it are comprised of a movement that unites fragments and residues, excrescences and relics. As such, the elements that have been excluded or rejected from a signifying structure call attention to the limits of that structure. We have seen how *La Recherche* articulates that limit as an allegory of the narcissistic desire motivating those narratives that organize themselves around the poles of totality versus fragmentation.

La Recherche is also the place where that which is repressed in the larger totality called *La Comédie* returns. The novel's structural irony, which is based upon a principle of repetition, subverts the clear boundaries between author and protagonist, character and character, Paris and Flanders, science and objects of desire. Irony reveals that such oppositions, which critics have so resolutely assumed to be absolute, are in fact contingent upon their positions in a representational structure. The novel questions the very project of searching for an imaginary *tout*, be it of the self, of a text, or of a literary cosmos, by calling attention to the (repressed) narcissistic structure of representation through which that *tout* emerges and to the violent *morcellement* [fragmentation] entailed in its construction. In this respect the novel is an *Étude philosophique,* not because it is about science, but because it conducts a transcendental inquiry—in the form of a self-reflexive allegory—into the grounds of its own (im)possibility. Hence the equivocal position of the novel (like its setting), both inside and outside *La Comédie:* it is one "philosophical" component that is within the literary cosmos yet not fully subsumable under its law. By sentencing Balthazar and Joséphine to death for their implication in an unselfconscious circuit of narcissistic projection, and even mocking their implication in this circuit, Balzac attempts to preserve the propriety of his own literary totality. Yet, as the two death scenes reveal, not even death affords the self-consciousness that would fracture the narcissistic configuration of self and other. Indeed, the inscription into those scenes of Balzac's desire for such totalizing self-consciousness marks the dangerous convergence of author and protagonist, *Comédie* and tragedy.

Four

The Secret of the Third Story in Charlotte Brontë's *Jane Eyre*

The inclusion of a reading of Charlotte Brontë's *Jane Eyre* (1847) in a study of literary realism requires some justification, as the novel is usually thought of as a version of the Gothic in literature. It is my contention that the concerns of the Gothic novel are not categorically distinct from those of the realist novel. Gothic conventions are themselves hyperbolic instances of tensions indigenous to the structure of the novel. More specifically, certain Gothic elements of *Jane Eyre,* in particular the telepathic cry from Rochester to Jane and the presence of Bertha, Jane's dark double, serve to dramatize the sustaining tension between the novel's mimetic claims and the subversion of mimesis, a tension that I see as a primary attribute of the genre of the novel.

The most heightened Gothic moment of dramatic intensity in *Jane Eyre* occurs in volume three, chapter nine. Jane has been attempting to reach a decision about her future with St. John, who would like to marry her and take her with him on his mission to India. On this particular evening, Jane has been listening to St. John read the twenty-first chapter of Revelation, the words of which "thrill" her with the immediacy of the picture they paint, their "vision of the new heaven and the new earth."[1] The reading is followed by the evening prayer, which also moves Jane profoundly: "I was excited more than I had ever been," she observes (424). As St. John utters the last words of the prayer while placing his hand on Jane's head, it is as if a current passes through her body, infusing it with the force of his vision. This is Jane's account of the event:

> I stood motionless under my hierophant's touch. My refusals were forgotten—my fears overcome—my wrestlings paralyzed. The Impossible—*i.e.* my marriage with St. John—was fast becoming the Possible. All was changing utterly, with a sudden sweep. Religion called—Angels beckoned—God commanded—life rolled

together like a scroll—death's gates opening, shewed eternity beyond: it seemed, that for safety and bliss there, all here might be sacrificed in a second. The dim room was full of visions. (423–24)

At this juncture, when Jane is on the threshold of the most crucial decision of her life (one that may even influence her afterlife), the text's verisimilitude, which hitherto had been faithfully upheld, breaks down. Jane recalls:

All the house was still; for I believe all, except St. John and myself, were now retired to rest. The one candle was dying out: the room was full of moonlight. My heart beat fast and thick: I heard its throb. Suddenly it stood still to an inexpressible feeling that thrilled it through, and passed at once to my head and extremities. The feeling was not like an electric shock; but it was quite as sharp, as strange, as startling: it acted on my senses as if their utmost activity hitherto had been but torpor; from which they were now summoned, and forced to wake. They rose expectant: eye and ear waited, while the flesh quivered on my bones.
"What have your heard? What do you see?" asked St. John. I saw nothing: but I heard a voice somewhere cry—
"Jane! Jane! Jane!" Nothing more. "Oh, God! what is it?" I gasped.
I might have said, "Where is it?" for it did not seem in the room—nor in the house—nor in the garden: it did not come out of the air—nor from under the earth—nor from overhead. I had heard it—where or whence, for ever impossible to know! (424)

In describing this moment of mystical communication, critics have for the most part either situated it within the tradition of Gothic literature—raising questions of typology as a strategy to avoid critical analysis—or seen it as an instance of unfortunate melodrama. Sandra Gilbert and Susan Gubar, by contrast, read the scene symbolically, arguing that the plot device of telepathic communion between Jane and Rochester should be understood in the context of the novel's narrative logic.

Her "presentiment" . . . is the climax of all that has gone before. Her new and apparently telepathic communion with Rochester . . . has been made possible by her new independence and Rochester's new humility. The plot device of the cry is merely a sign that the relationship for which both lovers had always longed is now possible, a sign that Jane's metaphoric speech of the first betrothal scene has been translated into reality: "my spirit . . . addresses your spirit, just as if both had passed through the grave, and we stood at God's feet, equal—as we are" (chap. 23). For to the marriage of Jane's and Rochester's true minds there is now, as Jane unconsciously guesses, no impediment.[2]

The notion that Jane "unconsciously guesses" what she goes on to discover as true is an intriguing if somewhat perplexing one, not only because it assumes that the unconscious is prophetic, but also because, up until this point in the novel, it has not been necessary to recast Jane's narrative in such patently metaphorical terms in order to adduce its significance. At the same time, insofar as Gilbert and Gubar understand the cry as a plot device prepared by Jane's "new independence," their analysis calls attention to the novel's central theme, namely, Jane's "march towards selfhood."[3] If the text's concern with this theme is what unites it with more realistic, that is, less patently Gothic texts, the fact that the achievement of selfhood is signaled by a moment of extravagant symbolic telepathy intimates something about the nature and possibility of the goal itself and the terms under which Jane's selfhood can be accomplished.[4]

By emphasizing that the origin of the cry is precisely what will remain "for ever impossible to know," Jane shrouds her telepathic experience in a cryptic secrecy that invites speculation even as it ostensibly wards it off. She heightens the sense of intrigue surrounding the agency of the communiqué by giving it a name, one that explicitly discourages us from understanding the call as an instance of the supernatural:

> "Down superstition!" I commented, as that spectre rose up black by the black yew at the gate. "This is not deception, nor thy witchcraft: it is the work of nature. She was roused, and did—no miracle—but her best."(425)

Jane's gloss on the telepathic voice proleptically discourages interpretations that would subsume this moment under the rubric of "the Gothic" in lieu of analyzing it in terms of the textual economy as a whole. That Jane has something to say about the origin of the voice— in spite of her earlier claim that it would remain "for ever impossible to know"—lends it an aura of uncanniness, precisely because it cannot be understood as an instance of the uncanny. Jane does not indicate in whose service the voice is an agency, only that, as a "work of nature," the voice is not miraculous but efficient. In what follows I suggest that

Jane's insistence that the "where or whence" of this "natural" voice remain a mystery derives from the threat its origin poses to the propriety of the novel's plot; and I argue that the completion of Jane's narrative depends upon the repression of the origin of the voice, because that origin calls into question the success, if not the desirability, of Jane's achievement of selfhood by exposing the narrowness of the social forms of identity available to her.

Jane's moment of epiphany, her recognition that she cannot marry St. John but must instead go to Rochester, has, as mentioned above, been understood as a sign of her newly achieved wholeness as an individual. Gilbert and Gubar point out that Jane aims at the achievement of a "wholeness within herself" through the exorcism of the "furies that torment her" by causing a "fragmentation of the self."[5] Only then, Gilbert and Gubar argue, can Jane become "an equal of the world Rochester represents" (368). The realization of such a bourgeois conception of the self as an autonomous and harmonious whole is not without its price, and in *Jane Eyre,* other characters pay for Jane's newfound identity. As Gilbert and Gubar point out, a concomitant physical fragmentation sets in at the novel's conclusion—Rochester, after all, is blind and maimed. In their analysis of Rochester's condition, Gilbert and Gubar do not address the violence with which Jane as narrator determines the fate of her male protagonist: they interpret Rochester's physical mutilation (like the scene of telepathic communion) symbolically.

> And surely another important symbolic point is implied by the lovers' reunion at Ferndean: when both were physically whole they could not, in a sense, see each other because of the social disguises—master/servant, prince/Cinderella—blinding them, but now that those disguises have been shed, now that they are equals, they can (though one is blind) see and speak even beyond the medium of the flesh. Apparently sightless, Rochester—in the tradition of the blinded Gloucester—now sees more clearly than he did when as a "mole-eyed blockhead" he married Bertha Mason (chap. 27). Apparently mutilated, he is paradoxically stronger than he was when he ruled Thornfield, for now, like Jane, he draws his powers from within himself, rather than from inequity, disguise, deception.[6]

It could just as plausibly be argued that Rochester's physical mutilation cannot be sublated through a symbolic reading that culminates in paradox; it may instead indicate that Jane's achievement of selfhood through unification occurs at the cost of a symbolic disembodiment or fracturing that, in her role as storyteller, she now displaces onto Rochester in the form of his physical impairment. Rochester's mutilation, then, might be the literalization of the symbolic violence—if not the violence of the symbolic—that underwrites the achievement of selfhood. In its displaced form, his mutilation might attest to a certain residual ambivalence born of such an achievement, given the loss that it entails.

Rochester is not the only character to suffer from Jane's metamorphosis. While Jane remains unscathed, other characters besides Rochester also succumb to illness and death. Indeed, one could go so far as to say that the deaths of significant individuals constitute the benchmarks of Jane's life: Uncle Reed's death gives Mrs. Reed license to mistreat Jane; Jane later befriends Helen Burns, who dies of consumption in the late spring of Jane's first year at Lowood; Jane might never have met St. John, Mary, and Diana if they had not congregated at their father's home upon his death; the death of Jane's uncle in Madeira enables Jane to assume her full identity as an "Eyre" by becoming an "heir," and it also brings about the disclosure that St. John, Mary, and Diana are themselves of the Eyre lineage; finally, the most significant death is Bertha's, because it frees Rochester to marry Jane.

While Jane is not in any way responsible for these deaths, her reactions to them are noteworthy. Not only does she display no outward remorse; even her private reflections betray no sense of loss. Consider, for example, her description of Helen Burns's death:

> When I awoke it was day: an unusual movement roused me; I looked up; I was in somebody's arms; the nurse held me; she was carrying me through the passage back to the dormitory. I was not reprimanded for leaving my bed; people had something else to think about: no explanation was afforded then to my many questions; but a day or two afterwards I learned that Miss Temple on returning to her own room at dawn, had found me laid in the little crib; my face against Helen Burns's shoulder, my arms round her neck. I was asleep, and Helen was—dead.
>
> Her grave is in Brocklebridge churchyard: for fifteen years after her death it was only covered by a grassy mound; but now a grey marble tablet marks the spot, inscribed with her name, and the word "Resurgam." (83)

Jane offers no reaction to her dear friend's death. Instead she provides a history of Helen's gravestone, as if the significance of Helen's death lay in the fact that it enables Helen's name eventually to be inscribed on the tombstone. The contrast between the intimate nocturnal scene, in which Jane is in bed with Helen, and the tremendous sense of temporal distance suggested by the mention of the fifteen years following Helen's death, bespeaks, on the one hand, Jane's proximity to death and, on the other hand, the force of her desire to separate herself from all direct contact with it.

Despite her attempt to distance herself from death, Jane, as narrator, actually seems to relish the scenes in which death is the issue, or better, relishes the definitiveness of death. For example, she writes about her uncle's death not once but twice, the first time when St. John receives word that he and his sisters have been excluded from the will, and the second time after it has been discovered that Jane is her uncle's legatee. The first episode follows Diana's comment, to which Jane refers twice in the text, that in some things St. John is "inexorable as death" (361, see also page 370).

> St. John passed the window reading a letter. He entered.
> "Our uncle John is dead," said he.
> Both the sisters seemed struck: not shocked or appalled; the tidings appeared in their eyes rather momentous than afflicting.
> "Dead?" repeated Diana.
> "Yes."
> She riveted a searching gaze on her brother's face. "And what then?" she demanded, in a low voice.
> "What then, Die?" he replied, maintaining a marble immobility of feature. "What then? Why—nothing. Read." (361–62)

In the above exchange Diana echoes her brother's words: she acknowledges St. John's statement that their uncle is dead by repeating the word *dead*. While she thereby conveys her appreciation of the potential import of the news (she, her brother, and her sister had been hoping to be included in their uncle's will), the reiteration is nevertheless gratuitous. St. John then utters Diana's nickname, "Die," which also makes reference to death. The use of the words *death* or *die* four times in such a short space suggests a strong narrative investment in the act or fact of dying. As such, the spelling of Diana's name may account for the reason she, and not Mary, is St. John's interlocutor in this dialogue. Moreover, as in the description of Helen Burns's tombstone, this scene makes mention of marble; and just as the earlier scene focused upon inscription or writing, here, the final word refers symmetrically to the act of reading. I will return to the implications of these similarities later.

Like the dialogue between St. John and Diana, the description of

Bertha's death also lingers on the word *dead*. In the passage below, the host of an inn near Thornfield Hall, relating to Jane the events that have transpired during her absence, tells the story of the fire that destroyed the house and was responsible for Bertha's death.

> "I witnessed, and several more witnessed Mr. Rochester ascend through the skylight on to the roof: we heard him call 'Bertha!' We saw him approach her; and then, ma'am, she yelled, and gave a spring, and the next minute she lay smashed on the pavement."
> "Dead?"
> "Dead? Aye, dead as the stones on which her brains and blood were scattered."
> "Good God!" (433)

The repetition of the word *dead* in Jane's reaction to the host's account is logically plausible and yet equivocal. On the one hand, her response may indicate her astonishment—surely she is shocked by the narrative she has just heard. On the other hand, it seems self-evident that someone who is lying "smashed on the pavement" would be dead, and the host's response to Jane's question—yet another, double repetition of the word "dead"—almost seems to mock Jane's incredulity. Moreover, this image of stones splattered with blood and brains figures a kind of grotesque form of inscription similar to the images of inscription in the two previous episodes. The scene that immediately follows this one substantiates the connection between the bloody stones and writing: Jane learns that Rochester is "stone-blind" (434), a condition that will later inspire her to conceive of her role as guide through a metaphor that again recalls the inscription on the marble tablets. She states of Rochester: "He saw nature—he saw books through me; and never did I weary of . . . impressing by sound on his ear what light could no longer stamp on his eye" (456).

Taken together, the scenes discussed above suggest that Jane, as narrator, derives a certain compensation, if not pleasure, from the act of writing the word *dead*. The most extreme example of her investment in scenarios of death occurs at the end of the novel. Jane has been reunited with Rochester, and, in her words, now knows "what it is to live entirely for and with what I love best on earth. I hold myself supremely blest—blest beyond what language can express; because I am my husband's life as fully as he is mine" (456). Although Jane claims that her happiness exceeds language, she of course continues to speak and write, although she never gives an account of the evolution of her literary talents. She finishes her narrative by engaging in a final moment of speculative imagining that reveals not only that she has been *subjected* to events that in some way concern death but also that she is now *actively engaged* in anticipating the death of someone who, to her knowledge, is still alive, namely St. John.

> St. John is unmarried: he never will marry now. Himself has hitherto sufficed to the toil; and the toil draws near its close: his glorious sun hastens to its setting. The last letter I received from him drew from my eyes human tears, and yet filled my heart with Divine joy: he anticipated his sure reward, his incorruptible crown. I know that a stranger's hand will write to me next, to say that the good and faithful servant has been called at length into the joy of his Lord. And why weep for this? No fear of death will darken St. John's last hour: his mind will be unclouded; his heart will be undaunted; his hope will be sure; his faith steadfast. His own words are a pledge of this:—
> "My Master," he says, "has forewarned me. Daily he announces more distinctly,—'Surely I come quickly;' and hourly I more eagerly respond,—'Amen; even so come, Lord Jesus!'" (458)

This final scene is the reverse of an earlier one in which St. John had nearly persuaded Jane to marry him, a prospect that compelled her to exclaim, "If I were to marry you, you would kill me. You are killing me now" (417). Here, at the conclusion of the book, Jane is doing the figurative killing, and her victim is her former oppressor. In foretelling St. John's death with utter assurance—"I know that a stranger's hand will write to me next"—Jane assumes that St. John will be content with his destiny. Its altruistic tone of piety notwithstanding, this moment of imaginative speculation, coming as it does at the novel's conclusion, bespeaks the premium Jane places on seeing, or imagining, St. John dead.[7] Moreover, instead of explicitly mourning the loss of St. John, Jane wishes him all the best in his afterlife and comments on his desire to embrace death. She thereby continues the pattern that has run throughout the book.

St. John's death, though, is qualitatively distinct from the other deaths in the novel, in that it is not narrated as an objective event but is a proleptic speculation that reveals more about Jane than about St. John. The ramifications of Jane's wish for St. John's death become manifest when we consider it in light of her relationship to her cousin/suitor.

The novel consistently emphasizes the rivalry that exists between the two. This rivalry is grounded in their mutual identification, which the text establishes through a series of parallels. St. John is Jane's namesake, his full name being St. John Eyre Rivers. Jane remembers having read the initial of his middle name in books she had borrowed from him, a fact that testifies to their common interest in reading. Like Jane, St. John is impelled by the "troubling impulses of insatiate yearnings and disquieting aspirations" (357). In the physical descriptions of the two characters, the eyes are the salient feature; at one point Jane refers to St. John's eyes three times within the space of two pages: they are "large and blue, with brown lashes" (349), "pictorial-looking" (350), and not very revealing. Jane writes, "St. John's eyes, though clear enough in a literal sense, in a figurative one were difficult to fathom" (350). Jane's eyes initially become noteworthy when Rochester mistakes their color for blue, mentioning Jane's "radiant hazel eyes," which prompts Jane to comment parenthetically "I had green eyes, reader; but you must excuse the mistake: for him they were new-dyed, I suppose" (260). Jane again calls attention to her eyes when she states, "He [St. John] wanted to train me to an elevation I could never reach: it racked me hourly to aspire to the standard he uplifted. The thing was as impossible as to mould my irregular features to his correct and classic pattern, to give to my changeable green eyes the sea blue tint and solemn lustre of his own" (403).

Both St. John and Jane value and embody originality.[8] She holds in reverence Rochester's "original . . . vigorous . . . expanded mind" (255) and is herself seen as original: "You *are* original," St. John tells her (380), while Rochester playfully asks, "Is she original? Is she piquant?" (271). St. John talks about his own "original qualities" and "original materials" (380).

In the past St. John had considered committing his originality to a literary career. In the following passage, he tells Jane of his former aspirations:

> A year ago, I was myself intensely miserable, because I thought I had made a mistake in entering the ministry: its uniform duties wearied me to death. I burnt for the more active life of the world— for the more exciting toils of a literary career—for the destiny of an artist, author, orator. (366)

St. John arrives at his decision not to write via a miraculous spiritual epiphany:

> I considered; my life was so wretched, it must be changed, or I must die. After a season of darkness and struggling, light broke and relief fell: my cramped existence all at once spread out to a

plain without bounds—my powers heard a call from heaven to rise, gather full strength, spread their wings and mount beyond ken. God had an errand for me; to bear which afar, to deliver it well, skill and strength, courage and eloquence, the best qualifications of soldier, statesman and orator, were all needed: for these all center in the good missionary. (366)

In tenor and magnitude, St. John's epiphany closely resembles Jane's later telepathic communication. Both hear a call—St. John from God, Jane from a force to which she prays in gratitude and which she calls "a Mighty Spirit" (425). Unlike Jane's experience, however, St. John's religious conversion is an instance of self-mastery through self-denial, the instability of which motivates his attempt to recruit Jane. He sees her as a kindred spirit—"I recognized [in you] a soul that revelled in the flame and excitement of sacrifice," he states—and on the basis of this identification attempts to compel her into sacrificing herself as he had done (408). Drastically confined by his own self-domination, St. John tries to dominate Jane.

The rivalry between St. John and Jane, which plays itself out as a struggle for intersubjective mastery, is closely bound up with the question of authorization, of who has the right to author, relate, and thereby control, the story of a person's life. Indeed, the struggle between Jane and St. John is inscribed within a larger theme running throughout the novel, concerning the opposition between, on the one hand, narrating or writing one's own story and, on the other hand, narrating or reading the stories of others; hence the images relating to writing in the physical descriptions of St. John and Jane.[9] Jane's own development as an autonomous individual corresponds to her shifting relation to literature and language. From the first scene in the novel, in which she is ordered to absent herself from the Reed family, she is depicted as a reader, or "Reeder," considering the name of her foster family. She takes great pleasure in the stories Bessie tells on winter evenings and also in the fairy tales and ballads Bessie relates from Richardson's *Pamela* and Wesley's abridgement of Brooke's *The Fool of Quality*. Indeed, one of her few positive childhood memories is of Bessie's "remarkable knack of narrative" (29). In fact, all of the women whom Jane admires and befriends are readers or storytellers, but the stories they tell are never autobiographical; they are always borrowed from someone else and at times no more profound than gossip. Jane first speaks to Helen Burns when Helen is absorbed in *Rasselas*. Then, once Helen is in confinement because of consumption, Jane spends her time with another student, Mary Ann Bates, who, while she has "a turn for narrative," tells stories that amuse but do not satisfy Jane's taste for the "higher things" (78). When Jane observes Diana and Mary for the first time, each is bent over a book just as Helen Burns was when Jane first saw her.

While the activity of reading is itself not necessarily a passive pursuit, with the exception of Jane, the women who do read or narrate stories never speak or write in an original, first-person voice of their own. The text emphasizes that these women are barred from the position of first-person narrator by presenting them as literal or figural captives who, in their own lives, are assigned powerless roles in narratives imposed by others: Bessie is a servant, while Helen and Mary Ann are incarcerated in Lowood Institution, whose director promotes the "spiritual edification" of his pupils "by encouraging them to evince fortitude under temporary privation" (63). Like Jane, Diana and Mary are original, "of a mak' of their own," but they are governesses and as such confined to a role that Jane, by contrast, has already outgrown (347).

As if to emphasize the difference between the passivity of reading, telling, or participating in the narratives of others versus the active nature of writing and living one's own story, Jane describes her near capitulation to St. John, in their critical scene of confrontation, through a metaphor whose homophonic resonance conjoins an image of weakness to one of reading: Jane writes, "Oh, that gentleness! how far more potent is it than force! I could resist St. John's wrath: I grew pliant as a reed [or read] under his kindness" (424). In a similar scene, when Jane almost capitulates to Rochester's plea not to leave Thornwood, Rochester says, "A mere reed she feels in my hand!" (322).

The relationship between Jane and St. John develops as a mutual struggle to command the other through the power of narrative. When Jane first meets St. John, she is immediately impressed by his oratorical prowess to the point that her own powers of expression are rendered ineffectual: "I wish I could describe that sermon: but it is past my power. I cannot even render faithfully the effect it produced on me" (356). We have seen how St. John uses his rhetorical skills to effect changes in Jane, practically convincing her to join him as his wife on his mission. He now also attempts to take control of Jane linguistically, forcing her to give up the study of German and instead learn "Hindostanee." In discussing why she could not oppose St. John's wishes, Jane invokes a metaphor of inscription: "St. John was not a man to be lightly refused: you felt that every impression made on him, either for pain or pleasure, was deep-graved and permanent" (402). While the image of St. John as a tablet upon which Jane engraves, or refuses to engrave, her impression seems to cast her in the role of active inscriber, it must be remembered that she assumes the role only in response to his demands.

The evening St. John conveys the news of Jane's inheritance to her, he repeatedly makes references to literature. He relates that he got tired of his "mute books and empty rooms," and that since the previous day, when he first discovered Jane's identity, he had "experienced the excitement of a person to whom a tale has been half-told and who is impatient to hear the sequel" (382). Now, in Jane's presence, he begins to fill in "the blank of a pause" with his tale, but not before he clarifies the terms in which he had portrayed his earlier excitement.

> I spoke of my impatience to hear the sequel of a tale: on reflection, I find the matter will be better managed by my assuming the narrator's part, and converting you into a listener. Before commencing, it is but fair to warn you that the story will sound somewhat hackneyed in your ear: but stale details often regain a degree of freshness when they pass through new lips. For the rest, whether trite or novel, it is short. (384)

Not content to be a mere listener, St. John assumes the narrator's part and in the third person tells Jane the story of her own life. He pulls out the key to his discovery of Jane's real identity, a piece of paper on which her name is inscribed in India ink, stating that "it is always more satisfactory to see important points written down, fairly committed to black and white" (385).

In the beginning of their relationship, St. John consistently assumes the role of active narrator/interpreter while Jane is the passive writing surface/listener.[10] Early in their relationship, Jane writes, "He looked at me before he proceeded: indeed, he seemed leisurely to read my face, as if its features and lines were characters on a page" (359). Similarly, in a comment whose play on the word "content" analogizes Jane to a text, St. John remarks, "I hope you feel the content you express" (365).

Once Jane learns of her inheritance, however, the roles of active inscriber and passive surface/listener become reversed. Now it is Jane who looks at "the blank wall" like the blank of St. John's pause, and finds inspiration (390). She decides to divide her inheritance between herself and her cousins and takes control of her future. With her financial independence comes recognition of her equality with her male cousin. She is willing to accompany St. John to India under the condition that she go "free," that is, unmarried. This proposition is unacceptable to St. John, who remains steadfast in his resolve to persuade Jane of the necessity of marriage. In the climactic moment of their confrontation, Jane reiterates her refusal to marry him: "If I were to marry you, you would kill me. You are killing me now" (417). St. John objects to Jane's sentiment by objecting to her language: "*I should kill you—I am killing you?* Your words are such as ought not to be used: violent, unfeminine, and untrue" (417).[11] The impropriety of her language derives from the fact that it signifies a redistribution of power between them. Now Jane is the active inscriber, while St. John is the passive surface:

> I had finished the business now. While earnestly wishing to erase from his mind the trace of my former offence, I had stamped on that tenacious surface another and far deeper impression: I had burnt it in. (417)

Her description of the voice that beckons her to Rochester underscores how her newfound power exists in contrast and contradistinction to St. John's forces: "I broke from St. John; who had followed, and would have detained me. It was *my* turn to assume ascendancy. *My* powers were in play, and in force" (425). Jane explicitly links her powers to the mysterious voice she hears:

> I recalled the voice I had heard; again I questioned whence it came, as vainly as before: it seemed in *me*—not in the external world. I asked, was it a mere nervous impression—a delusion? I could not conceive or believe it: it was more like an inspiration. (426)

Given the equivalence Jane has established between her own powers and St. John's—whose narrative proclivities have been emphasized all along—the above passage suggests that the internal, inspirational voice Jane hears is *literary*.[12] In other words, the telepathic communication between Jane and Rochester marks the inaugural moment of Jane's literary imagination, the moment when Jane engages in her first act of imaginative production.

As I discussed earlier, Jane's call has been read as a sign that she and Rochester are now in a position to come together as equals; but, given that such a miraculous moment of spiritual communion is coextensive with Jane's metamorphosis into a writer of fiction, it is impossible to decide whether her communion with Rochester is "real" or the upshot of her first literary endeavor. Is the novel's resolution the result of an inevitable turn of events that organically follows from the development of the plot or a testimony to the formal imperative of narrative closure, to the fact that the narrative requires a dénouement? In short, is the crisis that brings on resolution a fiction within a fiction? While the resolution Jane reaches suggests that she will be able to find self-fulfillment through marriage, Jane herself expresses the belief that complete happiness always expresses an imaginary reality:

> Human beings never enjoy complete happiness in this world. I was not born for a different destiny to the rest of my species: to imagine such a lot befalling me, is a fairy tale — a day dream. (261)

The telepathic cry of Rochester, I would suggest, signals the moment when Jane must depart from the principle of mimesis in order not to transgress the laws of novel form, which require every novel to arrive at a harmonious, "fairy tale" conclusion. Like the dream, the resolution of Jane's story does not express an objective reality but a wish-fulfillment.

The telepathic cry of Rochester thus commemorates Jane's transformation into a narrator by marking the breakdown of realistic verisimilitude that occurs when Jane attempts to impose closure upon a situation that would seem to demand more radical transformation, if at the expense of narrative coherence. Insofar as the cry originates in Jane's literary imagination, to expose its roots would be to call into question the forward trajectory of the events she purports to relate and thereby to undermine the coherence and objectivity of her narrative. Hence Jane's insistence that the origin of the telepathic cry must remain "forever impossible to know."[13]

We are now in a position to consider why death proliferates in the text as well as why the trope of inscription repeatedly substitutes for gestures of mourning. The aggressiveness with which Jane as narrator attempts to dispense with the characters in her story, whose lives represent alternatives to her own direction, suggests that these alternatives, however deficient, may be no less inadequate than the marriage she has chosen for herself. In fact, there are no indications that Jane has resolved the early ambivalence she felt about the prospect of marrying Rochester, who had formerly attempted to impose roles upon her that she would not accept.[14]

Jane claims that the crucial difference between St. John and herself concerns the significance of love in their lives. Whereas St. John "had put love out of the question, and thought only of duty," her own call to duty is the call of love itself (424). But that this call issues from the formal exigency of narrative coherence rather than from the internal evolution of the plot suggests that Jane's marriage to Rochester is as self-denying as St. John's decision to become a missionary.

The strong identification between Jane and St. John and the structural similarity between Jane's moment of telepathic intuition and St. John's call to serve God thus suggest that Jane's own epiphany is as precarious and unstable as St. John's. Her anticipation of his death thus attests to her desire to emphasize her otherness, to establish a vital difference between herself and her namesake in face of the possibility that such a difference might not in reality exist.

Ironically, the murderous force with which Jane repudiates Helen's self-abnegating piety, Bertha's incendiary violence, and St. John's resentful proselytizing testifies to Jane's affinity with St. John. These multiple deaths structurally replicate St. John's own will to power, which is manifest in his attempt to convert his own masochistic loss into sadistic appropriation. The creation of Jane's literary self occurs through a no less aggressive splitting of ambivalent tendencies into intersubjective oppositions, one pole of which must be repudiated (St. John) if not literally destroyed (Helen, Bertha) in order for Jane to establish her imaginary autonomy. The concomitant masochism of self-denial, so pointedly apparent in St. John's behavior, thus revenges itself through Jane's power as narrator to mutilate, even annihilate, her others. Acts of inscription thus displace acts of mourning, "real" events of death are conjoined with figures of writing, because writing enables Jane to construct an imaginary identity by expropriating her others while denying the loss that such expropriation entails.

Critics have stressed that the most pernicious of the identifications Jane must outgrow is with Bertha. Gilbert and Gubar, for example, see Jane's development as a gradual process of exorcism that culminates in the death of the madwoman, who is "the most threatening . . . avatar of Jane . . . Jane's truest and darkest double: she is the angry aspect of the orphan child, the ferocious secret self Jane has been trying to repress ever since her days at Gateshead".[15] Gilbert and Gubar regard Bertha's death as a clear indication that Jane

> had been irrevocably freed from the burden of her past, freed both from the raging specter of Bertha (which had already fallen in fact from the ruined wall of Thornfield) and from the self-

pitying specter of the orphan child (which had symbolically, as in her dream, rolled from her knee).[16]

While Bertha's death facilitates the resolution of the plot, like St. John, she continues to haunt the narrative in a way that Gilbert and Gubar fail to note. Not only does Jane's telepathic call reiterate St. John's divine call, it structurally echoes the call of Bertha's brother (who functions as Bertha's double) that Jane hears late one night at Thornfield Hall:[17]

> The night—its silence—its rest, was rent in twain by a savage, a sharp, a shrilly sound that ran from end to end of Thornfield Hall. . . . Indeed, whatever being uttered that fearful shriek could not soon repeat it: not the widest-winged condor on the Andes could, twice in succession, send out such a yell from the cloud shrouding his eyry. The thing delivering such utterance must rest ere it could repeat the effort.
> It came out of the third story; for it passed overhead—yes, in the room just above my chamber-ceiling—I now heard a struggle: a deadly one it seemed from the noise; and a half smothered voice shouted:—
> "Help! Help! Help!" three times rapidly.
> "Will no one come?" it cried; and then while the staggering and stamping went on wildly, I distinguished through plank and plaster:—
> "Rochester! Rochester! For God's sake, come!" (208)

Bertha utters the first shriek and her brother utters the ensuing exclamations. His cry of "Help! Help! Help!" is structurally parallel to the telepathic "Jane! Jane! Jane!" (424), while his appeal to God anticipates Jane's later appeal to God in her response to Rochester's plea: "Oh, God! what is it? . . . I am coming," she gasps (424–25). The cry from Rochester is thus a repetition of the earlier cry by Bertha's sane surrogate, who here speaks in the name of "the thing," that had to "rest ere it could repeat the effort."

If Rochester and Jane's telepathic communication signals the birth of Jane's literary imagination, its resonance with the cry of Bertha's double introduces the possibility that such a birth bears within itself certain unsettling ramifications. Bertha, after all, is literally dead, and yet figuratively she seems to live on, embodied in the cries of her relative, at the very moment when her death is requisite for the resolution of the plot. As the resolving element, the telepathic communication that supposedly occurs after Bertha's "exorcism" from the text can instead be read as an instance in which Jane is demonically possessed by that threatening presence.

Jane's metamorphosis into an author thus signals not her liberation from the madness of another, her double, but her introjection of the madwoman's identity. This accounts for the fact that encoded in the passage above are cryptogrammic and metaphoric references to Jane: the words *eyry* and *ere* echo Jane's name, while the figure of the condor continues a symbolic chain running throughout the text that links the "undomesticated" Jane to birds. In the opening pages of the novel, Jane is reading is Bewick's *History of British Birds* and is captivated by "certain introductory pages [that] . . . treat of the haunts of sea-fowl" (8);[18] Jane draws an analogy between her relation to Rochester before their marriage and a bird to its keeper when she writes "to taste but of the crumbs he scattered to stray and stranger birds like me, was to feast genially" (247); Rochester calls Jane "a wild, frantic bird that is rending its own plumage in its desperation" (256), noting how she opens her eyes "like an eager bird" (314); and in the scene following Rochester's disclosure of his marriage to Bertha, he speaks about the impossibility of capturing Jane's heart in this extended ornithological metaphor:

> Consider that eye: consider the resolute, wild, free thing looking out of it, defying me, with more than courage—with stern triumph. Whatever I do with its cage, I cannot get at it—the savage, beautiful creature. . . . Of yourself, you could come with soft flight and nestle against my heart, if you would: seized against your will, you will elude the grasp like an essence—you will vanish ere I inhale your fragrance. (322)

The metaphor of the bird is carried even further when St. John says of Jane, "My sisters, you see, have a pleasure in keeping you . . . as they would have a pleasure in keeping and cherishing a half-frozen bird, some wintry wind might have driven through their casement" (353).

Once Jane assumes control of her own narrative, she displaces the image of the captive bird onto Rochester. She writes of his appearance after the accident:

> I saw a change: that looked desperate and brooding—that reminded me of some wronged and fettered wild-beast or bird, dangerous to approach in his sullen woe. The caged eagle, whose

gold-ringed eyes cruelty has extinguished, might look as looked that sightless Samson. (436)

Jane also remarks that Rochester reminds her of "a royal eagle, chained to a perch . . . forced to entreat a sparrow to become its purveyor" (444).

Jane's identification with Bertha is not just metaphoric, but metonymic, inasmuch as both women occupy a common space, the name for which is associated with the writing of literature — the third story of Thornfield Hall. When Jane dreams of freedom, she walks the grounds of Thornfield and climbs to the third story, where she looks out over hills and fields and longs "for a power of vision which might overpass the limit" (110). In order to quell her discontent, she escapes to the third story:

> Who blames me? Many no doubt; and I shall be called discontented. I could not help it: the restlessness was in my nature; it agitated me to pain sometimes. Then my sole relief was to walk along the corridor of the third story, backwards and forwards, safe in the silence and solitude of the spot, and allow my mind's eye to dwell on whatever bright visions rose before it — and certainly they were many and glowing; to let my heart be heaved by the exultant movement which, while it swelled it in trouble, expanded it with life; and, best of all, to open my inward ear to a tale that was never ended — a tale my imagination created, and narrated continuously; quickened with all of incident, life, fire, feeling that I desired and had not in my actual existence. (110)

Significantly, Jane draws a distinction here between the "bright visions" of her imagination and her "actual existence," thereby suggesting that she sees narrative as a supplement to life rather than an imitation of it. Moreover, that the inner tale she hears diverges in its endlessness from her own written tale only underscores the fantastic nature of *Jane Eyre*'s closure.[19]

Jane's own discussion of sympathies and presentiments provides the terms with which we can delineate her identification with Bertha.

> Presentiments are strange things! and so are sympathies; and so are signs: and the three combined make one mystery to which humanity has not yet found the key. I never laughed at presentiments in my life; because I have had strange ones of my own. Sympathies I believe exist: (for instance, between far-distant, long-

absent, wholly estranged relatives; asserting, notwithstanding their alienation, the unity of the source to which each traces his origin) whose workings baffle mortal comprehension. And signs, for aught we know, may be but the sympathies of Nature with man. (222)

She accepts presentiments as plausible phenomena, suggesting that if sympathies exist it is because they share a common origin and that signs may be one instance of a sympathetic relationship between man and nature. What remains unarticulated in this passage is the relationship among presentiments, sympathies, and signs. I would suggest that the constellation of the three elements can be understood in terms of the relationship between Jane and Bertha: "not withstanding their alienation," Bertha and Jane exist in sympathy. They are "far-distant, long-absent, wholly estranged relatives," signs that share a common origin in Jane's aesthetic impulses. Insofar as Bertha threatens the propriety of narrative coherence, she is a force that must literally remain locked away in the third story of the house; but as the repressed element in the text, she escapes from her chamber only to return in the third story, or volume, of the text.

Bertha's constitutive significance is evident in her textual (dis)placement: the third volume of the novel structurally realizes the theme of the third story attic. Bertha figuratively lives on, transformed into the third and final volume of the tale, where the madness of textual closure is imposed upon the narrative. Read in this light, the description of the third story rooms of Thornfield pertains to the third volume of the novel as well. Inasmuch as the third story, understood as narrative space, commemorates the very tensions that were resolved only formally in the text, it is "interesting from . . . [its] air of antiquity . . . [It is] a shrine of memory" (106–7). Bertha's haunting presence in both the third story of Thornfield and the third story of *Jane Eyre* testifies to the purely symbolic nature of Jane's acts of exorcism and to the inevitable failure of her attempts to kill off her demonic doubles. As such, the epitaph on Helen's tombstone aptly pertains to the uncanny destiny of every "other" in *Jane Eyre:* "Resurgam."

Five

Domesticated Irony in Theodor Fontane's *Frau Jenny Treibel*

Theodor Fontane's theoretical writings on the novel bear a strong affinity to Lukács's theory of the novel. In his earliest literary-historical essay, *"Unsere Lyrische und Epische Poesie Seit 1848,"* Fontane discusses realism not as a stylistic tendency or historical movement in art but as the essence of art itself. Realism, he states, *"ist die Kunst"* [is art].[1] Fontane defines realism principally in terms of its formal requirements. He criticizes those works of art that display *"Überschwenglichkeit"* [effusiveness], and *"Phras[e]"* [empty phrases].[2] According to him, no choice of subject matter can correct such *"Mängeln in der Form"* [defects in form].[3]

Like Lukács, Fontane views mimetic representation as an expression of aesthetic subjectivity. Calling the process through which subjectivity inscribes itself into the text *Verklärung* [transfiguration],[4] Fontane praises Turgenev's photographic, documentary-like portrayals but criticizes the absence of *"Reflexionszuthaten, besonders wenn sie nebenher auch noch poetisch wirken sollen"* [the elements of reflection, particularly when they should at the same time achieve a poetic effect].[5]

Fontane cites two lines from Goethe's *"Vorspiel auf dem Theater"* that comprise an appropriate motto for his subjectivist realism: *"Greif nur hinein ins volle Menschenleben / Wo du es packst, da ist's interessant"* [You have only to catch hold of the fullness of human life / Where you seize it, there it is interesting].[6] The realist work is thus the product of a metaphorical hand that grasps its material. Fontane elaborates on the metaphor of the active hand, which calls up associations with the authorial hand, when he states immediately thereafter that the hand of the artist *"erweckt"* [awakens] the image from the raw material.[7] The truth of the work of art, then, which emerges through *Verklärung,* is neither within the raw material nor in the hand that works the material; rather, it derives from the interplay of the two. In the following passage Fontane explicitly joins the poetic to the work of art via the mediating link of the aesthetic subject:

> Es gibt kein Kunstwerk ohne Poesie, wobei nur zu bemerken bleibt, dass die *vollendete Wiedergabe der Natur* auch allemal einen höchsten Grad poetischer Darstellung ausdrückt. Nichts ist seltener als dieser höchste Grad, der absolute Gegenständlichkeit bedeutet. Die Regel ist, dass der Künstler in seinem Nachschaffen eben kein Gott, sondern ein Mensch, ein Ich ist und von diesem "Ich" in seine Schöpfung hineinträgt. Und von dem Augenblick an, wo das geschieht, dreht sich alles um die Frage: *"Wie ist dies Ich?"*

> There is no work of art without poetry, whereby it only remains to be noted that the perfect reproduction of nature always expresses an unsurpassed degree of poetic representation. There is nothing rarer than when this high degree of poetic representation signifies absolute objectivity. The rule is that the artist, in the process of recreating, is not a god but a human being, an "I," and carries himself forth from this I into his creation. And from the moment in which this happens, everything revolves around the question "How does this I work?"[8]

This passage sets up an opposition between two forms of the poetic, the absolute poetic, which is rare, and the relative poetic, which is "the rule." While the "unsurpassed" poetic form seems to be superior to the more humanly possible form and all but impossible to achieve, we could speculate that it might at times be realized in works that approach objectivity not by negating or denying the authorial *Ich* but rather by highlighting its presence in the work and thereby circumscribing any absolute claim to objectivity.[9]

In *Frau Jenny Treibel: Oder "Wo sich Herz zum Herzen find't"* (1892), the authorial hand makes itself felt in a complex play of irony composed of a double movement: a more traditional tropological movement, through which the narrative voice emphasizes its critical distance from the novel's protagonist, and a more radical form of structural irony that destabilizes the very grounds upon which the narrator's ironic perspective has been established.

I begin my analysis by examining the rhetorical irony deployed in the text and then discuss the character who has customarily been seen as Fontane's *porte-parole*. I demonstrate that the central conflict of the novel concerns a debate among the three principal female protagonists about ironic self-consciousness. The terms of this debate reflect two distinct conceptions of identity: identity conceived of as essence versus identity conceived of as theatrical performance and positioning. Finally, I discuss the structure of the novel in light of this debate and argue that the novel reveals the complicitous relationship between the narrative viewpoint and the object of its ironic scrutiny.

The novel's plot revolves around the conflict between Corinna, the daughter of Professor Wilibald Schmidt, and Jenny Treibel, the mother of Leopold, a weak-willed man from whom Corinna succeeds in soliciting a proposal of marriage. Jenny is unconditionally opposed to any marriage that will not enhance the Treibel's position in society and consequently views the daughter of a professor of modest means as an unacceptable candidate for the position of daughter-in-law. Aided by Helene, the wife of her oldest son, Otto, Jenny seems to prevail over Leopold, who never musters the courage to carry out his plan to elope with Corinna. As a result, Corinna grows impatient and breaks the engagement. Instead of Leopold she marries her cousin and childhood companion, Marcell, a young professor who has always loved her. Leopold, meanwhile, makes plans to marry Hildegard, Helene's younger sister, and cordial relations are restored between the Treibels and the Schmidts.

Writing after his turn towards Marxism, Lukács interprets this novel as an indictment of the *Besitzbürgertum* during the *Gründerjahre* of the nation. More recent studies of *Frau Jenny Treibel* have followed Lukács in their assumption that Fontane's depiction of Jenny Treibel is meant to expose the hypocrisy of the class to which she belongs.[10] David Turner notes that Fontane belongs to a tradition of social critics that includes Heinrich Heine, Gottfried Keller, and Carl Sternheim, all of whom share an aversion to "the mixture of sentimentality and materialism" that characterizes Jenny Treibel, the protagonist of the novel.[11] According to Turner, Fontane's critique of Jenny's bourgeois attributes emerges through the novel's rhetorical structure of ironic discrepancy. The following passage, in which Jenny uses the term *"Das Höhere"* both figuratively and literally, exemplifies this structure:

Der Gang mit Wilibald hatte so vieles wieder in ihr angeregt. Die Gewissheit, sich verstanden zu sehen—es war doch eigentlich das Höhere. . . . "Treibel ist gut, besonders auch gegen mich; aber die Prosa lastet bleischwer auf ihm, und wenn *er* es nicht empfindet, *ich* empfinde es. . . . Und dabei Kommerzienrätin und immer wieder Kommerzienrätin. Es geht nun schon in das zehnte

Jahr, und er rückt nicht höher hinauf, trotz aller Anstrengungen." (139)

The walk with Wilibald had stirred up so much in her. The certainty of seeing herself understood—that was really the higher thing. . . . "Treibel is good, particularly to me; but his prosaic nature weighs on him like lead, and if he doesn't feel it, I feel it. . . . And then Kommerzienrätin and forever Kommerzienrätin. It's been almost ten years now, and we don't seem to get any higher up, despite all the effort." [144–45]

Beginning at the second sentence, this passage expresses Jenny's sentiments through *erlebte Rede* and thereby suggests a certain confluence of attitude or identification between narrator and protagonist (I will address the reasons for such an identification later). This momentary identification is firmly interrupted through an ironic repetition: Jenny uses the word *"höher"* ["higher"] to lament her stalled progress up the social ladder after just having expressed her sensitivity to her poetic ideals, which she calls *"das Höhere"* ["the higher thing"]. A similar moment of rhetorical irony occurs when Jenny's imposing stature is revealed to be dependent on an inflatable object. During the dinner party, *"Alles ging infolge davon wie am Schnürchen, auch heute wieder, und ein Blick Jennys regierte das Ganze, wobei das untergeschobene Luftkissen, das ihr eine dominierende Stellung gab, ihr nicht wenig zustatten kam"* (26) ["Everything went like clockwork, today too, and Jenny's glance ruled the whole affair—helped not a little by the air cushion underneath her that gave her a dominating position," 22].

As Jenny's most articulate and outspoken critic, Professor Wilibald Schmidt serves as Fontane's *porte-parole*.[12] Consider, for example, the following passage in which Schmidt criticizes Jenny for her self-delusion:

Es ist eine gefährliche Person, und um so gefährlicher, als sie's selbst nicht recht weiss und sich aufrichtig einbildet, ein gefühlvolles Herz und vor allem ein Herz "für das Höhere" zu haben. Aber sie hat nur ein Herz für das Ponderable, für alles, was ins Gewicht fällt und Zins trägt. (79–80)

She's a dangerous person and all the more dangerous for not really knowing it herself, and she sincerely imagines she has a feeling heart, especially a heart for "the higher things." But she has a heart only for what has weight, for everything that counts and bears interest. [80]

In a letter to Paul Schlenther, Fontane refers to the novel in terms that echo Schmidt's. He describes it as *"eine humoristische Verhöhnung unserer Bourgeoisie mit ihrer Redensartlichkeit auf jedem Gebiet, besonders auf dem der Kunst und der Liebe, während sie doch nur einen Gott und ein Interesse kennen: das Goldene Kalb"* [a humorous mockery of our bourgeoisie with its hackneyed expressions in every area, particularly in art and love, while it actually knows only one god and one interest: the golden calf].[13] Similarly, Fontane writes to his son Theodor that the second half of the novel's title, *"Wo sich Herz zum Herzen find't,"*

> ist die Schlusszeile eines sentimentalen Lieblingsliedes, das die 50jährige Kommerzienrätin im engeren Zirkel beständig singt und sich dadurch Anspruch auf das "Höhere" erwirbt, während ihr in Wahrheit nur das Kommerzienrätliche, will sagen viel Geld, das "Höhere" bedeutet. Zweck der Geschichte: das Hohle, Phrasenhafte, Lügnerische, Hochmütige, Hartherzige des Bourgeoisstandpunkts zu zeigen, der von Schiller spricht und Gerson meint. (207)

> is the concluding line of a favorite sentimental love song that the fifty-year-old *Kommerzienrätin* constantly sings in intimate circles and thereby stakes a claim upon the "higher things," while in truth the "higher things" only signify what is entailed in holding the position of *Kommerzienrätin,* which is to say, lots of money. Purpose of the story: to show the hollowness, empty rhetoric, mendacity, arrogance, hard-heartedness of the standpoint of the bourgeoisie, who speaks of Schiller and means Gerson.[14]

As proof of Fontane's opposition to the bourgeoisie, critics frequently cite a line Schmidt utters immediately after Corinna's most openly antagonistic confrontation with Jenny, who pays a visit to the Schmidts in the hope of dissuading Corinna from her intention to marry Leopold. Upon Jenny's departure, Schmidt says, *"Corinna, wenn ich nicht Professor wäre, so würd' ich am Ende Sozialdemokrat"* (160) ["Corinna, if I weren't a professor, I'd become a Social Democrat in the end," 166]. While clearly an unabashed proclamation of political allegiance, Schmidt's comment poses an alternative—one is either a professor or a Social Democrat—that complicates the unequivocal significance attributed to the statement. Schmidt implies that his professional identity and his political inclinations do not coincide. Although we could understand his comment as a reflection of the political situation of the late nineteenth century—the antisocialist law of 1879 was in force until 1890—it is not clear why Schmidt could not have participated in some form of political activity, particularly given that, as Hajo Holborn points out, professors predominated in the *Verein für Sozialpolitik*.[15] In light of the following statement, Schmidt's remark acquires a slightly different meaning: *"Andererseits, so viel muss ich zugeben, hat Abstimmung immer was Totes, Schablonenhaftes und passt mir ausserdem nicht recht"* (71) ["But then again, I must admit, voting always had something dead, mechanical about it, and doesn't suit me that well besides," 72]. As an objection to the dead, mechanical quality of voting, Schmidt's comment suggests not that his profession precludes radical political activity, but that his role as professor may enable him to engage in an activity that, while incompatible with the dead and mechanical quality of voting, is nevertheless political in its own right.

Indeed, Schmidt's profession may even place him in a position to reflect critically on the voting process itself. In 1890, while writing *Frau Jenny Treibel*, Fontane states in a letter, "And now I must go out to put my ballot into the box, for the first time in many years. Why should it be? Finally I was reduced to counting my buttons. Only he who knows nothing knows without any doubt."[16] Fontane's comment implicitly elaborates on the reservations introduced by Schmidt. The ambivalence he voices towards voting suggests that he objects to the premises of political choice, namely, a reductive logic of opposition, the claim that every choice can be resolved into a number of mutually exclusive propositions, and the assumption that the voter possesses epistemological certainty that, as the notion of button counting suggests, in fact dissimulates the element of chance in every political decision as well as the potential exchangeability among the objects of choice. While Fontane's (and Schmidt's) reservations about the democratic process do not mitigate their critique of the bourgeoisie, they do suggest that voting may not be the only political forum. The political activities of both Fontane and his fictional double may consist precisely in their critiques of the grounds of political judgment and the structure of opposition—both among choices and between the chooser and the choices—that subtend the vote. This does not imply that the text vindicates the transgressions of the bourgeoisie but rather that its uniquely literary quality may reside in its capacity to examine a mode of political expression, voting, that, while in substance may be critical of the bourgeoisie, structurally preserves and even conspires with the object it purports to critique. The question that must be raised is not simply whether Schmidt (as Fontane's double) is politically engaged, but how his position encourages us to rethink our understanding of political engagement as such.

The epistemological critique of the logic of opposition underwriting political choice, a logic that attributes radical distinctiveness to each pole of an opposition, is played out in the novel in two debates, the first about the nature of the poetic and the second about the basis of institutional power. Both debates expose the connection between the bourgeois notion of identity as essence and the assimilation and preservation of social privilege. The aesthetic debate occurs between Jenny and Corinna. Jenny tells Corinna that she values absolute aesthetic forms because they enable the essence of the poetic to emerge. This essence discloses the superior value of the eternal over the transitory, the ideal over the mundane, the spiritual over the material: *"Mir gilt die poetische Welt, und vor allem gelten mir auch die Formen, in denen das Poetische herkömmlich seinen Ausdruck findet"* (29) ["I value the poetic world, and above all I also value the forms in which the poetic is traditionally expressed," 29]. But Jenny can afford to entertain such exalted notions of the poetic only because she herself already occupies a socially prominent position, and she in fact expresses these notions in order to protect this position, which she sees as threatened by Corinna's designs on Leopold. The performative force of her musings on the aesthetic consists in her attempt to convince Corinna that she should cease to be a social climber and surrender herself to the eminently superior world of spiritual gratification.

Schmidt disputes Jenny's notion of the poetic. He remarks, *"Das Poetische—vorausgesetzt, dass man etwas anderes darunter versteht als meine Freundin Jenny Treibel—, das Poetische hat immer recht; es wächst weit über das Historische hinaus"* (70) ["Poetry—assuming one understands it in a way other than does my friend Jenny Treibel—poetry is always right; it far exceeds history," 70].[17] Although critical of Jenny's conception of the poetic, Schmidt's assertion that the poetic is superior to the historical appears to come close to Jenny's disparagement of the transitory. This turns out not to be the case, however. The poetic is superior to the historical not because it departs from history but because it is metahistorical; it exposes the principles impelling history. For example, Schmidt's poetic understanding of Jenny reveals that her own history is based on the forgetting of her past: *"Jenny Treibel hat ein Talent, alles zu vergessen, was sie vergessen will"* (79) ["Jenny Treibel has a talent for forgetting whatever she wants to forget," 80]. In order to idealize the poetic, with its privileging of spirit over matter, Jenny must repress the fact that her own former desire to escape her petit bourgeois background is now mirrored in Corinna's desire for a materially rich way of life. Yet, she advises Corinna that *"Geld eine Last ist, und dass das Glück ganz woanders liegt,"* (12) ["money is a burden and happiness lies in an entirely different direction," 7]. Moreover, her refusal to recognize herself in Corinna suggests that the aggression she harbors towards Corinna is also self-directed. In opposing Corinna, she implicitly renounces her former self. In a similar manner, she condemns her childhood self when she sharply criticizes the way Helene is raising Lizzi. According to Jenny, Lizzi is *"die grösste Puppe..., die man nur sehen kann"* (85) ["the greatest doll to be seen anywhere," 87]. Yet in recalling her own childhood, she takes great pleasure in describing her former doll-like appearance and her ability, like Lizzi, to attract the gazes of others: *"Ich [war] ein halbwachsen Ding... mit kastanienbraunen Locken, die meine Mutter, soviel sie sonst zu tun hatte, doch immer mit rührender Sorgfalt wickelte... die Leute sahen mich auch immer darauf an"* (10) ["I was just a half-grown young thing with chestnut curls, which my mother—with all that she had to do—still always rolled up with touching care.... people always noticed me for it," 4].

Corinna makes an observation about Jenny's memory in terms that directly suggest the aesthetic implications of her willful amnesia; she states that Jenny can only prefer the poetic to the prosaic because she forgets, and *"verklärt"* ["transfigures"], her own past (13) [7]. Corinna's choice of words suggests that her critique of Jenny's understanding of the poetic may be related to the issue of the text's construction, given that it, as well, is based upon the principle of *Verklärung*. Her comment raises the possibility that the historical unfolding and resolution of the plot might be the effects of a similar process of repression, a point I will return to later.

The notion that aesthetic form preserves and discloses essences that are transhistorical and unchanging is based upon assumptions about identity that also underlie the beliefs of Schmidt's colleagues, who defend the importance of character in maintaining institutional power. Diestelkamp, the director emeritus of the gymnasium, mistrusts self-criticism because it undermines the basis of authority. He tells Schmidt,

> Lieber Schmidt, das Entscheidende bleibt doch immer der Charakter, nicht der eitle, wohl aber der gute, ehrliche Glaube an uns

selbst. Bona fide müssen wir vorgehen. Aber mit unsrer ewigen Kritik, eventuell auch Selbstkritik, geraten wir in eine mala fides hinein und misstrauen uns selbst und dem, was wir zu sagen haben. Und ohne Glauben an uns und unsere Sache keine rechte Lust und Freudigkeit, und auch kein Segen, am wenigsten Autorität. Und das ist es, was ich beklage. (62)

My dear Schmidt, the decisive factor will always be character; not vain, but good, honest faith in ourselves. *Bona Fide*—we must proceed in good faith. But with our eternal criticism, even self-criticism, we get into a *mala fides* and mistrust ourselves and what we have to say. And without faith in ourselves and our purpose, there is no genuine pleasure and joyfulness, nor any blessing, least of all authority. And that's what I'm lamenting. [62]

Schmidt disputes the grounding of power in character:

Du willst alles auf den Charakter zurückführen und denkst, wenn du es auch nicht ausspricht: "Und wenn ihr euch nur selbst vertraut, vertrauen euch auch die anderen Seelen." Aber, teurer Freund, das ist just das, was ich bestreite. Mit dem blossen Glauben an sich oder gar, wenn du den Ausdruck gestattest, mit der geschwollenen Wichtigtuerei, mit der Pompösität ist es heutzutage nicht mehr getan. An die Stelle dieser veralteten Macht ist die reelle Macht des wirklichen Wissens und Könnens getreten. (63)

You want to trace everything back to character and you think, even if you don't say it, "if you just have faith in yourself, other souls will have faith in you too." But, my good friend, that is just what I'm disputing. Mere faith in oneself or, if you'll permit the expression, swollen self-importance, pomposity, doesn't do anymore. This obsolete power has been replaced by the actual power of real knowledge and ability. [62]

The replacement of obsolete power by real knowledge and ability and old forms by new forms— *"Es ist vorbei mit den alten Formen"* ["It is over with the old forms"]—rests upon the power of self-questioning (63) [63, trans. modified]. The authentic forms of knowledge and ability to which Schmidt refers challenge the conception of the self as a monolithic essence. Such knowledge emerges from a process of self-irony, which enables the self to achieve the *"denkbar höchst[e] Standpunkt"* ["the highest conceivable standpoint"] (57) [56, trans. modified]. One verbal form that Schmidt's self-irony takes capitalizes upon the polysemous quality of language. For example, Schmidt names the group of professors who meet weekly *'die Sieben Waisen."* *Waisen* signifies both that the members of the group are wise—*weise*—and that they are orphans—*Waise*—who only attend the weekly gatherings for want of a better engagement.

Schmidt praises his daughter Corinna's ability to ironize herself:

> Das Schmidtsche strebt in ihr nicht bloss der Vollendung zu, sondern, ich muss das sagen, trotzdem ich ihr Vater bin, kommt auch ganz nah ans Ziel. Nicht jede Familie kann das ertragen. Aber das Schmidtsche setzt sich aus solchen Ingredienzien zusammen, dass die Vollendung, von der ich spreche, nie bedrücklich wird. Und warum nicht? Weil die Selbstironie, in der wir, glaube ich, gross sind, immer wieder ein Fragezeichen hinter der Vollendung macht. Das ist recht eigentlich das, was ich das Schmidtsche nenne. (74–75)

> The Schmidt in her not only strives towards perfection, but—I must say it even though I am her father—comes very near the goal. Not every family can bear that. But a Schmidt is composed of such ingredients that the perfection I'm speaking of never becomes oppressive. And why not? Because the sense of irony, in which we, I believe, are great, always puts a question mark after this perfection. That is essentially what I call the Schmidt quality. [75]

Since *"Vollendung"* means both perfection and completion, the above statement suggests that the "Schmidt irony" calls into question any completed form. As such, the near perfection of a Schmidt is a product of his or her continual self-questioning.

Schmidt's belief in the importance of self-irony is thematically central to the novel. I would suggest that the threat Corinna poses to Jenny and Helene concerns her ability to expose through self-irony the emptiness of Jenny's belief (with which Helene concurs) that aesthetic form expresses unchanging essences that comprise the basis of identity. Corinna by contrast understands form not as the disclosure of static essence but as a mode of performance that creates the illusion that essential differences exist as givens. She deploys her understanding of identity as performance to manipulate Leopold by strategically positioning herself within the economy of his desire. In this way Corinna hopes to gain access to the class to which Jenny belongs, a class that attempts to define itself through the exclusion of parvenues like the aspiring Corinna in spite of the fact that it is largely comprised of such individuals.

Jenny, Helene, and Corinna display their respective notions of identity in a forum that is consistent with what Schmidt says about the significance of detail: *"Das Nebensächliche, soviel ist richtig, gilt nichts, wenn es bloss nebensächlich ist, wenn nichts drin steckt. Steckt aber was drin, dann ist es die Hauptsache, denn es gibt einem dann immer das eigentlich Menschliche"* (70) ["The incidental, that much is right, doesn't count if it is merely incidental, if there is nothing in it. But if there is something in it, then it's the main thing, because it always reveals the human essence," 70]. In the novel as a whole, the "incidental" element that reveals the "essence" of Fontane's validation of self-irony emerges through a series of allusions that refer to the prosaic, and hence, by Jenny's standards, unworthy, domestic activity of ironing. Specifically, the novel establishes a correlation between the degree to which the principle female characters are aware of the dependence of identity upon theatrical representation and their attitudes towards ironing. The exploration of irony is thus based on the literalization of a bilingual pun on the German *"Ironie"* — and the English homonym "ironing." Such interlinguistic punning seems appropriate in a novel whose characters (specifically Helene, Mr. Nelson, and Corinna) speak English at various points and in which the authorial voice is represented by a character who considers word play the highest form of self-irony. Even with its prosaic connotations, the word *Plätten* [ironing] suggests reasons for its privileged position in the text. It belongs to a vocabulary of dialect, the name of which is legible in the word: *Platt*, or Low German. In one sense, then, *Plätten* is a figure for linguistic figuration or troping.

The character of the ironer first appears in a climactic scene of confrontation. After the outing to Lake Halen, during which Corinna and Leopold have secretly become engaged, Jenny is resting in her room, losing herself in *"süsse Selbsttäuschungen"* ["sweet self-deceptions"] (140) [145]. She walks to the window and looks out:

Drüben, im Hause gegenüber, hoch oben in der offenen Mansarde, stand, wie ein Schattenriss in hellem Licht, eine Plätterin, die mit sicherer Hand über das Plättbrett hinfuhr — ja, es war ihr, als höre sie das Mädchen singen. Der Kommerzienrätin Auge mochte von dem anmutigen Bilde nicht lassen, und etwas wie wirklicher Neid überkam sie. (140)

> In the house opposite, high up in the open garret, like a silhouette in bright light, someone stood running an iron over the board with a sure hand—why, it seemed to her she could hear the girl singing. The Kommerzienrätin could not take her eye off the charming picture, and something like genuine envy came over her. [145]

This is the only instance in which the narrator alerts us to the fact that Jenny is experiencing *"etwas wie"* ["something like"] genuine feeling. A silhouette against the light in the attic window across the street captivates her attention and triggers her desire. As the prosaic activity of ironing cannot itself be the source of Jenny's envy, the satisfaction of the image may well derive from the predominance of its formal self-containment: the figure of the ironing woman is an *"anmutige[s] Bild"* ["a charming image"], characterized by the play of contrasts, dark against light, delimited by the frame of the mansard window. When Jenny animates the image with a voice, she engages in a moment of imaginative production, inscribing her own desire onto the silent form.

Jenny experiences the allure of the *Bild* a second time. Leopold has come into his mother's bedroom to announce his engagement. Outraged by his decision, Jenny feigns a swoon and vows to prevent the marriage. Leopold has barely left the room, when Jenny stands up from the sofa and begins to pace: *"Jedesmal, wenn sie wieder in die Nähe des Fensters kam, blieb sie stehen und sah nach der Mansarde und der immer noch in vollem Lichte dastehenden Plätterin hinüber, bis ihr Blick sich wieder senkte"* (144) ["Every time she came near the window again she stood still and looked over at the garret and the woman still ironing in the full light until her glance would drop again," 149]. Despite the calamitous news she has just received, Jenny is still compelled by the image of the ironer. It is as if the ironer's *"sichere Hand,"* along with the firmly delimited borders of the silhouette, now function as a compensatory fantasy of totality for Jenny as she faces the immediate challenge to her authority. Moreover, that she returns to the window with an almost compulsive persistence reveals the significance of this image, which vies for her attention and even seems to distract her from the explicit drama; indeed, her fantasy takes the form of a structural rupture—a *(Schatten)riss*—that stalls the momentum of the plot.

The *Plätterin* proves to be more than a fortuitous figure in the text. A series of allusions to ironing, washing, and the related domestic art of invisible weaving elaborates on the issues raised in the episode in Jenny's bedroom, in particular the allure of representational closure.

The first scene of the novel mentions an incident pertaining to Helene's ironing day, which, *"nach ihrer Meinung allem anderen vorgeht, sogar im Geschäft"* (11) ["to her mind comes before anything else, even business," 5]. Just as the ironer draws Jenny away from an emotionally intense situation, so, too, does ironing compete with and even overshadow Helene's other concerns; she is willing to forego the opportunity to host a dinner party for an English business associate of her husband in order to supervise the *Plättag* in her home. The text repeatedly underscores the importance to Helene of ironing. Jenny sardonically says that Helene entertained the Englishman, Mr. Nelson, *"bloss damit ihr die Plättbolzen nicht kalt werden"* (84) ["just so that her irons don't get cold," 86]. She later writes in a letter to Helene's sister that if Helene wanted to visit her family in Hamburg she would tell Helene, *"Reise, Helene, reise heute, reise morgen, und sei versichert, dass ich mich, wie des Wirtschaftlichen überhaupt so auch namentlich der Weisszeugplätterei nach besten Kräften annehmen werde"* (150) ["Go, Helene, go today, go tomorrow, and be assured that I'll see to the household in general and to the linen ironing particularly," 156].

Helene's concern with ironing is part of her more general preoccupation with the upbringing of her daughter, Lizzi. Lizzi's first appearance in the text bespeaks the results of her mother's care. As Helene and her husband, Otto, are having breakfast one morning, Lizzi and her governess appear:

> Lizzi, trotz früher Stunde, war schon in vollem Staate. Das etwas gewellte blonde Haar des Kindes hing bis auf die Hüften herab; im übrigen aber war alles weiss, das Kleid, die hohen Strümpfe, der Überfallkragen, und nur um die Taille herum, wenn sich von einer solchen sprechen liess, zog sich eine breite rote Schärpe, die von Helenen selbstverständlich nie "rote Schärpe," sondern immer nur "pink-coloured scarf" genannt wurde. Die Kleine, wie sie sich da präsentierte, hätte sofort als symbolische Figur auf den Wäscheschrank ihrer Mutter gestellt werden können, so sehr war sie der Ausdruck von Weisszeug mit einem roten Bändchen drum. (87)

> In spite of the early hour Lizzi was already all dressed up. The child's slightly wavy blond hair hung down to her waist; everything else was white, the dress, the long stockings, the turn-downed collar. Around her waist, if it could be called that, she wore a wide red sash, which Helene never called a "red sash" in German but rather a "pink-colored scarf" in English. The way

she was, the little one could immediately have been placed on top of her mother's linen closet as a symbolic figure, a pure expression of freshly bought linen with a red ribbon around it. [89, trans. modified]

The terms in which Lizzi is presented install her in an economy of maternal desire: she is a *"symbolische Figur"* and an *"Ausdruck."* The importance of symbolic forms to Helene is further suggested by her attempt to control the names of things. As an expression, *"Ausdruck,"* Lizzi does not represent a presence but articulates a desire, the phallic contours of which are indicated by her symbolic placement on the linen closet of her mother, both because *"Schrank"* ["closet"] figures an enclosed feminine space and because the whiteness of Lizzi's outfit suggests that the closet contains underclothing.[18] The reference to Lizzi as *"die Kleine"* [the little one"] strengthens her phallic identity.

Lizzi is a model child whose exemplary normality reveals the abnormality of the obsessively normal: *"Alles normal und beinah über das Normale hinaus"* (87) ["Everything was normal and almost better than normal," 89]. The elements of her appearance embody not just the adorability of small children but forms of femininity as such. Her flowing hair, her midriff, which is described as a waist, and her character as a symbol of her mother's linen all suggest that the significance of her excess of normality bears generally upon the question of the representation of feminine identity. Lizzi's excessive normalcy reveals what Mary Ann Doane, drawing on the writings of Jacqueline Riviere, has described as the masquerade of femininity. According to Doane, this masquerade

> constitutes an acknowledgement that it is femininity itself which is constructed as a mask—as the decorative layer which conceals a non-identity. . . . The masquerade, in flaunting femininity, holds it at a distance. Womanliness is a mask which can be worn or removed. Masquerade . . . involves a realignment of femininity, the recovery, or more accurately, simulation, of the missing gap or distance. To masquerade is to manufacture a lack in the form of a certain distance between oneself and one's image. . . . The masquerade doubles representation; it is constituted by a hyperbolisation of the accoutrements of femininity.[19]

As a hyperbolic spectacle of her mother's femininity, Lizzi's appearance attests to the contingency of Helene's sex upon representation. Not that Helene is aware of this contingency. On the contrary, Lizzi's feminine appearance functions for Helene as a categorical denial of the fact that femininity is a masquerade, even while it reduplicates the split between the mask and the self in the form of the intersubjective distinction between mother and daughter. Insofar as Helene spectates on the spectacle of her own femininity, she occupies a position identical to that of the male fetishist, who both accepts and denies the "reality" of female castration.[20] Hence the phallic overtones of the image of Lizzi as a symbolic expression of maternal desire.

Helene's investment in the (denial of the) spectacularity of feminine identity, with its dependence on representation in general and the visual image in particular, accounts for her unwillingness to nurse her infant on the grounds that it is *"unschön"* ["unsightly"] (87) [89, trans. modified]. Her reluctance to nurse is an interesting reversal of what Karl Abraham and Maria Torok have described as the opposition between the *"relation maternelle d'une part et accession au sexe dans le social d'autre part"* [maternal relation on the one hand and accession to one's sex in the social realm on the other].[21] The *"prolongation excessive du maternage"* [excessive prolongation of mothering][22] interrupts accession into sexuality and the social order, which are themselves coterminous with *"le passage de la bouche pleine de sein à la bouche plein de mots s'effectue au travers d'expériences de bouche vide"* [the passing from the breast-filled mouth to the mouth filled with words is carried out through the experience of the empty mouth].[23] In refusing to breast feed Lizzi, Helene commits the crime not of excessively prolonging mothering but of doing the opposite: Lizzi's mouth prematurely becomes filled with words without the transitional experience of the empty mouth. That is, she prematurely accedes to her sex without sufficiently experiencing the stage in which the distance between the signifier and the signified, the self and its representation, can be perceived. Abraham and Torok describe this transitional stage as follows:

> Apprendre à remplir de mots le vide de la bouche, voilà un premier paradigme de l'introjection. On comprend qu'elle ne peut s'opérer qu'avec l'assistance constante d'une mère, possédant elle-même le language. Sa constance—comme celle du Dieux de Descartes—est le garant nécessaire de la signification des mots. Lorsque cette garantie est acquise, mais alors seulement, les mots peuvent remplacer la présence maternelle et donner lieu à de nouvelles introjections. D'abord la bouche vide, puis l'absence des objets deviennent paroles, enfin les expériences des mots elles-mêmes se convertissent en d'autres mots.

Learning to fill the empty mouth with words is the first paradigm of introjection. This process can only take place with the constant assistance of a mother, who herself possesses language. Her constancy—like that of the God of Descartes—is the necessary guarantee of the significance of words. Once this guarantee is acquired, and only then, can words replace maternal presence and give rise to new introjections. First the empty mouth, then the absence of objects becoming words, finally the experience of the words themselves converting into other words.[24]

The importance of the maternal presence as the guarantor of meaning is emphasized here. The mother provides the closeness and linguistic compensation necessary for the child's experience of the oral void. In Lizzi's case, the wet-nurse who takes the mother's place executes the feedings *"mit grosser Gewissenhaftigkeit und mit der Uhr in der Hand"* (87) ["with great conscientiousness and with a watch in her hand," 89]. The wet-nurse, while the paragon of efficiency, does not appear to provide the maternal supplement that facilitates accession into the symbolic order. On the contrary, the perfunctoriness of her attitude is suggested by the fact that Lizzi, left under her supervision, cuts her finger with a knife (the wet-nurse is consequently dismissed on account of her negligence). Because Helene forces Lizzi to incorporate symbolic forms of femininity prematurely, without the experience of the *"bouche vide"* ["empty mouth"] Lizzi can never experience the reassuring gap between identity and its symbolic embodiment.

If Helene occupies the position of the male fetishist with respect to Lizzi, Lizzi's grandfather, Komerzienrat Treibel, inversely occupies the feminine position. Whereas Helene is anxious for Lizzi to enter the symbolic order, Treibel is relieved to see evidence of the difference between the child and her symbolic identity. That is why the incident with the knife greatly relieves him. He states, *"Gott sei Dank, soviel ich sehen kann, es ist wirkliches Blut"* (88) ["Thank God, as far as I can see, it's real blood," 90]. His words evoke and reverse Helene's thankfulness towards God for the gifts of nature that she believes God *"sichtlich"* ["visibly"] (88) [89] bestowed on her in the form of her model child. Moreover, the act of self-mutilation figures the violence of Lizzi's (premature) accession into the symbolic, just as the blood recalls the sash that Lizzi wears in her capacity as symbol of maternal desire.

The child's fantasies of rebelling against her fetishization emerge in her play activities. In play, Lizzi steps out of her mother's orderly linen closet to become the instigator of disorder:

Ordnungsmässig hatte Lizzis Leben begonnen, und ordnungsmässig war es fortgesetzt worden. Die Wäsche, die sie trug, führte durch den Monat hin die genau korrespondierende Tageszahl, so dass man ihr, wie der Grossvater sagte, das jedesmalige Datum vom Strumpf lesen konnte. "Heut' ist der Siebzehnte." Der Puppenkleiderschrank war an den Riegeln numeriert, und als es geschah (und dieser schreckliche Tag lag noch nicht lange zurück), dass Lizzi, die sonst die Sorglichkeit selbst war, in ihrer, mit allerei Kästen ausstaffierten Puppenküche Griess in den Kasten getan hatte, der doch ganz deutlich die Aufschrift "Linsen" trug, hatte Helene Veranlassung genommen, ihrem Liebling die Tragweite solchen Fehlgriffs auseinanderzusetzen. (88)

Lizzi's life had begun in an orderly fashion, and it was continued in an orderly fashion. The undergarments she wore bore the corresponding number of the day throughout the month, so that, as her grandfather said, one could always read the date from her stockings. "Today is the seventeenth." Her doll's wardrobe had numbered hooks, and all the containers in her doll's kitchen were clearly labelled. When it happened (and this dreadful day was not far past) that Lizzi, otherwise care personified, had put seminola in the container very clearly marked "Lentils," Helene had taken the occasion to explain to her darling how far-reaching such a blunder was. [90, trans. modified]

The description of the doll's wardrobe implicitly elaborates on Lizzi's identity, both because she is frequently referred to as a *Puppe* [doll] and because the numbered hooks double Lizzi's numbered stockings. Lizzi asserts herself against her imposed image by striking out against the signifier, by refusing to read the word. Her act of rebellion expresses her desire to be other than a symbol or personification.

For Helene, whose own sense of identity depends upon her narcissistic investment in her daughter, Lizzi's lexical oversight is a veritable act of anarchy, the destruction of *"das Kleine"*: *"Wer Grosses hüten will, muss auch das Kleine zu hüten verstehen"* (88) ["Whoever wants to take care of great things must also know how to take care of small things," 90]. To illustrate the importance of protecting the phallic little one, Helene tells a story whose significance exceeds its intended meaning.

Bedenke, wenn du ein Brüderchen hättest, und das Brüderchen wäre vielleicht schwach, und du willst es mit Eau de Cologne bespritzen, und du bespritzest es mit Eau de Javelle, ja, meine Lizzi, so kann dein Brüderchen blind werden, oder wenn es ins

Blut geht, kann es sterben. Und doch wäre es noch eher zu entschuldigen, denn beides ist weiss und sieht aus wie Wasser; aber Griess und Linsen, meine liebe Lizzi, das ist doch ein starkes Stück von Unaufmerksamkeit oder, was noch schlimmer wäre, von Gleichgültigkeit. (88)

Just think, if you had a little brother, and the little brother seemed faint, and you wanted to spray him with *eau de cologne* and you sprayed him with *eau de javelle.* Why, Lizzi, then your little brother could become blind or if it went into his blood he could die. And that would still be easier to excuse because both are clear and look like water; but seminola and lentils, my dear Lizzi, that's a strong case of inattentiveness or, which would be even worse, of indifference. [90]

Helene's didactic tale justifies the necessity of reading signs carefully in terms of a fantasy of phallic power: she equates confusing cologne and chlorine with an act—blinding—that we could read as the symbolic equivalent of castration or even murder. As such, the fantasy bespeaks Helene's desire to see Lizzi, who already is the phallus for her mother, here *possess* the phallus. The patent aggressiveness of this fantasy accounts for the reason the imaginary little brother might feel faint: it is as if he had caught sight of the female phallus and then reacted in a stereotypically feminine way—by losing consciousness.

I have described Helene's preoccupation with Lizzi's appearance—which accounted for the importance of the *Plättag*—in terms of a logic of fetishistic identification. Helene's femininity establishes itself through a phallocentrism designed to repress the fact that femininity is constructed as a masquerade. But insofar as Lizzi is the essence of normality, her identity as a maternal fetish suggests that the process of feminine identity-constitution as such conforms to the logic of the fetish and that the success of the process depends upon repression of the knowledge of the symbolic underpinnings of feminine identity.

Jacqueline Riviere stresses the synonymity of the masquerade and femininity: "The reader may now ask how I define womanliness or where I draw the line between genuine womanliness and the 'masquerade.' My suggestion is not, however, that there is any such difference; whether radical or superficial, they are the same thing."[25] The universality of this fetishistic moment of feminine identity-constitution is further suggested by the fact that the emblem of fetishistic identification, *"Plätten,"* plays a significant role not only for Jenny and Helene, but also for Corinna, who invokes her domestic skills as proof of her femininity.

At the outset of the novel Jenny and Helene view each other antagonistically. Jenny disapproves of Helene's insistence on the superiority of customs in Hamburg over those in Berlin. Jenny attributes Helene's snobbism in part to Hamburg Anglophilia. As Jenny deridingly remarks, *"Das ist so hamburgisch, die kennen alle Engländer, und wenn sie sie nicht kennen, so tun sie wenigstens so"* (11) ["That's so like the Hamburgers, they know all the English, and if they don't know them, they at least act as if they did," 5].[26] Helene is angry with Jenny because she refuses to acknowledge and act upon her desire to see her younger sister, Hildegard, engaged to Leopold. Jenny claims she has had enough with one daughter-in-law from Hamburg and thus opposes a second marriage to a Munk daughter. But after the engagement of Leopold and Corinna, Jenny and Helene put aside their disagreements to join forces against their common enemy. Helene adds a note to the letter Jenny is sending Hildegard inviting her to pay the Treibels a visit. Helene

> war so bei der Sache, dass nicht einmal ein triumphierendes Gefühl darüber, mit ihren Wünschen für Hildegard nun endlich am Ziele zu sein, in ihr aufdämmerte; nein, sie hatte angesichts der gemeinsamen Gefahr nur Teilnahme für ihre Schwiegermutter, als der "Trägerin des Hauses," und nur Hass für Corinna. (153)

> was so absorbed in her task that it never occurred to her to feel triumphant because Hildegard had been invited at last. No, in view of the common danger, she only felt in sympathy with her mother-in-law as the "support of the house" and full of hatred for Corinna. [159]

Helene reconciles with Jenny for reasons independent of her interest in seeing her sister married to Leopold. The great danger Corinna poses to both women overshadows the issue of a second Hamburger daughter-in-law. Helene identifies with Jenny's threatened position as the symbolic *Trägerin* [supporter], precisely because it is the power of the symbolic that Corinna threatens to disrupt by ironically exposing, even flaunting, its theatrical underpinnings.

In contrast to Jenny and Helene, Corinna is not only aware that she plays a certain role when she attempts through storytelling to solicit a proposal of marriage, she does not try to dissimulate her histrionics. Marcell accuses her of playing a comedy, but this does not bother her. She remarks, *"Und wenn ich es tue, so doch so, dass jeder es merken kann"* (52) ["And if I do, then in such a way that everyone can tell," 51]. While all three women are invested in the image of totality as exemplified by the figure of the ironer and by ironing, only Corinna ironizes her investment. On the one hand, she shares Helene's and Jenny's desire for the totalized image: she justifies her wish to attend the Treibel dinner party by saying, *"Ich sehne mich manchmal nach Ungescheitheiten"* (16) ["I sometimes yearn for something unintelligent (undivided)," 10, trans. modified].[27] On the other hand, she exposes the imaginary quality of that undivided totality by acknowledging the theatricality of her desire. For example, when walking home with Marcell after the dinner party, she comments on the *"entzückende Bild"* ["enchanting view"] from the bridge they are crossing (51) [49–50]:

> Dünne Nebel lagen über dem Strom hin, sogen aber den Lichterglanz nicht ganz auf, der von rechts und links her auf die breite Wasserfläche fiel, während die Mondsichel oben im Blauen stand, keine zwei Handbreit von dem etwas schwerfälligen Parochialkirchturm entfernt, dessen Schattenriss am anderen Ufer in aller klarheit aufragte. "Sieh nur," wiederholte Corinna, "nie hab' ich den Singuhrturm in solcher Schärfe gesehen. Aber ihn schön finden, wie seit kurzem Mode geworden, das kann ich doch nicht; er hat so etwas Halbes, Unfertiges, als ob ihm auf dem Wege nach oben die Kraft ausgegangen wäre. Da bin ich doch mehr für die zugespitzten, langweiligen Schindeltürme, die nichts wollen als hoch sein und in den Himmel zeigen." (51–52)

> Thin mists were lying across the stream, but they did not completely absorb the gleaming lights that fell on the wide water surface from left and right, while the crescent moon stood above in the blue expanse, not two hands' breadth distant from the somewhat ponderous tower of the Parochial Church silhouetted very distinctly on the other bank.
> "Look at that," Corinna repeated, "never have I seen the singing clock tower so sharply. But to find it beautiful, as has become the fashion recently, that I can't do; there's something half or unfinished about it, as if it had lost its strength on the way up. I'd rather have the tapered, ordinary shingled spires that just want to be tall and point into heaven." [50]

Jenny and Helene would certainly share Corinna's attraction to the phallic figure (even if it is not as erect as it might be), and, like Corinna, prefer a more complete form. Indeed, this scene anticipates the one in Jenny's bedroom discussed earlier, in that the object of Corinna's gaze here is a *Schattenriss* [silhouette], as is the figure in the attic window. But whereas Jenny and Helene unreflectively desire phallic wholeness, Corinna is conscious of the theatricality of her desire. When Marcell asserts that her utterance is an empty rhetorical gesture, she does not disagree. He says, *"Sprich doch nicht so von dem Turm und ob er schön ist oder nicht. Mir ist es gleich, und dir auch; das mögen die Fachleute miteinander ausmachen"* (52) ["Don't talk about the tower like that, and whether it's beautiful or not. It's all the same to me, and to you too; let the experts decide that among themselves," 50].

Corinna considers herself an artist and calls her skills of invisible weaving an art. Her talents are in fact doubly textual: first, because weaving is itself an art that is etymologically linked to the production of texts (in Latin *texere:* to weave); and second, because she tells stories about her weaving. While Schmidt may be Fontane's *porte-parole,* Corinna has a uniquely allegorical function in the text. An artist and practicer of self-irony, she is both the dramatic agent of the narrative as well as the figure who stages the narrative strategy of the text as a whole. Her identity as an authorial double may also account for her preference for tea that tastes like ink, ink being a metonym for the authorial hand (131) [136].[28] Given Corinna's role as authorial double, we can no longer assume that Fontane represented his viewpoint exclusively through Professor Schmidt. Moreover, Corinna, in her capacity as authorial *porte-parole,* attests to the mobility of sexual roles, based as they are upon symbolic constructions.

As an artist/narrator, Corinna is vitally aware of her audience, Leopold, and performs with an eye toward engendering a particular response in him, namely, the response of his gender. Unfortunately, Leopold has a frail constitution. As a young man he was not sufficiently healthy to serve in the army; his mother forbids him to have more than one cup of coffee per day; and he is repeatedly referred to as an infant or a *"Wickelkind"* [babe-in-arms], the implication being that he has not yet been weaned from his mother's influence.[29]

Leopold's impotence is equated with his inability to weave a cohesive narrative. He confines his attempts at self-expression to the scratching of isolated signifiers into the sand:

Er blickte ... vor sich hin, knipste mit seiner Reitgerte kleine Kiesstücke fort und malte Buchstaben in den frischgestreuten Sand. Und als er nach einer Weile wieder aufblickte, sah er zahlreiche Boote, die vom Stralauer Ufer her herüberkamen, und dazwischen einen mit grossem Segel flussabwärts fahrenden Spreekahn. Wie sehnsüchtig richtete sich sein Blick darauf. (98)

> He looked down and flicked little pieces of gravel away with his riding crop and drew letters into the freshly strewn sand. When he looked up again after a while he saw numerous boats coming over from the Stralau shore and in between them a Spree barge with a large sail traveling downriver. His glance seemed to follow it yearningly. [100]

Leopold's gaze expresses the desire motivating his tracing of the letters into the sand. Unlike Lizzi, who is coerced into assuming a position in the symbolic order, Leopold wants to assume his sex by appropriating the powers of language. His yearning glance towards the boats and the barge with the large sail manifest a fascination similar to what Doane has described in reference to a character who gazes at a train and thereby expresses his "fascination with its phallic power to transport . . . [him] to 'another place.'"[30]

Corinna knows that Leopold's future depends upon whether he will be able to take control of narrative. She attempts to rouse Leopold with a display of her own narrative powers. She reintroduces the theme of ironing as a means of ironically dramatizing her own assumption of femininity. Addressing Mr. Nelson, Otto's English business associate, she says:

> Und zum Zeichen, dass ich, trotz ewigen Schwatzens, doch eine weibliche Natur und eine richtige Deutsche bin, soll Mr. Nelson von mir hören, dass ich auch noch nebenher kochen, nähen und plätten kann und dass ich im Lette-Verein die Kunststopferei gelernt habe. Ja, Mr. Nelson, so steht es mit mir. Ich bin ganz deutsch und ganz weiblich, und bleibt eigentlich nur noch die Frage: Kennen Sie den Lette-Verein und kennen Sie die Kunststopferei? . . . der Lette-Verein ist ein Verein oder ein Institut oder eine Schule für weibliche Handarbeit. (35–36)

> And to show that in spite of my eternal prattling I still have a feminine nature and am a genuine German, Mr. Nelson should know that I can cook, sew, and iron besides, and that I've learned invisible weaving in the Lette Institute. Yes, Mr. Nelson, that's how it is with me. I'm completely German and completely feminine and that just leaves the question—do you know the Lette Institute and do you know what invisible weaving is? . . . The Lette Institute is an institution or a club or a school for feminine handicrafts. [32]

Corinna groups together her domestic skills—cooking, sewing, ironing, and invisible weaving—all of which function as signs, *Zeichen,* of her femininity. As such, these skills are signs of her ability to create a wholeness analogous to the phallic wholeness associated with Helene's preoccupation with symbols.

In the following scene, Corinna tells a story that parallels Helene's tale of blinding, in that its effects depend upon the verbal representation of violence:

> Aber lassen wir das, um uns mit dem weit Wichtigeren zu beschäftigen, mit der Kunststopfereifrage. Das ist wirklich was. . . . Sehen Sie, hier ist mein Freund Leopold Treibel und trägt, wie Sie sehen, einen untadeligen Rock mit einer doppelten Knopfreihe, und auch wirklich zugeknöpft, ganz wie es sich für einen Gentleman und einen Berliner Kommerzienratssohn geziemt. . . . Und nun, wenn wir aufstehen, Mr. Nelson, und die Zigarren herumgereicht werden—ich denke, Sie rauchen doch—, werde ich Sie um Ihre Zigarre bitten und meinem Freunde Leopold Treibel ein Loch in den Rock brennen, hier gerade, wo sein Herz sitzt, und dann werd' ich den Rock in einer Droschke mit nach Hause nehmen, und morgen um dieselbe Zeit wollen wir uns hier im Garten wieder versammeln und um das Bassin herum Stühle stellen, wie bei einer Aufführung. . . . Und dann werd'ich auftreten wie eine Künstlerin, die ich in der Tat auch bin, und werde den Rock herumgehen lassen, und wenn Sie, dear Mr. Nelson, dann noch imstande sind, die Stelle zu finden, wo das Loch war, so will ich Ihnen einen Kuss geben und Ihnen als Sklavin nach Liverpool hin folgen. Aber es wird nicht dazu kommen. Soll ich sagen leider? Ich habe zwei Medaillen als Kunststopferin gewonnen, und Sie werden die Stelle sicherlich *nicht* finden. (36–37)

> But let's drop that to occupy ourselves with something far more important, with the question of invisible weaving. . . . You see, here is my friend Leopold Treibel and he's wearing, as you see, a faultless coat with a double row of buttons, and really buttoned up too, as is proper for a gentleman and a son of a Berlin Kommerzienrat. And I would estimate that the coat cost at least a hundred marks. . . . And now when we get up, Mr. Nelson, and the cigars are passed around—I imagine you do smoke—I'll ask you for your cigar and I'll burn a hole into my friend Leopold Treibel's coat, right here where his heart is, and then I'll take the coat home in a cab, and tomorrow at the same time we'll all gather again in the garden and place chairs around the basin of the fountain, as for a performance. And then I'll make my entrance like an artist— which I indeed am—and will let the coat make the rounds, and if you, dear Mr. Nelson, are still able to find the spot where the hole

was, then I'll give you a kiss and will follow you to Liverpool as your slave. But it won't come to that. Should I say, unfortunately? I've won two medals for invisible weaving, and you'll surely not find the spot. [32–33]

While this scene may first appear to be a frivolous display of coquetry, the strategy of coquetry itself manifests a tightly knit logic of aggressive desire. The entire performance, ostensibly presented for Mr. Nelson, is designed to trigger Leopold's mimetic desire. Corinna intends to win Leopold from her rival, Jenny, through a plan of attack whereby she exercises her femininity as a soldier wields a weapon. The metaphor of combat is suggested by the proof of her skill, her medals, which are like military decorations, as well as by the price of her defeat: she would be taken captive and enslaved. Her strategy is to convince Leopold of her phallic power and thereby to stimulate his desire to co-opt that power from her. The sign of Corinna's success as a woman would thus be her failure as a phallic weaver of holes into wholes: were Mr. Nelson to find the hypothetical *Loch* [hole]—a sure sign of femininity—he would secure a kiss and the spoils of matrimonial bondage. When Corinna assures Mr. Nelson that it will not come to that, she does not necessarily mean that the hole will not be found, but that she does not want him to be the one to find it. It is Leopold's heart she attempts to win by first burning a hole in it, a task she would accomplish by borrowing the phallic power of Mr. Nelson's cigar. The word for the garment Corinna proposes to burn, *"Rock,"* means both jacket and skirt, a fact that introduces an additional element of sexual indeterminacy into Leopold's character and even carries the more violent implication that the burning of the jacket/skirt is commensurate with an act of symbolic castration.

Like Lizzi's normality, Corinna's coquetry is described as an excess that inspires horror. Marcell states, *"Ich habe dich beobachtet, sag' ich, und mit einem wahren Schrecken das Übermass von Koketterie gesehen, mit dem du nicht müde wirst, dem armen Jungen, dem Leopold, den Kopf zu verdrehen"* (50) ["I was watching you, I say, and I was genuinely horrified at the excesses of coquetry you tirelessly used to turn that poor boy's, Leopold's, head," 48]. If the horror of Lizzi's normality derives from the way it reveals the essence of femininity to be masquerade, the analogous horror of Corinna's excess consists in her willingness to expose the dependence of female masquerade upon the occult powers of narrative. Corinna comments to Leopold,

[Ich könnte] . . . mich vor Ihnen als Seherin etablieren. Aber ich werde mich hüten. Denn vor allem, was so mystisch und hypnotisch und geisterseherig ist, haben gesunde Menschen bloss ein Grauen. Und ein Grauen einzuflössen ist nicht das, was ich liebe. (124)

I could . . . establish myself as a seeress before you. But I'll beware of that. For healthy people have a dread of everything that's as mystical and hypnotic and spiritualist as that. And I don't like to instill dread. [127–28]

In her next performance, Corinna does in fact establish herself as a seeress before Leopold. She pretends to read Leopold's future by telling a story whose effect will be to incite him to action. She envisages a marriage, describing it in detail but withholding the identities of the bride and groom. Corinna narrates how the bride and groom of the imaginary scenario approach their honeymoon residence:

"Sie . . . halten . . . vor einem Triumphbogen, an dessen oberster Wölbung ein Riesenkranz hängt, und in dem Kranze leuchten die beiden Anfangsbuchstaben: L und H."
"L und H?"
"Ja, Leopold, L und H. Und wie könnte es auch anders sein. Denn die Brautkutsche kam ja von der Uhlenhorst her und fuhr die Alster entlang und nachher die Elbe hinunter, und nun halten sie vor der Munkschen Villa draussen in Blankenese und L heisst Leopold und H heisst Hildegard."
Einen Augenblick überkam es Leopold wie wirkliche Verstimmung. Aber, sich rasch besinnend, gab er der vorgeblichen Seherin einen kleinen Liebesklaps und sagte: "Sie sind immer dieselbe, Corinna." (126)

"They stop in front of a little villa before a triumphal arch with a giant wreath at its highest point, and in the wreath glow the two initials L and H."
"L and H?"
"Yes, Leopold, L and H. And what else could it be? For the bridal coach came from the Uhlenhorst and drove along the Alster River and afterwards down the Elbe, and now they're stopping in front of the Munk villa out in Blankenese, and L means Leopold and H means Hildegard."
For a moment Leopold seemed overcome with something like genuine ill humor. But quickly recollecting himself he gave the

pretended seeress a little love pat and said, "You're always the same, Corinna." [129, trans. modified]

As a seer, Corinna occupies the position in the economy of visual representation reserved for the male spectator. Her story is proffered to Leopold as a challenge to his masculinity, or more precisely, to challenge him into manhood. She invites him to displace her as reader of signs and thereby to assume his sex. Leopold rises to her challenge with a gesture of (loving) violence meant to upbraid Corinna for possessing the phallic ability to interpret the signs of the future. The description of Leopold's initial reaction to the story as something *"wie wirkliche Verstimung"* ["like genuine ill humor"] echoes the authentic feeling— *"etwas wie wirklicher Neid"* ["something like genuine envy"]—with which Jenny had reacted to the *"anmutiges Bild"* ["charming picture"]. This parallel suggests that both Leopold and Jenny respond to an image, only in opposite ways: the totalized image of the ironer affords Jenny reassurance, counters the anxiety she feels when Leopold tells her about his engagement. Her response indicates that the image is a comforting ideal to which she aspires, not something she takes as already realized. If Jenny's attitude towards the image makes explicit the discontinuity between it and the heterogeneous totality of the subject, Leopold's anxiety in face of Corinna's performance attests to the misperception at the basis of his absorptive identification with the image of totality. Like Jenny, Leopold can never *be* that whole. Self-identical totality is, finally, an aesthetic and not an existential principle. And yet, Leopold proceeds as if the aesthetic and the existential were one and the same. He identifies so completely with the phallic wholeness of the image that he feels threatened by Corinna's apparent possession of that same attribute. And so, to preserve his self-image, he must insist that Corinna is sexually other and identifiable: she is always the same—*"immer dieselbe"*—he says, referring to her constant weaving of tales, but also establishing that she is self-identical and hence knowable through the phallic terms of male desire.

Leopold cannot assign such a stable identity to his mother. During the outing to the Halensee, Jenny is walking ahead of Leopold and Corinna:

Ein paarmal schon war er nahe daran gewesen, eine wenigstens auf sein Ziel überleitende Frage zu tun; wenn er dann aber der Gestalt seiner stattlich vor ihm dahinschreitenden Mutter ansichtig wurde, gab er's wieder auf, so dass er schliesslich den Vorschlag machte, eine gerade vor ihnen liegende Waldlichtung in schräger Linie zu passieren, damit sie, statt immer zu folgen, auch mal an die Tête kämen. Er wusste zwar, dass er infolge dieses Manövers den Blick der Mama vom Rücken oder von der Seite her haben würde, aber etwas auf den Vogel Strauss hin angelegt, fand er doch eine Beruhigung in dem Gefühl, die seinen Mut beständig lähmende Mama nicht immer gerade vor Augen haben zu müssen. Er konnte sich über diesen eigentümlichen Nervenzustand keine rechte Rechenschaft geben und entschied sich einfach für das, was ihm von zwei Übeln als das kleinere erschien. (123–24)

A couple of times already he had been close at least to asking a question that would lead to his goal; but when he would see the stately figure of his mother striding on in front of him, he would give it up again. Finally he suggested that they cut diagonally across a clearing just now in front of them in order that they would be in the lead once instead of always following. He realized that as a result of this maneuver he would get Mama's glance from the back or from the side, but with something of the attitude of an ostrich, he found relief in the feeling of not having his mother before his eyes, constantly laming his courage. He wasn't able to account for this peculiar nervous state and simply chose what seemed to him the lesser of two evils. [127]

The eye is again the privileged organ of sense, and Jenny clearly monopolizes the active position: as the object of Leopold's view she lames him, and as viewer she makes her gaze felt, even when it is not frontal. The phrase *"an die Tête"* solicits particular attention; because it is an idiom of French derivation, it stands out from the body of the paragraph and thereby structurally evokes Leopold's fear of separation, decapitation, or even castration. The images of the ostrich as well as the *tête* in the idiom itself both underscore the medusan quality of the scenario. Jenny's power consists in her ability to bar Leopold from language. Indeed, her command over the language of others has already been illustrated in the bedroom scene when she lent a voice to the silent ironer.

Corinna and the Treibel women struggle for control of the narratives that determine identity. Insofar as Corinna ironically reveals that identity is not based on essence but on the ability to control narrative, she has the means to gain access to Jenny's social position and symbolically to contaminate it with Jenny's repressed, *verklärte* past. Jenny's struggle to exclude Corinna from the *Besitzbürgertum* is, finally, an exercise in self-hatred, an attempt to keep her own repudiated past, which Corinna symbolically represents, out of the present.

Critics have viewed Corinna's decision to break her engagement to Leopold as proof of Jenny's relentless hold on him, despite textual evidence to the contrary.[31] When, for example, Schmidt, a reliable authority in the novel, offers such an interpretation, Marcell convinces him that it is erroneous (174). It has also been suggested that Corinna's decision attests to her superior wisdom, to her realization that the life to which she aspired is empty.[32] But even after she has broken her engagement, Corinna maintains that she still feels the desires that initially motivated her and that she would have enjoyed the life she would have had with Leopold.

The critical scene in which Corinna calls off her pursuit of Leopold reveals that the resolution of the novel does not result from any radical change in Corinna's viewpoint. Rather, it is motivated by an external, meta-narrational exigency. In the scene, Corinna and Schmolke, the household servant, are preparing the midday meal. The question of the marriage still remains open, and Corinna's inclinations are unclear.

> Corinna war nicht zum Sprechen zu bewegen, wenn die Schmolke begann: "Ja, Corinna, was soll denn nun eigentlich werden? Was denkst du dir denn eigentlich?" Auf all das gab es keine rechte Antwort, vielmehr stand Corinna wie am Roulette und wartete mit verschränkten Armen, wohin die Kugel fallen würde. (164)

> Corinna couldn't be moved to speak when Schmolke began: "Well, Corinna, what's it actually going to be now? What do you actually think?" There was no real answer to all that, and instead Corinna stood as if at the roulette wheel and waited with her arms crossed for where the ball would stop. [171, trans. modified]

The first task we see Corinna performing is pounding cinnamon for the fruit dish Schmolke is preparing. The women begin discussing the benefits and hazards of eating unpeeled, unstemmed fruit. Corinna explains that the stem and peel contain *"das Adstringens"* ["the astringent"] (168) [176]:

> Das Adstringens, das heisst das, was zusammenzieht, erst bloss die Lippen und den Mund, aber dieser Prozess des Zusammenziehens setzt sich dann durch den ganzen inneren Menschen hin fort, und das ist dann das, was alles wieder in Ordnung bringt und vor Schaden bewahrt. (168–69)

The astringent, that means that which draws together—first the lips and the mouth, but this process of drawing together continues throughout the whole inside of a person, and that's what then puts everything in order again and protects from harm. [176]

Like Corinna waiting for the roulette ball to drop, the narrative seems to be in a state of suspension; it resembles the *inneren Menschen* [inside of a person] in need of being pulled together and having its *Ordnung* [order] reaffirmed. Indeed, the self-reflexivity of the description is suggested by the *"zusammenziehen"* ["draws together"], which also means to mend together and which consequently recalls the textual production associated with *Kunststopferei* [invisible weaving].

Corinna switches activities and begins grating rolls for breadcrumbs. She

begann nun ihre Reibetätigkeit mit solcher Vehemenz, dass die geriebene Semmel über den ganzen blauen Bogen hinstäubte. Dann und wann unterbrach sie sich und schüttete die Bröckchen nach der Mitte hin zu einem Berg zusammen, aber gleich danach begann sie von neuem, und es hörte sich wirklich an, als ob sie bei dieser Arbeit allerlei mörderische Gedanken habe.
Die Schmolke sah ihr von der Seite her zu. Dann sagte sie: "Corinna, wen zerreibst du denn eigentlich?"
"Die ganze Welt."
"Das is viel . . . und dich mit?"
"Mich zuerst." (169)

began her grating activity with such vehemence that the grated rolls scattered out over the whole blue wrapper. Now and then she interrupted herself and poured the crumbs together into a little mound in the center, but immediately afterwards she would begin anew, and it really sounded as if she were having all sorts of murderous thoughts during this work.
Schmolke watched her from the side. Then she said: "Corinna, who is it you're actually grating up there?"
"The whole world."
"That's a lot . . . and yourself with it?"
"Myself first of all." [176]

Corinna's murderous grating both displaces and repeats Jenny's aggression. Destroying herself and the world, Corinna imitates Jenny's repudiation of her earlier self as the hostile other.

And yet, in the moment in which Corinna decides to break her engagement, the narrative offers no explanation for Corinna's decision. It occurs in silence and is signified only by the shine in Corinna's eye. Schmolke says to Corinna,

> "Ja, Corinna, da kann ich dir bloss noch mal sagen, dann is es wirklich die höchste Zeit, dass was geschieht. Denn wenn du *ihn* nicht liebst und *ihr* nich hasst, denn weiss ich nich, was die ganze Geschichte überhaupt noch soll."
> "Ich auch nicht."
> Und damit umarmte Corinna die gute Schmolke, und diese sah denn auch gleich an einem Flimmer in Corinnas Augen, dass nun alles vorüber und dass der Sturm gebrochen sei.
> "Na, Corinna, denn wollen wir's schon kriegen, un es kann noch alles gut werden. Aber nu gib die Form her, dass wir ihn eintun, denn eine Stunde muss er doch wenigstens kochen." (171)

> "Well, Corinna, then I can just tell you once more that it's high time that something happens. Because if you don't love *him* and don't *hate* her, then I don't know what the whole business is about."
> "I don't either."
> And with that Corinna embraced the good Schmolke, and the latter saw in the glistening in Corinna's eyes that everything was over now and that the storm had broken.
> "Well, Corinna, then we'll make it all right, and everything can still come out fine. But now give me the form so we can put it in because it does have to cook an hour at least." [178, trans. modified]

The reconstitution of Corinna's fragmented self is based on neither a conscious act of judgment nor a discernible necessity. Like the game of roulette, the narrative hangs in a state of suspense—if not threatened suspension—for which there seems to be no apparent resolution. It is not as if Corinna now suddenly recognizes the superiority of her values over Jenny's, or of the *Bildungbürgertum* over the *Besitzbürgertum*. Rather, a narrative exigency speaks through her: as Schmolke states, it is time for something to happen in the story. The story must achieve closure, meet the requirements of form. Hence Schmolke's request for the baking *form*.

The novel's denouement, which is as random as a game of roulette, reveals that the narrative is structured according to the principle of self-irony that Professor Schmidt espouses and Corinna stages. Just as Corinna's self-irony emphasizes the theatricality or fictitiousness of identity, grounded as it is in an imaginary identification with an image rather than in an unchanging essence, so, too, does the text self-consciously reveal its resolution to be a literary legerdemain. Put in slightly different terms, Corinna's decision to give up her pursuit of Leopold marks the point in the text where the internal logic of the plot threatens to break down. It is only for the purpose of formal closure that Corinna renounces her desire to assimilate to the *Besitzbürgertum*, not because she no longer feels this desire but because the persistence of her desire is precisely what threatens to subvert the constitutive opposition between the *Besitzbürgertum* and the *Bildungsbürgertum* that enables the novel's sustaining conflict to develop.

We can now see a certain complicity between the novel's patently artificial resolution and the aesthetic procedure of Jenny's memory, which, as Corinna states, transfigures [*"verklärt"*] the past by repressing certain enduring correspondences between it and Corinna (13) [7]. In fact, the historicity of Jenny's self-understanding and the diachronic progress of the plot both evolve through a process that dissimulates the crucial similarities between the two principle female characters. Bourgeois subjectivity and aesthetic totality have their origins in the same process of repression.

The final scene of the novel, Corinna's wedding to Marcell, further underscores the manner in which the conclusion calls into question the oppositions founding the internal logic of the plot. Corinna and Marcell are on their way to Verona for their honeymoon, and Jenny has gone home. Only Kommerzienrat Treibel, Schmidt, and Krola, the former opera singer who customarily accompanies Jenny on the piano, remain. Schmidt asks Krola to perform Jenny's favorite song, claiming that the performance will be a kind of desecration: *"Unser Treibel wird es nicht übelnehmen, dass wir das Herzenslied seiner Eheliebsten in gewissem Sinne profanieren. Denn jedes Schaustellen eines Heiligsten ist das, was ich Profanierung nenne"* (186) ["Our Treibel won't take it amiss that this song, so dear to his beloved wife's heart, is profaned in a sense—for every exhibition of something sacred is what I call a profanation," 196].

The performance of the song does indeed profane it insofar as it reverses its customary significance. Whereas for Jenny the song embodies the poetic, in this performance it becomes a vehicle for the subversion of her notion of the poetics of essence. This subversion emerges through the interplay between the lyrics of the song and the event of its performance. The text reproduces the lyrics, even though they were already quoted earlier, and thereby encourages us to consider them in the specific context of their performance.

Glück, von allen deinen Losen
Eines nur erwähl' ich mir,
Was soll Gold? Ich liebe Rosen
Und der Blumen schlichte Zier.

Und ich höre Waldesrauschen,
Und ich seh' ein flatternd Band—
Aug' in Auge Blicke tauschen,
Und ein Kuss auf deine Hand.

Geben, nehmen, nehmen, geben,
Und dein Haar umspielt der Wind.
Ach, nur das, nur das ist Leben,
Wo sich Herz zum Herzen find't. (187)

Fortune, of your thousand dowers
There is only one I want.
What good is gold? I love flowers
And the rose's ornament.

And I hear the rustling branches,
And I see a flutt'ring band—
Eye and eye exchanging glances,
And a kiss upon your hand.

Giving, taking, taking, giving,
And the wind plays in your hair.
That, oh that alone is living,
When the heart to heart is paired. [197]

The scene of the performance is not confined to Krola's rendering of the song; it encompasses the actions of the characters who are witness to the performance as well. The poem presents a world of irenic understanding in which language is notably absent and communication takes place through the unmediated gaze. The communion between the lyrical subject and its addressee is expressed through a series of images that suggests even exchange or mutual reciprocity: *"Aug' in Auge Blicke tauschen"* ["eye and eye exchanging glances"], *"Geben, nehmen, nehmen, geben"* ["giving, taking, taking, giving"], and *"Herz zum Herzen"* ["heart to heart"].

As Schmidt walks towards the piano with Treibel, it becomes clear that the actions, gestures, and words of the two men have been scripted by the lyric itself. The narrator depicts their comradeship through an image that recalls the doubled eyes and hearts of the poem: *"Schmidt und Treibel [folgten ihm] Arm in Arm"* (186–87) ["Schmidt and Treibel followed him arm in arm," 196]. When asking Krola to perform the song, Schmidt says, *"Der Augenblick ist da"* ["The moment has come"] (186) [196], thereby anticipating the *"Aug' in Auge Blicke"* of the second stanza. A cognate of *to exchange, "tauschen,"* appears in the frame narrative and is accentuated through repetition: Schmidt says to Treibel, *"Hab' ich recht, Treibel, oder täusch' ich mich in dir? Ich kann mich in dir nicht täuschen. In einem Manne wie du kann man sich nicht täuschen"* (186) ["Am I right, Treibel, or am I deceived in you? I can't be deceived in you. By a man like you one can't be deceived," 196, trans. modified].[33]

The presentation of the lyric at the novel's conclusion is thus another vehicle for displaying the lyrical nature of the conclusion itself. The scene not only represents Krola's performance of the song, it also dramatizes the song's lyrics. Schmidt and Treibel are now impelled by the force of a poem; they act out a fiction in a novel whose resolution bespeaks the demands of literary form. This final *mise-en-scène* thus stages the artificial nature of the conclusion, which unfolds according to an authorial fiat that marks a rupture (like the *Schattenriss* of the ironer) in the novel's mimetic referentiality.[34]

There is even a suggestion at the conclusion of the novel that the subversion of the text's mimetic referentiality comprises its political significance. After hearing his lyric performed, Schmidt says of his writing career, *"Ich hätte doch am Ende dabei bleiben sollen"* (187) ["I should have in the end stuck to it," 197, trans. modified]. The gesture towards endings echoes Schmidt's remark, *"Corinna, wenn ich nicht Professor wäre, so würd' ich am Ende Sozialdemokrat"* (160) ["Corinna, if I weren't a professor I'd become a Social Democrat in the end," 166]. The similarity of these comments suggests that the lyrical and the political converge in their critiques of the essentializing logic of identity. This convergence, moreover, may begin to explain why Fontane, unlike Schmidt, in the end stayed with his literary career.

At the same time, the echo of Schmidt's earlier statement recalls the bourgeois implications of Schmidt's political critique and his choice — if it can be called one — of irony over politics as such. Indeed, Treibel and Schmidt's joining of arms ironically stages the proximity of the *Besitzbürger* and the *Bildungsbürger*. Inasmuch as he and Treibel are exchangeable *(tauschbar)*, Schmidt is deceived *(getäuscht)*, or deceives himself, even though he wants to be assured that Treibel could not deceive him. Moreover, this final manifestation of irony suggests yet another of its connotations that is implicit in *"Plätten"* — irony as a covering up or leveling of difference: *platt*, as in *"etwas platt drücken,"* also means to flatten something out.[35]

The critique of "conventional" political engagement is thus itself subject to critique in a manner that exceeds the intentionality of either Schmidt or Fontane. While Schmidt attempts to maintain a satirical distance from the bourgeoisie, the form of his flirtation with the Social Democratic position suggests the dependence of his views on bourgeois ideology. His restrained, hypothetical protest veils an ambivalence that prepares for the possibility of an ironic standpoint. This standpoint is itself indebted to the position of the bourgeois class; it is possible for Schmidt to refuse to make a political choice only as long as the bourgeoisie remain in a position of social power. (The belief that one could stand above political parties was expressed by late-nineteenth-century writers like Freilegrath, who wrote political poetry for the middle class.) Schmidt's affinity with the bourgeoisie is further manifest in the notion of the subject that informs his ironic position, which is based on the bourgeois view of the self as autonomous and free-floating. In a strict class analysis one would have to say that Schmidt's ambivalence towards politics is precisely the inscription of his (and Fontane's) objective class position into their critiques of the bourgeoisie; here, as always, class position helps determine the place from which Schmidt speaks, even when he intends to suggest the contrary.

In general terms, we could say that *Frau Jenny Treibel* reveals the structural relationship between Schmidt's form of irony and Jenny's notions of the aesthetic. Both entail a form of deception: while Schmidt's irony dissimulates the constellation of social power that authorizes the decision to abstain from political engagement, Jenny's notion of aesthetic form as disclosing essence veils the fact that identity is based on one's positioning in a narrative that always reflects a will to power. Moreover, the plot of the novel undermines the apparently free position of the ironist by revealing Corinna's free choice to be a novelistic construct, that is, to be wholly determined, as it were, by a roulette wheel that she is not spinning. In the end, she does not decide her fate; it is decided for her by an agency she cannot comprehend. And while art and politics literally and figuratively converge at the novel's conclusion, the final, subversive irony of the text, which exceeds all authorial intentionality and thereby attests to the novel's "rare" form of poetic *Verklärung,* suggests that such a convergence is possible in fiction alone.

Six

Orality, Aggression, and Epistemology in Walker Percy's *The Second Coming*

The Second Coming (1980) has been read as a celebratory affirmation of the restorative powers of love in the modern world. Like all of Percy's protagonists, Will Barrett, hero of both *The Last Gentleman* (1966) and *The Second Coming,* is a perennial seeker. But unlike Binx Bolling, Dr. Thomas More, and Lancelot Andrewes Lamar, Will actually discovers the objects of his pursuit.

When the novel opens, Will Barrett is experiencing spells of physical and psychic dislocation: he inexplicably falls down on golf courses and suffers extended fits of involuntary memory. Recently widowed, Will comes to recognize that he and his wife had been virtual strangers to each other and that he is equally estranged from his only daughter, Leslie, "a dissatisfied nearsighted girl whose good looks were spoiled by a frown which had made a heavy inverted U in her brow."[1] While Leslie quells her discontent through "new-style" Christianity, "giving her life to the Lord through a personal encounter with Him," Will rejects the dogmatic forms of both old- and new-style Christianity (152). Well into middle age, he finds himself detached from family, friends, and God and slowly losing hold of whatever tenuous connections to the world he had hitherto maintained.

A second line of narration, interwoven with Will's story, centers on Allie, a young woman tired of conforming to the demands of her parents and of attempting to achieve socially determined goals. Having made straight A's yet "flunked life," Allie has a breakdown and stops using rational discourse (99). She is committed to a mental hospital but eventually escapes with the intention of seeking legal counsel. She takes refuge in an abandoned greenhouse located on a piece of property she has recently inherited. The last thing she expects is that a man—a lawyer—will fall through the roof of her greenhouse. This is precisely what occurs when Will attempts to resolve his existential crisis by proving or disproving the existence of God. In order to do this, he descends into a cave that extends into the side of a mountain, where he will await a sign from God. If the sign appears, his reasoning goes, he will possess the certainty that God exists and thereby gain what he feels is necessary for continuing to live. If no sign is forthcoming, he will die, and others will profit from his death, which will attest to God's absence or at least to his unwillingness to make his existence known. Will's experiment is, however, interrupted by a toothache. Forced by nausea and excruciating pain to abort his plan, he climbs towards the mouth of the cave. On the way he falls through the roof of Allie's greenhouse, which abuts the cave. The events that follow certainly seem to suggest that Will and Allie each move from individual alienation to intersubjective union. She nurses her unexpected guest back to health, and they fall in love and plan to marry. While Allie intends to start a small business, a nursery, in her greenhouse, Will plans on returning to the practice of law. They will buy a garden home, have a child, and even employ the itinerant characters who have appeared at various points in the story (a detail that promotes the sense of narrative closure) — Kelso, a fellow patient at the mental hospital, Mr. Ryan, a contractor, and Mr. Arnold, a cabin notcher. The latter two are living in a rest home but are eager and fit enough to work. Will and Allie even seem to establish a kind of ideal discourse together; he understands every oblique comment she makes, follows the metonymic associations of her speech, and, because she does not always understand conventional language, promises to fulfill her need for an interpreter.

Critics have praised the relationship of Will and Allie in language verging on the rapturous. Jac Tharpe notes, "In love they are reborn, Allison immanent, Will transcendent, Allison speaking in tongues their holy idiocy, Will listening at last without deafness."[2] According to Patricia Lewis Poteat, theirs is "a quiet tale of love and life hard-won and finite and good."[3] Most recently, John Edward Hardy has written, "Percy's *The Second Coming* is in the first place a love story, a story of earthly love, and quite a beautiful love story. Beautiful love stories, plausibly 'affirmative' love stories, are extremely rare in fiction that purports to treat in any way realistically the life of our unhappy times."[4]

The majority of critics read the text as a *depiction* of the overcoming of existential alienation, lending authority to Percy's remark that *The Second Coming* "may be the first unalienated novel written since Tolstoy." (It should be noted that Percy explicitly states that this comment is intended "half-seriously.")[5] These critics identify Will Barrett as the agent of this overcoming of alienation and thereby tacitly assume that the narrative is a mimetic transcription of that event. Ted

Spivey writes, "For the first time in his work, Percy actually shows in detail what it means to live the ordinary life joyfully. . . . he portrays two characters who by finding the secret of communication through the shared discovery of themselves and of God are able to see ordinary life illuminated by joy."[6]

The popularity of the novel seems largely due to its didactic appeal. The novel holds out the promise of meaning to the reader, who is led to believe that he or she, too, can have access to significance in life. Will's experience is said to disclose "stratagems for being" that potentially apply to the world beyond the text, and Percy is accordingly seen as "tempting readers to identify with his people," a statement that would seem to suggest that Percy encourages his readers to use the novel as a manual for their own real-life situations.[7]

To my knowledge only one reader of Percy, Doreen Fowler, has expressed reservations about the novel's being successful in any sustained way. Her analysis is interesting because it implicitly raises questions about the relation between Will Barrett's quest for knowledge on the one hand and the project of the critic/reader on the other. Fowler points to an ambivalence in Percy's fiction that is particularly manifest in *The Second Coming*.

> Try as he will to offer constructive criticism, to suggest alternative modes of living, to root out the source of the modern malaise, Percy's very manner of presentation frequently seems either to defuse or to invalidate his answers. A fundamental ambivalence polarizes his fiction as Percy tries to make his art stretch to straddle two widely disparate views of life—a heroic, idealistic attitude and a more practical, empirical position. Because Percy refuses to commit himself entirely to one view, his answers are often contradicted by opposing suggestions in the novel, creating a precarious balance of opposites.[8]

The ambivalence Fowler identifies concerns the status in the novel of absolute knowledge. On the one hand, *"The Second Coming* counsels acknowledgement of man's inability to see."[9] On the other hand, even at the novel's conclusion, Will continues to pursue absolute knowledge.

Fowler believes that Will's retreat to the cave in pursuit of a sign from God is extremely resistant to interpretation. She provides a number of possible readings of the episode without deciding in favor of any single one. She first suggests that "Percy is implying a substitution of Allison for love of God. Will was looking for a manifestation of God and found Allison, who offers the possibility of love."[10] Or perhaps, she speculates, Percy is implying that absolute knowledge exists but remains inaccessible to man. She compares Will's search for knowledge to the Platonic allegory of the cave as well as to the flight of Icarus. Whereas the first analogy suggests that "man's inability to see the truth does not necessarily mean that the truth does not exist," the second association is a reminder of man's limitations and a lesson in acceptance of those limitations.[11]

The overdetermination of the cave experiment, laden as it is with possible meanings, does not lend itself to any one reading. Fowler is thus compelled to generate various alternatives that, upon closer consideration, appear mutually contradictory and raise further questions: if Will is reminiscent of the figure of man in Plato's epistemological allegory, but with the added hubris of Icarus, why is he not punished like Icarus when he attempts to approach the light of absolute knowledge? Why is he instead rewarded with the discovery of love? And if Fowler is correct in stating that Will learns that "one can act and must act despite limited understanding," why does Will not know this?[12] As Fowler notes, after Will finds his answer and is "asked what the answer was, he replies, 'I don't know.'"[13]

The scene in the novel in which "the answer" is apparently disclosed makes it increasingly clear not only that Will is ignorant of all solutions, but more importantly, that the urgency of his desire for knowledge is derailed through narrative irony. In that scene, Will says to Allie, "There is something . . . I want to tell you. About me. . . . It's what I learned in the cave and what I am going to do" (243). Instead of continuing, Will becomes quiet and watches the rain outside. Once he does begin to speak, the narrator relates not his words but Allie's reaction to them. When Allie has trouble understanding the meaning of his words, the narrator does not supplement her reaction with another perspective. The reader is thus compelled to rely on her perception alone. Furthermore, when Will finally addresses the issue of the cave and its significance, his voice is drowned out by an electrical storm. It is as if the tension Fowler identifies between two contradictory but discrete "views" in the novel is circumscribed in this scene by a series of narrative devices that displaces Will as the novel's epistemological center. While Fowler herself notes the divergence between narrator and protagonist, the terms of her own analysis compel her to override the competing narratorial presence. She does this by appealing to an unexamined norm of mental health. She writes, "We see the world through his [Will's] eyes, and the narrator tells us that Will is crazy. If we discount Will's views as psychotic, what view does the novel offer? We have

Will's world or none; there is no alternative. And despite the narrator's warnings, Will does not appear insane."[14] Fowler must silence this other narratorial voice, because it seems to pose a danger to interpretation: it threatens to revoke the one view proffered by the text and thereby to place the critic in the uneasy situation of having no firm grasp of the text's meaning.

A further, even more unsettling danger emerges when we consider Fowler's summary of the salient characteristic common to all of Percy's heroes.

> Like all of Percy's protagonists, he [Will] needs to know. He questions as naturally as he breathes; wonder is his nourishment. . . . He is determined to unveil the hidden truth, sharing with all of Percy's heroes a will to understand. . . . All of these characters are distinguished by the same quality—a formidable thirst for knowledge. They weigh, question, hypothesize, and interpret every word, gesture, and posture in an unending quest for meaning. For them, life is a search.[15]

In characterizing Will Barrett and the other Percyian protagonists, Fowler aptly, if inadvertently, describes the profile of the literary critic, who weighs, questions, hypothesizes, and interprets every word, gesture, and posture in an unending quest for meaning. And yet, it is precisely with respect to the search for knowledge or signs of presence that the narrator pronounces the following judgment on Will:

> Madness! Madness! Madness! Yet such was the nature of Will Barrett's peculiar delusion when he left his comfortable home atop a pleasant Carolina mountain and set forth on the strangest adventure of his life, descended into Lost Cove cave looking for proof of the existence of God and a sign of the apocalypse like some crackpot preacher in California. (186)

The narrator's comment about the madness of Will's hermeneutic inquiry also has implications for any literary analysis that views the text as supplying "answers" or "solutions" to existential problems. The comment calls into question the assumption, underlying such readings, that the novel provides an (ideal) imitation or mimetic transcription of predicaments common to fictional characters and nonfictional readers alike. It would be tempting, because reassuring, to draw a distinction between sane and mad forms of literary analysis; and yet, if we acknowledge that every reading is motivated by a will to understand, the narrator's comment renders *all* interpretation, regardless of its aim, mad as such. The question is not whether we can avoid this madness but whether the narrative of Will's quest can help us to recognize and understand the madness of understanding that impels this and every reading of the novel.[16] I will track, in what follows, the narrative voice whose presence Fowler senses but does not see articulated in the novel in any coherent way. It is this voice, speaking through an insistent strategy of ironic subversion, that lends insight into the madness of the hermeneutic enterprise.

Keeping in mind that Will's quest for meaning thus allegorizes the reader's, I'd like to begin my analysis by considering the connotations of Will Barrett's name. Fowler points out that it captures the hero's will to discover, to "bare it." An additional, more oblique play on the name intimates the nature of the impulse to reveal; the narrator queries, "Where does such rage come from? from the discovery that in the end the world yields only to violence, that only *the violent bear it away,* that short of violence all is in the end impotence?" (165, my italics). This passage suggests that the hermeneutic enterprise of "baring it" may itself entail a violence that cannot be dissociated from a certain phallic strength—short of this violence, all is impotence; I will return to the implications of this violence later.[17]

Certain details of Will's cave experiment outline the contours of the violence that may be indigenous to the uncovering of knowledge. The following passage describes the reasons Will was forced to abort his experiment:

> Unfortunately for the poor man awaiting the Last Days and raving away at God and man in the bowels of Sourwood Mountain directly below thousands of normal folk playing golf and antiquing and barbecuing and simply enjoying the fall colors—for on the following day at the height of his lunacy the cloud blew away and the beautiful days of Indian summer began, the mountains glowed like rubies and amethysts, and leafers were out in force—unfortunately things can go wrong with an experiment most carefully designed by a sane scientist. A clear yes or no answer may not be forthcoming, after all. The answer may be a muddy maybe. In the case of Will Barrett, what went wrong could hardly be traced to God or man, Jews or whomever, but rather to a cause at once humiliating and comical: a toothache. So in the end not only did he not get an answer to his peculiar question, not a yes or a no or even a maybe—he could not even ask the question. How does one ask a question, either a profound question or a

lunatic question, with such a pain in an upper canine that every heartbeat feels like a hot ice pick shoved straight up into the brain? The toothache was so bad it made him sick. He vomited.

There is one sure cure for cosmic explorations, grandiose ideas about God, man, death, suicide, and such—and that is nausea. I defy a man afflicted with nausea to give a single thought to these vast subjects. A nauseated man is a sober man. A nauseated man is a disinterested man. (199–200)

The author/narrator here assumes an ironic, omniscient position over his "poor" character. Speaking in the name of sanity and appealing to the values of immediacy and groundedness embodied by the prosaic activities of the world above the cave, he poses a rhetorical question at the end of the first paragraph that emphasizes the inevitability of Will's failure to ask the profound question. At the same time, the hyperbolic rhetoric of the second sentence in the second paragraph—"I defy a man"—ironically calls attention to the artifice of the situation he claims is inevitable: while it may be true that nausea "cures" cosmic explorations and grandiose ideas, it is also the case that the most natural, unpredictable, and prosaic of afflictions—a toothache—is, here, a fictive construct. Not God or man, Jews or whoever, but the author/narrator composes this "humiliating and comical scene." As such, the "cure" for Will's epistemological itch is as consciously constructed as the "natural" infirmity; it displays a narrative logic that emulates the principle of the vaccination, which cures the disease through the disease and thereby reveals the nature of the sickness. In Will's case, the toothache that cures belongs to a series of images that establish a relationship among three elements: orality, aggression, and the search for knowledge.

The orality associated with knowledge had already informed Will's entry into the cave, itself an obvious cavity. Before Will even ventures inside, he experiences the cave orally: "He opened his mouth. Clean ferrous ions blew onto his tongue" (196). Similar imagery recurs in the episode, as for example, when Will turns "past a lip of rock" (196).

Teeth and toothaches are also mentioned in connection with Allie's father. The author/narrator describes the anatomy of his smile, which extended "back to his eyeteeth . . . all his expressions, even frowns, occurred within the smile" (99). His salient attribute is an aggressiveness that manifests itself as the will to abuse the mouths of his patients with his instruments—he is, fittingly, a dentist—and their ears with his unsolicited speeches. In the following passage, Allie, who used to assist her father's dental hygienist, reflects upon her father and his medical practices.

> He had passionate and insane views on every subject. She was certain that one reason he had taken up dentistry was so he could assault helpless people with his mad monologues. In he'd come, smiling and handsome, hands scrubbed pink, breath sweet with Clorets, and while she kept the patient's mouth dry with a suction tube, he'd stuff the same mouth with hot wax and crowns and fillings and fingers and then he'd come out with it. (99)

The patients of Allie's father are victims of an aggression legitimated by his position of authority yet barely dissimulating his blatant sadism. While Allie is not directly in her father's line of fire, the silence to which she, as his assistant and daughter, is relegated doubles the silence imposed upon the patients. Nevertheless, even in their most inflamed manifestations, the attacks by Allie's father remain rhetorical, as for example when he declaims, "Do you know what I'd do with all of them? Line them up against that wall and go down the line with my BAR" (99), speaking of "coal miners, hippies, queers, Arab sheiks, Walter Cronkite, George Wallace . . . media Jews, Miami Jews . . . Ronald Reagan . . . Roosevelt(!), Carter, Martin Luther Coon, Kennedy, Nixon . . . the Mafia, Goldwater . . . J. Edgar Hoover" (99).

In contrast to Allie's father's verbal attacks, another scene of oral paternal aggression is more overtly physical. Will's father commits suicide in a way that marks the most emphatic intersection of orality and violence: he fires a double-barreled gun into his mouth. In an extended and graphic meditation on his father's death, Will attempts to come to terms with the significance of the suicide. The meaning of the death is perhaps the most difficult and knotted issue in the text; it conjoins questions of interpretation—what it means for Will to "bare" the significance of his father's death—with problems of inter- and intrasubjective aggression.

As an adult, reflecting upon the suicide, Will relates it to an event that preceded it. When he was a boy of thirteen, he had gone on a quail shoot with his father. His father misfired, wounding Will and himself. According to one reconstructed account, the father had been beset by a dizzy spell and lost his balance, accidentally discharging the double-barreled shotgun. Years later, Will realizes that this account is false. He reconstructs the chain of events, based on the number of shells retrieved by a Negro guide after the accident. This other account proves that his father had consciously intended to kill Will and then himself but had changed his mind at the last second and missed Will. The father eventually commits suicide, although he does not make another attempt to take Will's life. In his reconstruction, Will links sequentially the attempted filicide/suicide and the suicide. He sees the suicide as the belated execution of whatever his father was trying to accomplish on the quail shoot.

> The sorrow in your eyes when I came over and sat beside you in Georgia—were you sorry you did it or sorry you didn't. . . . Sorry you didn't do it. Because the next time you took no chances and did it right, used both barrels, both thumbs and your mouth. (143)

According to Will, his father achieves "the next time" what he did not get right the first time. While the second attempt takes only one life, the "overkill" apparent in the use of two barrels and two thumbs is also overdetermined, given that originally Will's father was going to shoot both Will and himself.

Will accounts for his father's shift in plans by incorporating the recollection of the hunting trip into a fantasy of epistemological transmission:

> *Ah then, so that was it. He was trying to tell me something before he did it. Yes, he had a secret and he was trying to tell me and I think I knew it even then and have known it ever since but now I know that I know and there's a difference.*
>
> He was trying to warn me. He was trying to tell me that one day it would happen to me too, that I would come to the same place he came to, and I have, I have just now, climbing through a barbed-wire fence. Was he trying to tell me because he thought that if I knew exactly what happened to him and what was going to happen to me, that by the mere telling it would not then have to happen to me? Knowing about what is going to happen is having a chance to escape it. If you don't know about it, it will certainly happen to you. But if you know, will it not happen anyway? (62–63)

Will's fantasy of epistemological transmission may have the effect of blocking out another possible meaning of the episode, namely, that the attempted filicide was a sign of the father's lack of love, a fear that could have been reenforced by Will's loss in childhood of his mother, who had died at a young age. The father's suicide would thus feel like a second act of parental abandonment. The fantasy prevents Will from arriving at such a conclusion. To Will's question, "Was it love or failure of love?" that made the father pull up at the last second, the fantasy answers, "love" (143). In the second paragraph of the above passage, Will poses a series of questions that reveals both his hope that the transmission of knowledge will foster immunity from "it" as well as his fear that even knowledge cannot change the course of events. Despite his hope, however, Will cannot but repeat his father's experience precisely in the act of believing his father has taught him a lesson. It will become evident that Will's acquisition of knowledge actually participates in a process of symbolic suicide that structurally replicates the real death of the father.

The "secret" Will believes he learns from the father's suicide pertains to the convolution of death-in-life. He thinks,

> The name of this century is the Century of the Love of Death. Death in this century is not the death people die but the death people live. Men love death because real death is better than the living death. That's why men like wars, of course. Bad as wars are and maybe because they are so bad, thinking of peace during war is better than peace. (252)

The confusion of death and life manifests itself in different forms of aggression, both inter- and intrasubjective. The following passage characterizes the relation of Will's grandfather to the other as intersubjectively aggressive, or sadistic, and that of his father to the other as intrasubjective, or masochistic: "Both his grandfather and his father had enemies. One, like Ivanhoe, had enemies he hated. The other had the guilts like [Lord] Jim and an enemy he hated, himself. And one had the shotgun, the other the Luger. What do you do when you are born with a love of death and death-dealing and have no enemies?" (141). While Will makes a genealogical distinction when he aligns sadism with his grandfather and masochism with his father, the two forms of aggression are not mutually independent; sadism turns out to be another manifestation of masochism. Will's father discovers his enemies in the external world. Will reflects,

> I was never so glad of anything as I was to get away from your doom and your death-dealing and your great honor and great hunts and great hates (Jesus, you could not even walk down the street on Monday morning without either wanting to kill somebody or swear a blood oath of allegiance with somebody else). (72)

Inasmuch as the self-hatred of Will's father compels him to assume a hostile position vis-à-vis an intersubjective other, his masochistic belligerence is in fact a version of sadism. Conversely, while Will's father wants to kill another, and does attempt to kill his son, he is not differentiated from the object of his aggression: *"You and I are the same,"* he says to Will just before the shooting incident (56). If we take the father's words *à la lettre,* they signify the absence of a defined identity, the merging of self and other in an imaginary moment characterized by the unstable polarities of love and aggression.

The confusion of self and other corresponds to a condition of semantic deficiency. Will's father attempts to account for the blurring of particular oppositions such as life/death and war/peace in terms of a lack in language:

> One night after the war and during the Eisenhower years the father was taking a turn under the oaks. The son watched him from the porch.
> "The trouble is," the man said, "there is no word for this."
> "For what?"
> "This." He held both arms out to the town, to the wide world. "It's not war and it's not peace. It's not death and it's not life. What is it? What do you call it?"
> "I don't know."
> "There is life and there is death. Life is better than death but there are worse things than death."
> "What?"
> "There is no word for it. Maybe it never happened before and so there is not yet a word for it. What is the word for a state which is not life and not death, a death in life?" (122–23)

If Will's father cannot find the proper word for the state of death-in-life, Will by contrast seems able to arrest the confusion by discovering the missing name. The following passage suggests that the acquisition of the name defines the border between death and life, self and other. Will muses,

> Ha, there is a secret after all, he said. But to know the secret answer, you must first know the secret question. The question is, who is the enemy.
> Not to know the name of the enemy is already to have been killed by him.
> *Ha,* he said, dancing, snapping his fingers, and laughing and

hooting, *ha hoo hee,* jumping up and down and socking himself, *but I do know. I know. I know the name of the enemy.*

The name of the enemy is death, he said, grinning and shoving his hands in his pockets. Not the death of dying but the living death. . . . I know your name at last, he said, laughing and hooting *hee hee hooooee* like a pig-caller. (251–52)

Will celebrates his discovery of the name, which he believes will save him from ending up like his father. He thereby gives a negative answer to the question he had posed earlier, "If you know, will it not happen anyway?" (63). Yet, it is precisely the identification of the forms of death through the discovery of the "name" of the enemy that reveals the scandalous connection between knowledge—"I know. I know. I know the name of the enemy"—and a particular mode of violence: knowing and naming, or knowing as naming, creates discrete identity—life versus death, enemy versus enemy—within the very economy of sadomasochism that Will had attributed to his father and grandfather. Will thinks,

Death in the form of death genes shall not prevail over me, for death genes are one thing but it is something else to name the death genes and know them and stand over against them and dare them. I am different from my death genes and therefore not subject to them. My father had the same death genes but he feared them. (254)

While Will believes that naming will engender the death of death, to the extent that the repudiated "gene" of death is a part of himself, the act of naming becomes inseparable from a masochistic splitting of the self into an aggressive opposition between self and other. A fundamental ambivalence is thus associated with naming: while it is an indispensable cognitive process, it functions by imposing hostile borders that displace and divide identity in representing it. When Will designates his other through a genetic metaphor, he engages in a fictionalizing act of projective expropriation that enables him to create his identity. This act ironically replicates the very antagonism he believes he is evading. In this respect, the "secret" answer to the "secret question" is yet another form of suicidal dissolution.[18] The "secret" reveals that the constitution of identity through naming is synonymous with a form of symbolic suicide. The meaning Will assigns to his father's death thus points to the *modus operandi* of the process of naming. In other words, within the logic of Will's fantasy of epistemological transmission, the suicide allegorically stages this process. Hence, the gesture of rejecting the father's death as other, as something from which Will can escape, expresses Will's desire to reject the process of naming itself. Seen in this way, Will's fantasy of epistemological transmission bespeaks his determination to make his father's death mean something as well as his desire to evade the divisive effects of the symbolic order.

In summation, Will makes himself audience to the scenario of naming by installing the death of his father in a narrative of epistemological transmission; he places himself in the role of recipient of "secret" knowledge, thereby attempting to contain the secret and protect himself from its effects. This gesture of containment actually replicates the very violence Will endeavors to elude, for to reject his father's death, and symbolically the act of naming, is to replicate structurally the very process of naming.

To the extent that Will's recollection of the hunt performs a psychic service, it functions like fantasy, as Abraham and Torok define it:

> Fantasy is in essence narcissistic: rather than make an attack on the individual, it attempts to transform the world. The fact that it is often unconscious indicates, not that it is irrelevant, but that its frame of reference is a *secretly maintained* topography.
>
> Thus the task of understanding a fantasy becomes specific: to pinpoint concretely what topographical change the fantasy is called on to resist.[19]

According to this logic of the fantasy, Will's narrative of epistemological appropriation protects his psychic constitution from the narcissistic loss suffered through the acquisition of the name, that is, through the accession into the symbolic order with its attendant intrapsychic splitting of the ego. Furthermore, Will's refusal of the loss, which he accomplishes by constructing a narrative about it, conforms to the pattern of one fantasy in particular that Abraham and Torok isolate and discuss, the fantasy of incorporation: "Whereas in the mechanism of introjection, language articulates and thereby supplements an absence, by *representing* presence . . . it is because the mouth cannot articulate certain words, cannot utter certain phrases . . . that in fantasy one will take into the mouth the unspeakable, the thing itself." According to Abraham and Torok, the words of introjection are available as long as the loss they signify can be recognized: there must be *"auto-apprehension"* of the absence of the object.[20]

The substitution of incorporation for introjection is thus the response to a verbal inhibition. To the extent that naming creates identity by dividing the non-identical, it is an act of symbolic suicide that enables self and other to become knowable entities, that is, knowable as entities. The efficacy of the act depends on the inhibition of the knowledge and articulation of its constitutive violence: were the created self to recognize the process of its differentiation in a moment of self-consciousness, the borders that divide and create the self would dissolve. The father's death can only stage the act of naming *for* Will, because the father himself cannot be subject and audience of the scenario in which he participates. Will, in turn, cannot comprehend that he repeats the self-divisive act his father performed. Since he cannot acknowledge through mourning the loss of the narcissistic object, he instead objectivizes the process of naming through a narrative of paternal suicide. Will's reconstruction thus superimposes the fantasy of rejecting representation, on the grounds of its "suicidal" violence, onto the real event of the hunting accident.

As if to underscore the fantasmatic nature of the reconstruction, Will confuses the object of mourning. The following two passages reveal that rather than mourn the loss of the father, Will mourns his own death:

> All these years he had thought he was in luck that it didn't happen and that he had escaped with his life and a triumphant life at that. But it was something else he had escaped with, not his life. His life—or was it his death?—he had left behind in the Thomasville swamp, where it still waited for him. (275)

> I thought he missed me and he did, almost, and I thought I survived and I did, almost. But now I have learned something and been surprised by it after all. Learned what? That he didn't miss me after all, that I thought I survived and I did but I've been dead of something ever since and didn't know it until now. (301)

Through his rupture with his father, Will attempts to assert his difference from him. The text signals the inevitable failure of Will's attempt to distance himself from his father by ironically reinscribing the rejected other into the object of Will's desire. The love of death characteristic of his father returns in the person of Marion, Will's late wife, who literally and figuratively incorporates the fatal relation between identity and death that Will attempted to reject:

> After he married Marion, she seemed happier than ever, gave herself to church work, doing so with pleasure, took pleasure in him—and suddenly took pleasure in eating. . . . She ate and ate and ate. She grew too heavy for her hip joint already made frail and porous by polio. The ball of her femur drove into the socket of her pelvis, melted, and fused. She took to a wheelchair, ate more than ever, did more good works. . . . She truly gave herself to others—and ate and ate and ate, her eyes as round and glittering as a lover's. (151)

The repetition of the phrase "she ate and ate and ate" suggests that Marion holds a kind of fascination for Will. It is as if he is encountering a specular double of himself, the recognition of which he must resist; hence the sense of distance he establishes from her by portraying the chronology of their relationship as divided by a mysterious rupture: "suddenly," and, by implication mysteriously, everything changed.

Marion's own attempt to reject internal alterity manifests itself in the role she assumes as perpetual, voluntary mourner: "When an old person died at St Mark's, often there was no one to claim the body. Marion would go to great lengths to trace the family and arrange the funeral. Yamaiuchi would chauffeur them in the Rolls, leading the way for the hearse to distant Carolina towns, Tryon or Goldsboro" (126). In becoming a custodian of the dead, Marion locates and thereby tries to confine death to a position outside of herself. This process of division and confinement cannot be arrested, however, since placement of the death "outside" generates a narcissistic urge to reappropriate the obliterated other, to exhume its corpse and consume it as part of the self that is lost in the process of delimiting inside from outside, death from life:

> After the funeral in an empty weedy cemetery they would head for the nearest Holiday Inn in time for the businessman's lunch. Marion, animated by a kind of holy vivacity, would eat the $2.95 buffet, heaping up mountains of mashed potatoes and pork chops, and go back for seconds, pleased by the cheapness and the quantity of food. Like many rich women, she loved a bargain. (126)

Like Will's father, Marion kills herself through a process of violent oral incorporation. A comparison of the descriptions of the deaths reveals their structural affinity. In the lurid rhapsody that follows, Will imagines his father's suicide:

> I remember now. I cleaned the gun when I got it back from the sheriff in Mississippi. Both barrels. Wouldn't one have been enough? Yes, given an ordinary need for death. But not if it's a love of death. In the case of love, more is better than less, two twice as good as one, and most is best of all. And if the aim is the ecstasy of love, two is closer to infinity than one, especially when the two are twelve-gauge Super-X number-eight shot. And what samurai self-love of death, let alone the little death of everyday fuck-you love, can match the double Winchester come of taking oneself into oneself, the cold-steel extension of oneself into mouth, yes, for you, for me, for us, the logical and ultimate act of fuck-you love fuck-off world, the penetration and union of perfect cold gunmetal into warm quailing mortal flesh, the coming to end all coming, brain cells which together faltered and fell short, now flowered and flew apart, flung like stars around the whole dark world. (143)

The rhetorical force of this passage derives from the dense overlay of themes and images that are held together by an almost incantatory rhythm and sequence of repetitions. The passage fantasizes the violent event of suicide in figural language borrowed from the rhetoric of intimate self-enclosure. It thereby communicates the interrelation of perfect self-union or identity and infinite multiplication, identity as the non-identical. The violent combination of the rhetoric of intimacy and the theme of suicide also reflects the double edge of the experience Will reconstructs: in describing his father's death, he is also fantasizing his own symbolic death. To indicate that the suicide exhibits an extraordinary desire for death is not to suggest that there are other, more ordinary suicides; the extraordinariness and scandalousness of the father's death resides in its very ordinariness. The perversity of the desire for death is not exceptional. Rather, the suicide is "the logical and ultimate act" of a universal process that the father's death makes visible.

In the gun's doubleness condense the masochism of the samurai and the aggression of fuck-you love that doubles back on the self. This redoubling is stressed through the chain of syncopated repetitions of numbers and consonants (particularly "b," "f," and "g") that impels the narrative forward while making it fold back upon itself. The cold steel extension of gun into mouth engenders a chilling union of self, an encircling or creation of identity that is at once an explosion whose ambivalent volatility emanates from the chiastic conjunctions of imagery—death in germination, the dissolution of the self in its uniting depicted as a flowering and scattering of stars around the world. "This coming to end all coming" reads as a self-reflexive allusion to the novel's title, thereby suggesting that an ambivalent violence, a death in flowering, marks the production of the text as well, a point I will return to later. As if to emphasize that the quail shoot is a pretext, in both senses of the word, for the allegorization of the constitutive process of naming, the narrative reinscribes the bird of the filicidal hunt into the father's suicidal target, the "quailing mortal flesh."

In terms of the logic of incorporation, the "unspeakable" process of naming is here taken back into the mouth in the form of the gun.[21] The method of the father's suicide dramatizes the interrelation of death and the constitution of the self: the orality of taking a double-barrel gun into the mouth reflects both the desire to reincorporate the lost part of the self that has been split through the creation of identity, to take it back into oneself, and the sadomasochistic aggressiveness of the self vis-à-vis its expropriated other, which is stimulated by the need to keep the other out of bounds of the self.

Neither the phallocentricity of the suicide nor its ambivalence should be taken as issues of gender. Rather, the act of naming, to which both sexes are subject, is itself gendered. Both Will and Allie react against this phallocentricity, Will by repudiating the suicidal act of naming, and Allie by experiencing discomfort when she sees the gun/phallus:

> He [the policeman] had a large high abdomen. From a wide black cartridge belt a heavy revolver in a holster was suspended. The belt crossed his abdomen just below its fullest part. The position of the belt and the weight of the pistol created in her a slight discomfort. She wished he would hitch up his pants. (39)

A pattern of ejection and incorporation structures Marion's death as well. The following passage begins by describing Marion as a monstrous object of Will's fascination. The description condenses detail upon detail in its documentation of Marion's shopping list, gathering momentum as it mimetically expands to her appetite:

> It had been a pleasure for him to please and serve her. Only he, she said, had the strength and deftness to lean into the Rolls, take her by the waist while she took him by the neck, and in one quick powerful motion swing her out and around and into the wheelchair. . . . To the A & P, then push her by one hand and the cart by the other while she snatched cans off the shelves, Celeste pizzas, Sara Lee cream pies, bottles of Plagniol, brownies, cream,

butter, eggs, gallons of custard ice cream. . . . She ate more. She grew bigger, fatter, but also stronger. She ate more and more: Smithfield hams, Yamaiuchi's wife's shirred eggs, Long Island ducks. Cholesterol sparkled like a golden rain in her blood, settled as a sludge winking with diamonds. A tiny stone lodged in her common bile duct. A bacillus sprouted in the stagnant dammed bile. She turned yellow as butter and hot as fire. There was no finding the diamond through the cliffs of ocherous fat. She died. (151–52)

This passage resonates with references to the death of Will's father: the reference to Yamaiuchi's wife establishes an implicit link, via a common cultural denominator, to the samurai self-love of death; the sparkling golden rain of cholesterol winking like diamonds in sludge recalls the stars flung in the dark universe; and just as in the passage on the suicide the force of the image of destruction through vital growth derives from its chiastic pairing, here, as well, the productive conjunction of bacillus and stagnant bile renders fatal disease in terms of life-affirming proliferation. The cold rain of cholesterol and the heat of jaundice echo the confluence of cold gun metal and warm quailing flesh, while the onanism of the double-barrelled fellatio, the "taking oneself into oneself," finds its counterpart in the images of the driving, fusing and melting of the ball of Marion's femur into the socket of her pelvis and her glittering lover's eyes. At the same time, the erotic imagery in the two scenes retains a sense of violent self-abuse. The masochism of naming is inscribed into these images of flesh: Will's father turns his rifle on himself in an act that punishes flesh, and Marion amasses flesh, thereby destroying her own skeleton and poisoning her own blood.[22]

If Will believes that his knowing about knowing, his consciousness of death-in-life, will enable him to master the violence of the process of naming, Allie rejects the process entirely.[23] She recognizes the non-identity between word and thing and within the word itself. According to her, "words often mean their opposite" (81). The non-identity of language provides the occasion for others to co-opt meaning from her or to assign her their meanings: "No matter what she said or did, her mother would make her own sense of it" (100). And so she protests, "Stop trying to make sense of my nonsense" (92). In the following passage, which reads like an American counterpart to Kafka's *The Penal Colony,* the letter is incised into Allie's body. Allie reflects on her past life of conformity:

Sarge: spending a week with him at Nassau doing what I pleased or what I thought of as doing as I pleased. Sarge, a thin mustachioed blond Balfour Salesman (fraternity and sorority jewelry) from Durham, who knew his catalogue of pins and drop letters and crests so well that he had won a salesman-of-the-month trip to Nassau. Tickets for two. I, not a sorority sister, Sarge not a fraternity man, but he "pinned" me with four different pins, Chi O, Phi Mu, KD, Tri Delt, and we thought that was funny. Sarge always going by the book, usually the catalogue but in Nassau another book, Sarge and I in bed looking at a picture book and he doing the things in the book with me he thought he wanted to do and I doing the things I thought he wanted me to do and being pleased afterwards then suddenly knowing that the main pleasure I took was the same as doing well for my father: look at my report card, Daddy, straight A's, A Plus in music. (92)

The violent imposition of the name is figured here as a quadruple pinning of the fraternity letters onto the body. These Greek letters, like the alienating picture-book images that function as blueprints for erotic experience, inscribe the demands of representation upon the self.

Allie chooses to reappropriate self-control by rejecting linguistic convention. She withdraws into her own private language. In the hospital her doctor administers a variety of treatments and insists on the therapeutic value of the joke. He tells Allie jokes "to give her a 'language structure' so that she, who had stopped talking because there was nothing to say, would have a couple of easy lines, straight man to his comic" (85). The word Allie uses to describe the shock treatment that is supposed to jolt her back to meaningful discourse recalls the violence of the name embodied by Ewell McBee, the allegorical figure for the word: she calls the process a "buzzing" (89) (see note 18).

After Allie escapes from the hospital, she must relearn how to communicate with others. This is no less than a rediscovery of herself, because in rejecting language she has rejected identity as such. Much of the novel traces her reacquisition of language, beginning with her rediscovery of the name:

She gazed at the photograph on the license. She read the name. Earlier in the Gulf rest room she had looked from the photograph to the mirror then back to the photograph. The hair was shorter and darker in the photograph, the face in the mirror was thinner, but it was the same person.
She uttered her name aloud. At first it sounded strange. Then she recognized it as her name. Then it sounded strange again but

strange in a different way, the way an ordinary word repeated aloud sounds strange. Her voice sounded rusty and unused. She wasn't sure she could talk. (26–27)

Upon meeting Will, her resistance to language temporarily returns: "What to call *him*? Mr. Barrett? Mr. Will? Will Barrett? Bill Barrett? Williston Bibb Barrett? None of the names fit. A name would give him form once and for all. He would flow into its syllables and junctures and there take shape forever. She didn't want him named" (231). But contrary to her previous experience, the effects of Will's language upon her are not negative. When he is speaking to her, his language has a tactile but positive effect: "Even though he was not touching her, his words were a kind of touching" (245). Allie wonders, "Was he saying the words for the words themselves, for what they meant, or for what they could do to her" (243). The ideal nature of their communication is suggested by the contrast between the inscriptive Greek letters and the gentle gaze, which seems to be a means of transcendent communication. Unlike the Greek letters that impale, pierce, and control, Will's "looks did not dart, pierce or impale. They did not control her" (220). Similarly, the first time Will meets Allie, he notices her "fond hazed eyes" (76); reflecting later on the encounter he remembers "her soft dazed eyes" (77).

Insofar as the novel has a "happy ending," the introduction of the love story seems to mark a turning point.[24] And yet, certain details of the novel's conclusion cannot help but generate a sense of déjà vu in the reader. The life Allie and Will envisage together bespeaks a reclusive self-enclosure reminiscent of the father and Marion's deadly self-encirclings: the couple plans on developing a self-sufficient colony, a community outside of the community. When they venture out of the greenhouse together for the first time, they check into the Holiday Inn, a site strongly associated with the death-in-life they supposedly have overcome but which haunts the description of a meal Allie eats there: Will "fetched two plates from the buffet, Tennessee pork sausage, sweet potatoes, butter beans, corn on the cob, ten pats of butter, corn bread, buttermilk, and apple pie. . . . She began to eat. She ate fast and ate it all" (308). The accumulation of detail, the repetitive syntax of the final two sentences and the lipoid yellowness of the foods cannot but evoke the memory of Marion's deadly feasts.

Perhaps the most remarkable quality of the relationship concerns an unresolved question that a comment by John Hardy registers, albeit as a denegation; Hardy writes that while Will's feelings towards others carry "insistent and frequently sinister sexual overtones," the love affair *"redeems"* these other relationships.[25] This statement is extraordinary, in light of the numerous references in the text to the possibility that Allie and Will could be father and daughter. When Will first meets Allie, the narrator relates, "For one moment she was as familiar to him as he himself" (76). Allie has the same thought. She asks herself, "Was he someone she had known well and forgotten?" (106), and then immediately thereafter nearly asks Will if he is her father:

"Are you—?"
"Am I what?"
"Are you my—?"
For a moment she wondered if she had considered saying something crazy like "Are you my lover?" Or "Are you my father?" (106)

Kitty, Allie's mother, blatantly suggests to Will that Allie may be his daughter: "Sometimes I have the strongest feeling that you could be or ought to be her father—ha! fat chance, yet there is a slight chance, remember?" (161). Allie eventually poses the question of incest explicitly:

"Could you be my father?"
"Hardly."
"Remind me to look up hardly."
"Okay."
"How do you know you're not my father?"
"If I were I wouldn't be here."
"Then why is it I seem to have known you before I knew you. We are different but also the same."
"I know. I don't know."
"Then why does it seem I am not only I but also you?"
"I don't know." (242)

While the circular logic of Will's answer—the fact that he is there proves that he is not Allie's father—seems to invalidate his credibility, the text offers no reason to doubt Will. Had Will's relationship with Allie been incestuous, it is unlikely that it would have been discussed so explicitly in the novel. Will's ambiguous "Hardly," which is barely a yes or almost a no, suggests that the theme of incest may function as a decoy dissimulating another transgression that cannot be articulated within the discursive logic of the plot and that instead disrupts that logic.[26]

This unspeakable transgression is registered as a rupture in the following scene, in which Will discloses an important piece of information to Allie: "Because your mother and I are old friends, among other reasons, she has asked me if I will be your legal guardian—God I hate this beard, I meant to ask you to buy me a razor" (242). An odd disjunction, in the form of a dash, separates two apparently unrelated and peculiarly incongruous thoughts: the serious question of Allie's future and the comparatively insignificant remark about the stubble on Will's face. Nevertheless, a connection emerges if we consider a secondary meaning of the word "beard." A beard is "a person used as an agent to conceal the principal's identity."[27] It is also the pubic hair. In colloquial usage, a beard is a woman who poses as the heterosexual partner for a homosexual male. The pubic overtones of the name of Allie's mother, Kitty, suggest the possibility that she is the hateful beard who, by appointing Will to be Allie's legal guardian, plays cover or beard to a certain unarticulated sexual relation. Details in the text seem to support this possibility: the first time Will sees Allie, he mistakes her for a young boy, and even after he realizes that she is a girl dressed in oversize man's clothes, he mentions that her haircut makes him think of the expression "boyish bob" (76). At the end of the novel Will thinks of Allie's "lean muscled boy's arms" (334), and lest Will's desire be mistaken for an indeterminate homoeroticism, Allie's full name specifies the identity of the desired object: she is Allison, Alli-*son*. This reinscription of the father/son relationship into that of the lovers ironically undercuts the linearity of the plot; the resolution of the novel becomes an imaginary inversion and repetition of the attempted filicide which itself was replaced by the intrasubjective aggressiveness of naming. We traced this same structure of ironic repetition in Will's narrative of epistemological transmission: Will attempts to reject the splitting of the self, and the narrative ironically reinscribes it into the act of rejection.

If the acknowledgment of the taboo on filicide reflected the necessity of becoming (a) subject to and through the symbolic order, the possibility of incest registers the desire to evade that order. Moreover, the suggestion of incest occupies a pivotal position in the text: Will's remark that he could "hardly" be Allie's father indicates the point where the mimetic and self-reflexive lines of narrative converge. In this respect, Will's remark is overdetermined. In a literal sense, he is not Allie's father, so "hardly" in this context means no. At the same time, within the novel's symbolic economy the relationship is yet another version of the desire to reappropriate the loss accrued to the self in its constitution. As such, the suggestion of incest is the final element in a series of substitutions: it stands in for the homoerotic bond between father and son that in turn substitutes for and symbolically reverses the attempted filicide, which itself is an allegorical staging of the scenario of naming. Thus Will is Allie's father—just a little, "hardly," to the extent that genealogical relations in the novel express linguistic predicaments.

Insofar as the father insures both the creation and rupture of the self—the creation of the self as ruptured—he becomes the object of an ambivalence expressed through the figure of the Negro guide. Will explicitly acknowledges the struggle between the Negro guide and the father; he notes that when the father shot the dog on the hunting trip, he "could as easily have shot the guide" (165), and that "his father, known as a nigger-lover, cursed the guide like a nigger-hater" (164). The Negro guide also discovers the evidence, the empty shells, that help to establish that Will's father had attempted to kill him. The notable absence of Will's mother in the text suggests another attempt to preserve the presymbolic dyadic relation. In addition, the mother is mentioned only once in the novel, by a figure who metonymically lines up with the Negro guide: D'Lo, the black servant who cared for Will as a child, says, "You poor little old boy, you all alone in the world. Your mama dead, your daddy dead" (255).

As a figure of social marginality, the Negro guide can be said to pose a challenge to the symbolic order from the margins of that order itself. This function also extends to another socially marginalized character, the Jew. Throughout the novel Will is haunted by the question of the Jew's significance. He constantly asks himself and others, "Are the Jews a sign?" The narrator makes the following comment about this question: "It is not at all uncommon for persons suffering from certain psychoses and depressions of middle age to exhibit 'ideas of reference,' that is, all manner of odd and irrational notions about Jews" (15). If the narrator does not dispute that the Jews may be signs, he does label as delusive the idea that these Jews refer to something outside of themselves. Like the Negro guide, the Jews embody the desire to exceed or repudiate the symbolic order and for this reason signify something about that order. Ethel Rosenblum is the primal Jewish figure in the text:

> Suddenly he knew why he remembered the triangular patch of woods near the railroad tracks where he wanted to make love to Ethel Rosenblum. It was the very sort of place, a nondescript weedy triangular public pubic sort of place, to make a sort of love or to die a sort of death. (156)

The significance of Ethel is, from the very beginning, ambivalent, to the extent that Will's desire for her occupies the same space as death.

Ethel becomes the object of desire at the moment Will literally falls onto a text whose title indicates the nature of that shared space:

> Once in his life had he set foot on this unnamed unclaimed untenanted patch of weeds, and that was when he saw Ethel Rosenblum and wanted her so bad he fell down. So keen was his sorrow at not having his arms around her, his fingers knotted in her kinked chalk-dusted hair, that he flung himself down in a litter of algebra books, ring binders, *Literature and Life,* down into the Johnson grass and goldenrod, onto the earth smelling of creosote and rabbit tobacco. (11)

Deprived of Ethel, Will falls onto *Literature and Life*. The action of flinging recalls the "brain cells flung like stars" in the description of the suicide and thereby reaffirms the continuity between death and the fall into language.

Will's desire derives from his fascination with Ethel's ability to create unity out of difference:

> She could factor out equations after the whole class was stumped, stand at the blackboard, hip hiked out, one fist perched cheerleaderwise on her pelvis, the other small quick hand squinched on the chalk, and cancel out great a^2-b^2 complexes *zip zip slash,* coming out at the end: $a/a = 1, 1 = 1!$ Unity! . . . No matter how ungainly the equation, ugly and unbalanced, clotted with complexes, radicals, fractions, *zip zip* under Ethel Rosenblum's quick sure hand they factored out and canceled and came down to unity, symmetry, beauty. (11)

Ethel's mathematical abilities are the specular inversion of the suicidal multiplication of the self. Whereas that process moved towards infinity and expansion, Ethel reduces and cancels difference. Just as the alternative to the paternal suicide was filicide, which was characterized by the lack of differentiation between self and other and which was prior to the act of naming, so too is Ethel's unity prelinguistic. Will's recollection of Ethel expresses his desire for unity and not his state of being; indeed, as Ethel's surname, Rosenblum, intimates, this desire is bound up with the death-in-flowering of the father's suicide. Moreover, the images of her hip hiked out, her pelvis, and her fist (through its roundness) recall the fusing of the ball of Ethel's hip into the socket of her pelvis and thus align Will's desire for Ethel with his desire for Marion. It also suggests a continuity between Marion's fatal attempt to reincorporate her lost self and Ethel's ability to create unity.

I mentioned earlier that the description of the father's suicide contained a self-reflexive allusion—"the coming to end all coming"—to the novel's title. It suggested that an ambivalent violence, a death-in-flowering, pertained to the novel's production as well. The connection between the suicidal dispersion of naming and *The Second Coming* is more explicit in the passage in which Will holds an imaginary dialogue with his dead father, who seems to beckon him from the grave to follow his example. In that dialogue the father refers to suicide as "the second, last, and ultimate come to end all comes" (312).

In the context of the self-reflexive references, the scene of the attempted filicide/suicide is significant, because it not only narrates the logic of naming, it is itself implicated in that very logic and stages this implication. The scene returns repeatedly, even compulsively, in the novel and with great clarity. It appears to have the status and significance of a kind of primal scene; it was the only event that "had ever happened to him [Will] in his life. Everything else that had happened afterwards was a non-event . . . nothing else had ever happened to him" (53). If we consider that the shooting is presented as a *reconstruction*, a tension emerges, analogous to that surrounding the discussion of incest, between the traumatic nature of the material and the form in which it is presented. The reconstruction is coherent, precisely detailed, and fully accessible to Will's consciousness. It is subject to neither the distortions nor the displacements that typically alter traumatic memories, which raises the possibility that this crime, like the issue of incest, might be an alibi for another, more unspeakable transgression that is not so readily narratable. A repetition links the attempted filicide to another incident and thereby strengthens the possibility that the "real," reconstructed event is a symbolic displacement or screen memory for the other scene.[28] When the novel opens, Will is playing golf and slices out-of-bounds: "As he searched for the ball deep in the woods, another odd thing happened to him. He heard something and the sound reminded him of an event that had happened a long time ago. It was the most important event in his life, yet he had managed until that moment to forget it" (7). The "most important event" he immediately refers to is not the hunting incident, which the narrator states was the only event "that had ever happened to him in his life" (53). There are thus *two* events that are supposedly of primary and unmatched significance. The only way to reconcile these competing claims is to assume that the separate events are, in fact, identical.

The other event with the same status as the attempted filicide concerns the piece of land that was the site of Will's desire for Ethel. Will's memory of the land is triggered by a sound. The memory returns "as if the scene lay before him" (10). Its uncanny vividness further establishes its affiliation with the memory of the shoot, since that recollection also displays the heightened presence typical of a screen memory:

> Instead of the brilliant autumn-postcard Carolina mountains, he seemed to see a weedy stretch of railroad right-of-way in a small Mississippi town. It wasn't even part of the right-of-way, but no more than a wedge-shaped salient of weeds angling off between the railroad tracks and the back yards of Negro cabins. It was shaped like a bent triangle, the bend formed by the curve of tracks. Perhaps it was owned by the railroad or perhaps by the utility company, because in one corner there was a small metal hut. Or perhaps it was owned by the city, because at the end of this narrow vista of weeds rose the town water tower. Or perhaps it belonged to no one, not even the Negroes, a parcel of leftover land which the surveyors had not noticed on their maps. (10)

Despite the narrator's claim that this land is unremarkable, the persistence with which he returns to it belies the claim itself. The narrator refers to the land as a "nondescript sector of earth . . . this unnamed unclaimed untenanted patch of weeds . . . [a piece of] leftover land . . . this non-place . . . this surveyor's interstice . . . [and] the only place not Jew or Gentile, not black or white, not public or private" (11–12).

The overdetermination of the triangular plot of land as well as its topography comprise an intertextual reference to "The Delta Factor," which is the introductory essay in Percy's collection of writings on semiotics entitled *The Message in the Bottle*. "The Delta Factor" opens with the following passage:

> In the beginning was Alpha and the end is Omega, but somewhere between occurred Delta, which was nothing less than the arrival of man himself and his breakthrough into the daylight of language and consciousness and knowing, of happiness and sadness, of being with and being alone, of being right and being wrong, of being himself and being not himself, and of being at home and being a stranger.[29]

In the above passage, Percy inserts the Greek letter delta, which according to him signifies irreducibility, between alpha and omega. He emends God's word as recorded by John, thereby identifying the biblical text of Christ's Second Coming as the site of Delta. This semiotic rewriting of the sacred text implies that the arrival of man is coterminous with the Second Coming of Christ; it turns the Revelation to John into an allegory of the appearance of man, a profane inversion that the novel substantiates by depicting Will's fall into the greenhouse as the arrival of Christ:

> Except for the golfer's tan of his face and arms, his skin was white, with a faint bluish cast. The abdomen dropping away hollow under his ribs, the thin arms and legs with their heavy slack straps of muscle, cold as clay, reminded her of some paintings of the body of Christ taken down from the crucifix, the white flesh gone blue with death. The closed eyes sunk in their sockets and bluish shadow, the cheekbones thrust out like knees. (219)

Bearing the same name as Christ's arrival (which Percy anthropomorphizes), *The Second Coming* can thus be read as an allegorical performance of the "arrival of Man" into the "daylight of language." As such, Percy's writings on the Delta Factor theoretically articulate the intersubjective phenomenon of naming or symbolizing staged in *The Second Coming*.

The Delta Factor designates the process whereby the individual receives a sensory message as well as a symbol that designates or names that message and couples the two, message and symbol. The act of coupling is astonishing in Percy's opinion, because the relation between the thing named and the name itself is not internally motivated but sanctioned by the authority of a namer. The namer's power to authorize the pairing of word and thing underscores the nonbinarity of the sign even as it insures that pairing.

In discussing the authority of the namer, Percy invokes scenarios of the discovery of language that involve individual subjects already constituted and installed within the symbolic realm. This should not overshadow the fact that the intersubjective process he analyzes is not restricted to an exchange between discrete, self-contained subjects; the Delta phenomenon pertains to the act of delimitation that occurs when subjects not only intersect in language but are intersected by language. As the opening quotation from "The Delta Factor" suggests, the breakthrough into the daylight of language is simultaneous with the birth of consciousness, whose structure it also indicates: happiness/sadness, being with/being without, being right/being wrong, being oneself/being not oneself, being home/being a stranger—are all defined by a structure of opposition, which the novel relates to the constitution of identity.

A second intertextual reference in *The Second Coming* attests to the "presence" of Percy's theoretical writings in the novel. While playing golf, Will sees a strange bird,

> undoubtedly some kind of hawk, fly across the fairway straight as an arrow and with astonishing swiftness, across a ridge covered by scarlet and gold trees, then fold its wings and drop like a stone into the woods. It reminded him of something but before he could think what it was, sparks flew forward at the corner of his eye. He decided with interest that something was happening to him. (49)

Resuming his golf game, he compares himself to the hawk, which in turn engenders a further association:

> He was of two minds, playing golf and at the same time wondering with no more than a moderate curiosity what was happening to him. Were they [the other golfers] of two minds also? . . . The hawk was not of two minds. Single-mindedly it darted through the mountain air and dove into the woods. Its change of direction from level flight to drop was fabled. That is, it made him think of times when people told him fabulous things and he believed them. Perhaps a Negro had told him once that this kind of hawk is the only bird in the world that can—can what? He remembered. He remembered everything today. The hawk, the Negro said, could fly full speed and straight into the hole of a hollow tree and brake to a stop inside. He, the Negro, had seen one do it. It was possible to believe that the hawk could do just such a fabled single-minded thing. (49–50)

The perception of the hawk's single-mindedness contrasts with Will's contrary sense of self-division. This contrast, moreover, is related to another difference that emerges between bird and man: the bird's single-mindedness is literally the stuff of fables whose persuasive force belongs to a time in Will's past. Will's sense of self-division, on the other hand, is not a fable but a reality of his present.

The hawk and the Negro guide also appear in the opening passage of Percy's essay "Metaphor as Mistake":

> I remember hunting as a boy in south Alabama with my father and brother and a Negro guide. At the edge of some woods we saw a wonderful bird. He flew as swift and straight as an arrow, then all of a sudden folded his wings and dropped like a stone into the woods. I asked what the bird was. The guide said it was

a blue-dollar hawk. Later my father told me the Negroes had got it wrong: It was really a blue darter hawk. I can still remember my disappointment at the correction. What was so impressive about the bird was its dazzling speed and the effect of alternation of its wings, as if it were flying by a kind of oaring motion.[30]

The incident of the hawk occasions the boy's discovery of the cognitive power of metaphor. Percy accounts for the boy's disappointment when the father corrects *blue-dollar* to *blue darter* by claiming that the phrase *blue darter* describes something *about* the bird—its color, what it does—whereas *blue-dollar* promises to disclose what the bird *is*. According to Percy, when one being is conceived of in terms of another, an essential distance must be preserved between name and thing to protect the freedom of the viewer's private apprehension. Percy calls this "the ontological pairing . . . or 'error' of identification of word and thing."[31] This is the mistake of metaphor. Since *blue-dollar* refers to something other than the bird that nevertheless has the same ontological status as the bird, the boy's delight derives from the disclosure of being that is afforded by the name *blue-dollar*. The efficacy of this metaphor is two-fold: in disclosing the being of the thing through the name, the metaphor simultaneously sanctions the selfhood of the naming, viewing subject. Citing Cassirer, Percy writes that the ability to name, to identify a thing, organizes the self through a process of projection in which "subjective impulses and excitations [are resolved] in definite object forms and figures."[32]

But what happens when the self submits to the mistake of metaphor, that is, when the self is both subject and object of language? Percy calls attention to the more violent counterface of the metaphoric process in "Symbol as Hermeneutic Existentialism," in which he writes:

> The whole objectizing act of the mind is to render all things *darstellbar*, not "proper" but presentable, that is, formulable. . . . The naming judgment . . . is both existential and figurative. It affirms that this *is* something, but in so rescuing the object from the flux of becoming, it pays the price of setting it forth as a static and isolated entity—a picture-book entity. But at any rate it is the requirement of consciousness that everything *be* something and willy-nilly everything *is* something—*with one tremendous exception*! The one thing in the world which by its nature is not susceptible of a stable symbolic transformation is *myself*. I, who symbolize the world in order to know it, am destined to remain forever unknown to myself.[33]

The self thus resists symbolic transformation. And yet it cannot avoid it either, since consciousness requires that everything *be* something. The self paradoxically appears as what it is not. Representation functions not as a revealing of being but as its concealing or distortion.

According to Percy, there is only one way in which the nonhypostatic being of the self can be recognized, namely, through the intersubjective gaze of another. In a passage reminiscent of the opposition between the letters that impale Allie's and Will's nonpiercing gazes, Percy writes, "What is revealed . . . in the discovering look of another . . . is literally my unspeakableness (unformulability). . . . I am exposed—as what? not as a something—as *nothing,* as that which unlike everything else in the world cannot be rendered *darstellbar.*"[34] Just as the authority of the namer insures the connection between word and thing, the gaze of the other acknowledges the distance between the forms the self assumes and the self's resistance to form. By perceiving the limits of the stabilized form of the self, the intersubjective gaze recognizes the limits of the representation or *Darstellung* that the self assumes in fulfilling "the requirements of consciousness that everything *be* something." It is significant that the other reveals the "unspeakableness" of being through its gaze and not through the word: "The look is of the order of pure intersubjectivity without the mediation of the symbol. . . . It is not formulable."[35] The truth of the self's unformulability cannot be spoken, because such an articulation would have to adopt the hypostatic formulations of the symbolic process whose limits it is attempting to expose.

Like all representations, Percy's essays are fully subject to the distortions of symbolization. The accuracy of Percy's theory is thus ironically attested to by the displacements that are legible in its presentation. Specifically, the *Darstellung* of the process of metaphor arrests the ambivalence of that process, insofar as it separates positive from negative effect: when metaphor represents an object to the subject, the subject experiences the pleasure of discovery (the child's jubilant reaction); when metaphor represents the objectizing subject, the subject is dehumanized (becomes a picture-book entity). To the extent that both moments depend on the silent recognition of the intersubjective other, who interrupts the dyadic pairing of word and thing, their separation cannot be taken at face value but must be seen as the result of metaphoric projection.

When Will Barrett associates the hawk with the world of fable, he implicitly relegates the possibility of self-identification to the past world of fiction. He sees himself, in contrast to the hawk, as divided, dual-minded. The chronological disjunction Will posits between self-identity and self-division in fact signifies a temporalization of a difference within the process of metaphor, inasmuch as Percy's theory of metaphor seems to imply that self-identity and self-division are inextricable and simultaneous effects of the constitutive power of metaphor. It would thus be a fiction to believe either that fables are the proper place of self-identity or that there was a time in the past when self-identity was not fabulous. The divisions of fable versus fact, present versus past, and self-identity versus self-division are not extra-textual realities but rather effects of the metaphoric process that organizes being into a representable form.[36]

Generally speaking, the difference Will establishes between himself and the hawk signifies a structural disjunction necessary to the generation of the fictional narrative. Moreover, given that the hawk is a Percyian icon for the constitutive process of metaphor, Will's gesture of temporal distantiation reveals how the constitutive effects of metaphor depend upon the dissimulation of the linguistic nature of the process. While Will's experience may represent this process, Will himself cannot comprehend its meaning. In terms of the novel's symbolic economy, the figure of the triangle of land as well as the hunting scene are images of narrative condensation that signify texts that are literally and figuratively out of bounds of the novel; literally, because they belong to Percy's theory of language—the wedge of land through its metaphoric similarity to delta and the hunting scene because of its appearance in "Metaphor as Mistake"—and figuratively, because they are metonymies for texts that call into question the basis for the linearity of the plot of *The Second Coming*. Percy's essays on semiotics pose the most radical challenge to the temporal and substantive oppositions structuring *The Second Coming* by theorizing how narrative temporalization derives from the necessity of splitting and isolating the ambivalence of the metaphoric process.

Critics who have written on Percy's theoretical writings as well as those who have noted the correspondence between Percy's fiction and his theory tend to overemphasize two points: they focus on the communicative intentionality of language to the exclusion of the question of the subject's formation in language, and they assume that Percy operates within a dualistic schema without recognizing that his writings are concerned with the process that generates these oppositions.[37] Fowler's comments about the problem of knowledge in *The Second Coming* are typical of this latter assumption. She locates the source of the problem in the individual when she reads the following statement by Allie as a comment on "innate human blindness":[38] "Imagine being born with gold-tinted corneas and undertaking a lifelong search for gold. You'd never find it" (42). What Fowler calls an image of blindness can be characterized more accurately as an image of the paradox of attempting to see the medium of sight. The person with gold-tinted corneas is not blind; it is just that everything he or she sees is tinted, as it were, with the subjective instruments of perception, which themselves cannot be isolated and viewed as discrete objects.

Allie's comment is a version of a passage from "The Delta Factor" that further specifies the medium of perception.

> The truth is that man's capacity for symbol-mongering in general and language in particular is so intimately part and parcel of his being human, of his perceiving and knowing, of his very consciousness itself, that it is all but impossible for him to focus on the magic prism through which he sees everything else.
>
> In order to see it, one must be either a Martian, or, if an earthling, sufficiently detached, marooned, bemused, wounded, crazy, one-eyed, and lucky enough to become a Martian for a second and catch a glimpse of it.[39]

In this passage, the magic prism, which is structurally analogous to the gold corneas, specifies through its deltic triangularity the intimate relation between language and perception, cognition, and consciousness. The one-eyed figure who can see this magic prism fittingly frames *The Second Coming:* during his golf game, Will "paused for several seconds, wood still held in both hands, fingers overlapped, and seemed to listen for something. He gazed up at the round one-eyed mountain, which seemed to gaze back with an ironical expression" (9–10). As if to have the last word, the one-eyed figure appears on the final page of the novel as well: "Will Barrett stopped the old priest at the door and gazed into his face. The bad eye spun and the good eye looked back at him" (334). Both the silent one-eyed mountain, not an earthling but a personification of the earthly, and the one-eyed priest embody the *modus operandi* of the novel's irony. This irony does not speak but gazes at Will Barrett in order to produce a silent but legible commentary on the limits of the text's own *Darstellung*. This voiceless irony inscribes process into effect, repetition into change, theory into fiction. It enables us to recognize that the text offers no solutions or answers to the search but instead figures the discursive and dispersive structure of language that makes the search conceivable in the first place.

Conclusion

Whereas the Greek world seems, from the perspective of modernity, to embody the concept of totality, in the post-Hellenic world, novelistic form compensates for the apparent loss of the objective totality. Lukács argues that such a loss signifies the disappearance of the conditions under which mimetic art is possible. Thus, rather than reflecting objective reality, the form of the novel manifests the modern subject's desire for totality. By examining the relationship between fetishism and the ambivalence that I argue is associated with formal totality, my analysis has attempted to suggest that the historical difference between mimetic and postmimetic art must itself be understood within the process of identity-constitution staged in the novel. Indeed, to assume that the novel is a mimetic form analogous to a mirror would be not only to deviate from Lukács's literary-historical schema but also to fall prey to a deception structurally analogous to the systematic deception of the fetish.

I have attempted to show how fetishism shares several of its primary attributes with one rendering of the realist aesthetic. For this reason it has been a recurrent topic in this study and constitutes what I consider to be my most salient contribution to the study of the novel. Freud's analysis of the fetish reveals the constitutive role of mimetic representation, or more accurately misrepresentation, in the process of identity-constitution. In this process, the representation of a totality becomes the model for the self, who then attributes non-identity to the other. The fetishistic moment depends for its effectiveness upon a confusion of the image with that which it supposedly represents: the perceiving subject does not recognize that its knowledge of self and other depends upon a form of narcissistic projection that construes identity in terms of totality and fragmentation. In the novels I have considered, the emphasis upon the visual register of perception, the locus of the fetishistic configuration, has been linked to an antagonistic relation between subject and object. For example, in *La Recherche de l'Absolu,* Joséphine is the symbolic equivalent of the tulips, which are nearly blinding; and in *Frau Jenny Treibel,* Lizzi enacts the threatening masquerade of femininity. The attempt to assimilate to totalizing forms turns out to be inseparable from a desire to domesticate the intra- and intersubjective other.[1]

In *La Recherche* and *The Second Coming,* Balthazar Claës and Will Barrett—like many critics of realist texts—entertain a concept of truth as that which needs only to be bared or unveiled. Such a notion of truth as an occluded but nevertheless accessible presence is contested in the novels themselves through a structural irony that enables the concomitant logic of domination characteristic of the visual, fetishistic metaphor to emerge. For example, in *The Second Coming* the relation between the search for visible, empirical, embodied truth on the one hand and aggression on the other is articulated in terms of a thematics of orality and a relation of sadomasochism that alternates between gestures of incorporation and of expulsion.

The novels I have analyzed do not avoid the logic of domination that they expose, and yet they do not simply replicate it either. We have seen how the structural irony of the novels subverts the authority not only of the protagonists but also of the narrative voices. My readings have identified switch points where the mimetic and reflexive lines of narrative converge, and I have argued that this convergence destabilizes the mimetic grounding of each text. In *La Recherche* Balthazar's deadly search for the absolute bears witness to the precariousness of creating the totality of the literary cosmos, *La Comédie Humaine;* in *Frau Jenny Treibel,* Professor Schmidt and Corinna embody the ideal standpoint of self-irony, and yet this standpoint itself turns out to be the expression of a class (the *Besitzbürgertum*) they consider to be antithetical to their own (the *Bildungsbürgertum*). *Jane Eyre* stages, while dissimulating, the violence inherent in both the creation of the domesticated female subject as well as in the writing of her story. Similarly, *The Second Coming* exposes the divisiveness of the process of naming. By figuring theory as out of bounds of fiction, the novel attempts to expropriate or deny that divisiveness.

While my readings have suggested the similarity between the structure of the fetish and the structure of the mimetic narratives I have analyzed, there are major differences between them concerning their degrees of critical reflexivity. The texts I have considered stage and thereby call attention to the initial, deceptive moment of identity-constitution. In *Die Theorie des Romans,* this staging takes the form of a displacement of the mytho-historical narrative into an allegorical narrative of identity-constitution. Lukács's literary-historical account of the development of the novel performs the process of creating a subject, who, furthermore, is by no means self-identical. In each of the four novels I have analyzed, mimetic referentiality, which requires a diachronic progression of the plot, is interrupted by a supplementary narrative that underscores the formal, nonorganic nature of the textual totality and the constitutive expulsions that subtend it.

Read in these terms, the theoretical and fictional works I have considered compel us to rethink the critical opposition that separates mimetic from nonmimetic discourse and indeed to postulate a relation of intratextual supplementarity between these putatively distinct modes of representation. In addition, they propose a conception of the subject as identical and yet divided, or divided because identical, and thereby complicate any firm demarcation between pre- and postmodernist conceptions of the literary subject. Finally, they suggest that the critique of operative notions of literary realism that I have been developing in these pages is in a sense anticipated by the very texts that have been classified under that rubric. This is the most radical inversion of all, if only because it makes it impossible to know in the end who reads and who is being read.

Notes

Introduction

1. Aristotle, *Poetics,* trans. Ingram Bywater, in *Introduction to Aristotle,* ed. Richard McKeon (New York: Random House, 1947), 661–62.

2. For a discussion of the *Poetics* in the context of Renaissance aesthetic theory, see Stephan Kohl, *Realismus: Theorie und Geschichte* (Munich: W. Fink, 1977), 50–51. In *A History of Literary Criticism in the Renaissance* (New York: Columbia Univ. Press, 1908), Joel E. Spingarn analyzes how the imitation of the classics affected the development of literary history; see especially chap. 5, 77–96. The amount of subsequent literature on imitation in the Renaissance is immense. See, for example, Thomas Greene, *The Light in Troy* (New Haven: Yale Univ. Press, 1982).

3. See Herbert Dieckmann, "Die Wandlung des Nachahmungsbegriffs in der französischen Aesthetik des 18. Jahrhunderts," in *Nachahmung und Illusion,* ed. Hans Robert Jauss (Munich: Eidos Verlag, 1964), 28–59. Dieckmann links the eventual decline of *imitatio* to the initial elevation of reason by the rationalistic and scientific currents that united in the *Querelle des anciens et des modernes.*

4. Quoted in Kohl, 69. The transition from *imitatio* to mimesis was in effect a double shift, inasmuch as the notion of mimesis itself evolved from meaning an imitation that had nature as its object *(natura naturata)* to meaning an imitation whose author or creative subject was identified with nature *(natura naturans).* As such, nature became more closely associated with the subject of representation, while the mimetic object became more dependent on that subject.

5. Lukács's later theory of *Widerspiegelung* seems to return to a notion of mimesis by emphasizing the reflective capacity of a work of art. While Lukács attends to the subjective dimension of *Widerspiegelung* and believes with Lenin that in the modern world no work can ever present an objective totality, at times he makes statements that contradict this latter notion. See *Ästhetik Teil I: Die Eigenart des Ästhetischen,* vols. 11–12 of *Werke* (Neuwied: Luchterhand, 1963), esp. vol. 12, 193–266.

6. Lukács, "The Old Culture and the New Culture," *Telos* 5 (Spring 1970); reprinted in *Marxism and Human Liberation,* ed. E. San Juan, Jr. (New York: Dell, 1973) 10–11; quoted in *Marxism and Totality,* by Martin Jay (Berkeley: Univ. of California Press, 1984), 101.

7. David Carroll's analysis of *Die Theorie des Romans* is interesting in

that it emphasizes the nonmimetic thrust of Lukács's theory. Carroll stops short of considering the performative aspect of Lukács's discourse and hence ends up reading the theory too referentially, that is, as a documentary account of the real history of the novel form. See David Carroll, *The Subject in Question* (Chicago: Univ. of Chicago Press, 1982), 88–109.

8. Erich Auerbach, *Mimesis* (Princeton: Princeton Univ. Press, 1953; first pub'd, Berne: A. Francke, 1946).

See also Peter Brooks, *Reading for the Plot: Design and Intention in Narrative* (New York: Vintage Books, 1984). Brooks's study of narrative plotting also takes up the question of narrative subjectivity in terms of the desire motivating the act of plotting. Whereas Brooks suggests that "the desire of the text is ultimately the desire for the end, for that recognition which is the moment of the death of the reader in the text" (108), and emphasizes "desire in its plastic and totalizing function" (37), my study examines the attitude of ambivalence towards closure, which I see as much more fundamental.

9. Auerbach, 551. Auerbach wrote *Mimesis* during World War II, in exile in Istanbul, while Lukács wrote *Die Theorie des Romans* in the atmosphere engendered by what he called the "war psychoses" of World War I. These circumstances may be significant to understanding the respective attitudes of these authors towards the disintegration of the objective social totality.

10. Stephen Halliwell discusses the two views of poetic mimesis—mimesis as imagemaking and mimesis as enactment—and argues that these two views coexist in Aristotle's text, although they are fundamentally incompatible. See Stephen Halliwell, *Aristotle's Poetics* (London: Duckworth, 1986), 109–37. For a recent study of mimesis in the novel, which emphasizes mimesis as an expressive rather than imitative mode, see Andrew Gibson, *Reading Narrative Discourse: Studies in the Novel from Cervantes to Beckett* (London: Macmillan, 1990). Gibson is interested in the nonmimetic tendencies in the novel that compete with the mimetic ones, whereas my study concerns itself with the implications of such tendencies for an understanding of novelistic subjectivity.

11. John D. Lyons and Stephen G. Nichols, Jr., eds., *Mimesis: From Mirror to Method, Augustine to Descartes* (Hanover, N.H.: Univ. Press of New England, 1982), 1.

12. See, for example, Walter Benjamin, "Über das Mimetische Vermögen," in *Gesammelte Schriften,* ed. Rolf Tiedemann and Hermann Schweppenhäuser (Frankfurt: Suhrkamp, 1977), vol. 2, part 1, 110–13, and the discussions of mimesis in Theodor Adorno, *Ästhetische Theorie,* in *Gesammelte Schriften*, vol. 7, and Theodor Adorno and Max Horkheimer, *Dialektik der Aufklärung* (Frankfurt: Fischer, 1969).

13. Mihai Spariosu, ed., *Mimesis in Contemporary Theory* (Philadelphia: John Benjamins, 1984), 35. Spariosu quotes from Adorno's *Ästhetische Theorie* (Tiedemann and Schweppenhauser, 7:169).

One
Mimesis and Subjectivity in Lukács's
Die Theorie des Romans

1. Georg Lukács, *Die Theorie des Romans* (hereafter cited as *TR*) (1920; reprint, Neuwied: Luchterhand, 1971), 21; Georg Lukács, *The Theory of the Novel*, trans. Anna Bostock (Cambridge: MIT Press, 1971), 29. Throughout, English translations of this work are from Bostock; references to pages in the translation appear in brackets.

2. Augustine, *Letters,* 137, v, 18, as cited by Tzvetan Todorov in *Theories of the Symbol,* trans. Catherine Porter (Ithaca: Cornell Univ. Press, 1982), 77.

3. Martin Jay, for example, reads *Die Theorie des Romans* according to the first view. He argues that Lukács traces a "process of decay" in the history of literary forms. According to Jay, Lukács takes the "highly idealized image of the Homeric Greeks as his standard" and thus sees this history ending in a form that expresses the "dismal reality" of the modern era. See Martin Jay, *Marxism and Totality* (Berkeley: Univ. of California Press, 1984), 95.

In a similar vein Fredric Jameson asserts that Lukács's understanding of the novel depends "on what is a kind of literary nostalgia, on the notion of a golden age or lost utopia of narration in Greek epic." Fredric Jameson, *Marxism and Form* (Princeton: Princeton Univ. Press, 1971), 179. Jameson, who wants to save Lukács's model, proposes to exclude the Greek paradigm from narrative analysis. However, as the following passage from Jameson's book reveals, the image of idealized reconciliation returns in his proposal.

> Any change in the framework [of *The Theory of the Novel*] will entail a far-reaching reevaluation of the empirical history of the novel itself. Obviously the ultimate realization of a reconciled universe will now be projected into the future, and with such a shift in perspective we are already well within a Marxist theory of history. But more than this, we would expect the removal of the idea of a golden age to result in a new interpretation of modern literature as well, and to allow for the possibility of at least partial moments of reconciliation in modern times, of at least isolated examples of genuinely concrete works of art, in a way which the overall historical schema of *The Theory of the Novel* seemed to preclude. (179–80)

Jameson's excision of a golden age of narration is, in fact, a displacement of that age from past to future. His hope for "partial moments of reconciliation" expresses the residue of nostalgia within his own thought.

4. J. M. Bernstein, *The Philosophy of the Novel: Lukács, Marxism, and the Dialectics of Form* (Minneapolis: Univ. of Minnesota Press, 1984), 69.

5. Ibid., 75.
6. Ibid., 71.
7. Ibid., 70.
8. Ibid., 71.

9. Ibid., 64.

10. Paul de Man, "Georg Lukács's *Theory of the Novel*," in *Blindness and Insight*, 2nd ed. vol. 7 of *Theory and History of Literature* (Minneapolis: Univ. of Minnesota Press, 1983), 52–53.

11. See Georg Lukács, *Die Seele und die Formen* (hereafter cited as *SF*) (1911; reprint, Neuwied: Luchterhand, 1971), 23–24; Georg Lukács, *Soul and Form*, trans. Anna Bostock (London: Merlin Press, 1974), 13. Bracketed page numbers refer to the translation.

12. Georg Lukács, letter to Paul Ernst, 14 April 1915, in *Briefwechsel 1902–1917*, ed. Eva Karáde and Eva Fekete (Stuttgart: Metzler, 1982), 348, my translation.

13. Lukács, *Briefwechsel*, 175, my translation.

14. Jacques Lacan, "Aggressivity in Psychoanalysis," in *Ecrits, A Selection*, trans. Alan Sheridan (New York: Norton, 1977), 21.

15. In the opening essay of *Die Seele und die Formen*, entitled "Über Wesen und Form des Essays" Lukács alludes to the principle that was later to become the centerpiece of *Die Theorie des Romans*, namely, structural irony. The irony of the essay, according to Lukács, lies in its performative dimension. The explicit themes treated in essays are pretexts that serve another purpose. As Lukács explains:

> Die Ironie meine ich hier, dass der Kritiker immer von den letzten Fragen des Lebens spricht, aber doch immer in dem Ton, als ob nur von Bildern und Büchern, nur von den wesenlosen und hübschen Ornamenten des grossen Lebens die Rede wäre; und auch hier nicht vom Innersten des Innern, sondern bloss von einer schönen und nutzlosen Oberfläche. So scheint es, als ob jeder Essay in der grösstmöglichen Entfernung von dem Leben wäre, und die Trennung scheint um so grösser zu sein, je brennender und schmerzlicher die tatsächliche Nähe der wirklichen Wesen beider fühlbar ist. (*SF* 18–19)

> The irony I mean consists in the critic always speaking about the ultimate problems of life, but in a tone which implies that he is only discussing pictures and books, only the inessential and pretty ornaments of real life—and even then not their innermost substance but only their beautiful and useless surface. Thus each essay appears to be removed as far as possible from life, and the distance between them seems the greater, the more burningly and painfully we sense the actual closeness of the true essence of both. [9]

To what is Lukács referring when he mentions the "ultimate problems in life"? He relates, *"Jetzt muss der Essayist sich auf sich selbst besinnen, sich finden und aus Eigenem Eigenes bauen. Der Essayist spricht über ein Bild oder ein Buch, verlässt es aber sogleich"* (*SF* 28) ["The essayist must now become conscious of his own self, must find himself and build something of his own out of himself. The essayist speaks of a picture or a book, but leaves it again at once," 15]. The irony of the essayist, then, consists in the fact that the ostensible topics of his attention are occasions for accomplishing his primary task as we have identified it, namely the construction of self-consciousness. In *Die Seele und die Formen* Lukács does not elaborate the precise method of this ironic self-construction.

16. Apropos of this passage, Bernstein observes that Lukács at times borrows his materials directly from Schlegel. "For example," Bernstein writes, "Schlegel states that the complexly structured literary work, what he called 'the arabesque,' presents to the reader 'artfully ordered confusion, a charming symmetry of contradiction, this wonderfully perennial alteration of enthusiasm and irony which lives even in the smallest part of the whole'" (Bernstein, 190–91). According to Bernstein, Lukács weakens his own theory by borrowing from Schlegel. He believes the material from Schlegel goes against the implicit, if unmistakable, Marxist spirit in which Lukács wrote *Die Theorie des Romans*. Bernstein writes,

> Lukács's arabesque ignores the difference between his project and Schlegel's. Thus: (i) for Lukács it is discrete experience and conceptual form which stand opposed to one another, not the finite and the infinite considered as metaphysical elements of the world; (ii) conceptual form is unable to totalise social experience, not because the finite and the infinite are forever in contradiction with one another, but because the imagination cannot resolve by itself a contradiction that has been historically caused, i.e. ultimately, conceptual form and social reality can be brought into harmony only through social change; (iii) technically, it is form not irony which corrects the world's fragility; irony corrects the willfulness of form. (191)

According to Bernstein, Lukács contradicts his main lines of argument by appropriating Schlegel; and so, as a critic, Bernstein feels he is justified in omitting the objectionable parts of the text on the grounds that they "infect the rest of his account" (Bernstein, 191). He stresses the social basis of the split between subject and object. According to him, in following Schlegel, Lukács misconstrues this split in metaphysical, hence reified, terms. Significantly, however, Bernstein's contention that Lukács should understand this split historically depends upon an interpretative interpolation by the English translator of *Die Theorie des Romans* that Bernstein chooses not to modify (although at other times he does alter the standard translation): *"Diese Ironie ist die Selbstkorrektur der Brüchigkeit,"* is translated as, "The irony of the novel is the self-correction of the world's fragility." Nowhere in the German text do we find reference to the fragility of the world. On the contrary, the *"Selbstkorrektur"* appears to refer to the correction of the fragility of the subject, since it follows the passage in which irony is associated with the *Aufhebung* of subjectivity, which we understood as the ambivalent process of recognition and annihilation that emphasizes the fragility of the self's identity.

17. As cited by Lukács. The Goethe quotation can be found in Johann

Wolfgang von Goethe, *Werke,* ed. Erich Trunz (Hamburg: Christian Wegner, 1960), 10:175.

18. Goethe, 183, my translation.

19. The unmasking of convention, or "second nature," anticipates Lukács's famous analysis of reification, later developed in *History and Class Consciousness.*

20. Friedrich Schlegel writes:

> So wie man aber wenig Wert auf eine Transzendentalphilosophie legen würde, die nicht kritisch wäre, nicht auch das Produzierende mit dem Produkt darstellte, und im System der transzendentalen Gedanken zugleich eine Charakteristik des transzendentalen Denkens enthielte: so sollte wohl auch die Poesie die in modernen Dichtern nicht seltnen transzendentalen Materialien und Vorübungen zu einer poetischen Theorie des Dichtungsvermögens mit der künstlerischen Reflexion und schönen Selbstbespiegelung . . . vereinigen, und in jeder ihrer Darstellungen sich selbst mit darstellen, und überall zugleich Poesie und Poesie der Poesie sein.
>
> Just as one would place little value on a transcendental philosophy that was not critical, that did not represent the producer with the product and thereby include in the system of transcendental thought a trait of transcendental thinking, so should transcendental poetry . . . unite with artistic self-reflection and beautiful self-mirroring the transcendental material and preliminary exercises for a poetic theory of aesthetic capacity which are frequently present in modern works, and represent itself in each one of its representations, and everywhere be both poetry and poetry of poetry.

Friedrich Schlegel, "Athenäum Fragment 288," in *Kritische Ausgabe,* ed. Ernst Behler (Munich: Ferdinand Schöningh, 1962), 2:204, my translation.

21. Ibid., 183, my translation.

22. Paul de Man develops the intrasubjectivity of irony in his discussion of Baudelaire's "De l'essence du rire," in "The Rhetoric of Temporality," in *Blindness and Insight,* 211ff.

23. See Sigmund Freud, "Fetischismus," in *Gesammelte Werke*, 18 vols. (Frankfurt: S. Fischer Verlag, 1940–68), 14:309–17 (English ed.: "Fetishism," in *The Standard Edition of the Psychological Works of Sigmund Freud,* ed. James Strachey et al., 24 vols. [London: Hogarth, 1953–74], 21:147–54).

Two
Mimesis in a Two-way Mirror: Freud's *Totem und Tabu*

1. Sigmund Freud, *Totem und Tabu* (hereafter cited as *TT*), in *Gesammelte Werke*, 18 vols. (Frankfurt: S. Fischer Verlag, 1940–68), 9:88; Sigmund Freud, *Totem and Taboo*, in *The Standard Edition of the Complete Psychological Works of Sigmund Freud*, ed. James Strachey et al., 24 vols. (London: Hogarth, 1953–74), 13:71, trans. modified. Bracketed page numbers refer to the translation.

2. This notion of the splitting of the self is reiterated in Freud's comment that *"das sexuelle Bedürfnis einigt die Männer nicht, sondern entzweit sie"* (*TT* 173) ["the sexual need does not unite men but divides them," 143, trans. modified].

3. Freud elaborates upon this notion of play in his discussion of the Fort/Da game in *Jenseits des Lustprinzips*, in *Gesammelte Werke*, 13:9–15 (*Beyond the Pleasure Principle*, in *The Standard Edition*, 18:12–17).

4. Samuel Weber, "Ambivalence, the Humanities, and the Study of Literature," *Diacritics* 15, no. 5 (Summer 1985): 22.

5. Sigmund Freud, "Aus der Geschichte einer infantilen Neurose," in *Gesammelte Werke*, 12:131; Sigmund Freud, "From the History of an Infantile Neurosis," in *The Standard Edition*, 17:97. Bracketed page numbers refer to the translation.

6. Freud, "Geschichte," (72) [45].

7. Ibid., (74) [47].

8. Ibid., (73) [46].

9. Ibid., (72) [46]. Freud's reliance on the work of Wilhelm Wundt in his discussion of the taboo might in this context also be considered an interesting coincidence, given Wundt's name (*Wunde* means wound). Freud relates that Wundt's *Elemente der Völkerpsychologie* was both a stimulus for his essays and a methodological contrast to his own work.

10. Freud, "Geschichte," (116) [84].

11. Ibid.

12. Strachey's translation glosses over this difference by stabilizing the dominance of cognition. He writes,

> When we, no less than primitive man, project something into external reality, what is happening must surely be this: we are recognizing the existence of two states—one in which something is directly given to the senses and to consciousness, and alongside it another, in which the same thing is *latent* but capable of re-appearing. In short, we are recognizing the co-existence of perception and memory, or, putting it more generally, the existence of *unconscious* mental processes alongside the *conscious* ones.

Three
Dreadful Discovery in Balzac's
La Recherche de l'Absolu

1. Honoré de Balzac, *La Recherche de l'Absolu,* in *La Comédie humaine,* ed. Pierre-Georges Castex, (Paris: Gallimard, Bibliothèque de la Pléiade, 1979), 10:662; Honoré de Balzac, *The Quest of the Absolute,* in *The Novels of Honoré de Balzac,* trans. G. Burnham Ives, (Philadelphia: George Barrie and Son, 1899), 45:298. Bracketed page numbers refer to the translation.

2. Albert Béguin, *Balzac lu et relu* (Paris: Éditions du Seuil, 1965), 235.

3. Madeleine Fargeaud, Introd. to Balzac, *La Recherche de l'Absolu,* 636.

4. Josué Harari, "The Pleasures of Science and the Pains of Philosophy: Balzac's *Quest for the Absolute,*" *Yale French Studies* 67 (1982): 155.

5. For a discussion of the Romantic influence upon the Balzacian notion of genius, see Gretchen R. Besser, *Balzac's Concept of Genius* (Geneva: Librarie Droz, 1969). For a reading that emphasizes the sublime nature of Joséphine's marital devotion see Arlette Michel, *Le Mariage et l'amour* (Paris: Librarie Honoré Champion, 1976).

6. Peter Brooks, *The Melodramatic Imagination* (New Haven: Yale Univ. Press, 1968), 205.

7. Madeleine Fargeaud, *Balzac et* La Recherche de l'Absolu (Paris: Hachette, 1968), 20, my translation.

8. Indeed, Balzac's interest in science is well documented. In order to write *La Recherche,* he familiarized himself with recent developments in chemistry, botany, and biology, even seeking the counsel of two members of the Academy of Science. The works of Fargeaud and Harari provide valuable information about the text's scientific references. See also Fargeaud's "Balzac, homme de science(s)," published under her maiden name, Ambrière, in *Balzac: L'Invention du roman*, ed. Claude Duchet and Jacques Neefs (Paris: Pierre Belfond, 1982), 43–55.

9. Harari, 138.

10. See Harari, 141.

11. Balzac, *Lettres à l'étrangère* (Paris: Calman-Lévy, 1899), 1:180, my translation.

12. Harari, 149.

13. Ibid., 151.

14. Ibid., 151 (quoted from Collection Lovenjoul, man. 157, fol. 83).

15. [Honoré de Balzac], "Préface des études de moeurs au XIXe siècle," in *La Comédie humaine,* ed. Pierre Citron (Paris: Éditions du Seuil, 1965), 1:597, my translation. The introduction, though signed by Félix Davin, was in fact written by Balzac. See the editor's note to the preface, as well as Fargeaud, *Balzac et* La Recherche de l'Absolu, 597, for the history of the introduction.

16. This is worth noting, because critics have emphasized the nonlinguistic nature of the Balthazarian and Balzacian "Absolutes." As Peter Brooks writes, *"La Recherche . . .* elaborates most fully the figure who neglects the

vehicle of representation in the search for an effable tenor. Balthazar Claes is the very opposite of those young lions who invest everything in representation, hoping that it will of itself create and impose significance" (Brooks, 116).

Harari has argued this point by addressing the question, "Does Balzac's novel attempt to demonstrate that the Absolute is a reality which is not of the order of language? This hypothesis would at least explain why the Absolute cannot be named, cannot be articulated, in the text of *La Recherche"* (Harari, 155).

17. The play in *déshonoré* on *Honoré de* raises the possibility that issues of sexual identity pertain as well to Balzac's authorial identity.

18. For a discussion of the significance of similar imagery in dreams, see Sigmund Freud, *Traumdeutung,* in *Gesammelte Werke,* 18 vols. (Frankfurt: S. Fischer Verlag, 1940–68), 3:374–76 (English ed.: *The Interpretation of Dreams,* in *The Standard Edition of the Complete Psychological Works of Sigmund Freud,* ed. James Strachey et al., 24 vols. [London: Hogarth, 1953–74], 5:369–71).

19. Joséphine's need to have the connection between herself and the holistic image certified recalls Lacan's analysis of the child's need to have its mother acknowledge its identification with its mirror image. See Jacques Lacan, "Le stade du miroir comme formateur de la fonction du Je," in *Écrits* (Paris: Éditions du Seuil, 1966), 89–109.

20. Samuel Weber, *Unwrapping Balzac* (Toronto: Univ. of Toronto Press, 1979), 22.

21. *Langenscheidts Enzyklopädisches Wörterbuch* (Berlin: Langenscheidt KG, 1975).

22. Bernard Vannier, *L'Inscription du corps* (Paris: Éditions Klincksieck, 1971), 70–71, my translation.

23. Balzac, *Pensées, sujets, fragments,* ed. J. Crépet (Paris: Blaizot, 1910), 45, cited in Vannier, 174, n. 17, my translation.

24. In the "Avant-propos" of *La Comédie,* Balzac refers to the writer as *"un peintre"* [a painter] who creates *"le tableau de la Société"* [a tableau of society]. See "Avant-propos," in Pierre Citron's edition of *La Comédie humaine* 1:52–53.

25. Honoré de Balzac, *Les Proscrits,* in *La Comédie humaine* (10:547) [46:157].

26. *Grand Larousse de la langue française* (Paris: Librairie Larousse, 1971).

27. See Sigmund Freud, *Drei Abhandlungen zur Sexualtheorie,* in *Gesammelte Werke,* 5:87 (*Three Essays on the Theory of Sexuality* in *The Standard Edition,* 7:186). Also in *Gesammelte Werke* see Freud's essays "Über Triebumsetzungen, insbesondere der Analerotik," 10:401–10, and "Charakter und Analerotik," 7:23–30 (in *The Standard Edition,* "On the Transformation of Instinct, as Exemplified in Anal Eroticism," 17:127–33, and "Character and Anal Eroticism," 9:169–75).

28. For a discussion of the constitutive nature of narcissism, see "A Problem of Narcissism," in Samuel Weber, *The Legend of Freud,* trans. Samuel Weber (Minneapolis: Univ. of Minnesota Press, 1982), 8–16; orig. pub. as "Die Auseinandersetzung" in *Freud-Legende. Drei Studien zum psychoanalytischen Denken* (Olten, Switzerland: Walter Verlag, 1979), 201–9.

29. See Madeleine Fargeaud, "Les Sources Vivantes," in *Balzac et* La Recherche de l'Absolu, 53–86.

30. See Paul de Man, "Autobiography as De-facement," in *The Rhetoric of Romanticism* (New York: Columbia Univ. Press, 1984), 67–81. See also Cynthia Chase's discussion of de Man's definition of prosopopoeia in "Giving a Face to a Name," in *Decomposing Figures* (Baltimore: Johns Hopkins Univ. Press, 1986), 82–112.

31. Honoré de Balzac, *Lettres sur la littérature*, in *Oeuvres diverses* (vols. 38–40 of *Oeuvres complètes*) (Paris: Louis Conard, 1912), 3:320, my translation.

32. Balzac, *Lettres à l'étrangère*, 1:163–64, my translation.

33. Ibid., 1:180, my translation.

34. Balzac, "Préface des études de moeurs au XIXe siècle," 597, my translation.

Four
The Secret of the Third Story in Charlotte Brontë's *Jane Eyre*

1. Charlotte Brontë, *Jane Eyre* (Oxford: Oxford Univ. Press, 1975), 422. Subsequent page references to this work will be found in the text.

2. Sandra Gilbert and Susan Gubar, *The Madwoman in the Attic* (New Haven: Yale Univ. Press, 1979), 367.

3. Ibid., 362.

4. Robert Heilman sees Brontë's text as a reworking of the Gothic tradition. As an instance of the "new Gothic," *Jane Eyre*, he argues, explores the realm of human passion that exists apart from social convention. One feels the influence of Heilman's analysis in ensuing interpretations (like Gilbert and Gubar's) that have focused on the concept of individual subjectivity at work in the novel. My own reading of *Jane Eyre* is similarly indebted to Heilman, but I agree with Eve Kosofsky Sedgwick's critique of Heilman's reading. Sedgwick takes issue with Heilman's psychological understanding of the self as portrayed in Gothic literature. Whereas he argues that Gothic literature identifies an interior or deep psychological realm that remains somehow cut off from the external or more superficial social realm, Sedgwick sees the relationship between depth and surface or interior and exterior as marked by specular repetition and correspondence. My reading will emphasize how the development of Jane's identity can be read not as a realization of her passionate self in an acceptable form of Victorian femininity but as the exploration of the madness of those external forms. See Robert Heilman, "Charlotte Brontë's 'New Gothic,'" in *From Jane Austen to Joseph Conrad: Essays Collected in Memory of James T. Hillhouse*, Robert Rathburn and Martin Steinmann, Jr., eds. (Minneapolis: Univ. of Minnesota Press, 1958), 118–32; excerpted in *Jane Eyre*, Norton Critical Edition, Richard J. Dunn, ed. (New York: Norton, 1987), 458–62. See

also Eve Kosofsky Sedgwick, *The Coherence of Gothic Conventions* (New York: Methuen, 1986).

5. Gilbert and Gubar, 362, 368.

6. Ibid., 369.

7. Maggie Berg reads the "inexplicable and awkward" conclusion of the novel in which Jane imagines St. John's death as signifying Jane's indictment of St. John on the grounds that he refuses to engage in introspection and gain self-knowledge thereby. See Maggie Berg, *Jane Eyre: Portrait of a Life* (Boston: Twayne, 1987), 110-11. According to Judith Williams, St. John's presence at the end of the novel disturbs the harmonious resolution represented by Jane's marriage to Rochester. See Judith Williams, *Perception and Experience in the Novels of Charlotte Brontë* (Ann Arbor: UMI, 1988), 51-52.

8. For another discussion of the significance of originality see Rosemarie Bodenheimer, "Jane Eyre in Search of Her Story," in *The Brontës*, ed. Harold Bloom (New York: Chelsea House, 1987), 155-68; orig. pub. in *Papers on Language and Literature* 16, no. 3 (Summer 1980).

9. For a reader response–oriented analysis of the role of reading in *Jane Eyre*, see Mark M. Hennelly's article in which he considers the emblematic significance of scenarios of reading in terms of the text's consistent indeterminacy, the presence of which engenders the necessity of constant rereading and reinterpretation. Mark M. Hennelly, Jr., "*Jane Eyre*'s Reading Lesson," *ELH* 51, no. 4 (Winter 1984): 693-717.

10. Paul Pickrel contends, in opposition to Gilbert and Gubar, that St. John is not named after St. John the Baptist but after St. John the Divine, author of the book of Revelation. This strengthens the authorial nature of St. John's identity. Interestingly, the final page of the novel includes a passage from a letter St. John has written that, as Pickrel points out, coincides with the ending of Revelation, thereby further underscoring the role of St. John as writer. See Paul Pickrel, "*Jane Eyre*: The Apocalypse of the Body," *ELH* 53, no. 1 (Spring 1986): 165-82.

11. Jane's identification with Bertha is played out in similar sexual terms; Bertha introduces elements of the "unfeminine" into Jane's proper self. Her physical masculinity matches the masculinity of Jane's own demonic voice, about which Jane's aunt states, "I could not forget my own sensations when you thus started up and poured out the venom of your mind: I felt fear, as if an animal that I had struck or pushed had looked up at me with human eyes and cursed me in a man's voice" (241).

The voice as sexual other becomes the locus of Jane's identification with Bertha: Bertha's voice not only penetrates Jane; at times it becomes impossible to know whether it emanates from Bertha or from Jane herself. Jane makes it clear that she is drawn to Bertha's laugh:

> [Bertha's laugh] when first heard had thrilled me: I heard, too, her eccentric murmurs; stranger than her laugh. There were days when she was quite silent; but there were others when I could not account for the sounds she made . . . her oral oddities. (111)

At other times, Bertha's laugh and Jane's own movements seem synchronized to each other. In the following passage, Jane halts in the hallway, and so does the laugh, as if movement and laughter "originate in but one": Jane is lingering in the long hallway.

> While I paced softly on, the last sound I expected to hear in so still a region, a laugh, struck my ear. It was a curious laugh; distinct, formal, mirthless. I stopped: the sound ceased, only for an instant; it began again, louder: for the first, though distinct, it was very low. It passed off in a clamorous peal that seemed to wake an echo in every lonely chamber; though it originated in but one, and I have pointed out the door whence the accents issued. (108)

Perhaps the strongest oral/aural confusion of Bertha and Jane occurs when Jane is awakened from her sleep by a sound, the proximity of whose source to Jane's own mouth (and the inclusion of the word "ere," which echoes Eyre) suggest that the sound emanates from her:

> This was a demoniac laugh low, suppressed, and deep uttered, as it seemed, at the very key-hole of my chamber-door. The head of my bed was near the door, and I thought at first, the goblin-laughter stood at my bedside—or rather, crouched by my pillow: but I rose, looked round, and could see nothing; while, as I still gazed, the unnatural sound was reiterated: and I knew it came from behind the panels. My first impulse was to rise and fasten the bolt; my next, again to cry out, "Who is there?"
>
> Something gurgled and moaned. Ere long, steps retreated up the gallery towards the third story staircase: a door had lately been made to shut in that staircase; I heard it open and close, and all was still. (149)

    12. Peter J. Bellis reads Jane's assumption of authorship in psychoanalytic terms as an appropriation of the masculine gaze. See Peter J. Bellis, "In the Window Seat: Vision and Power in *Jane Eyre*," *ELH* 54, no. 3 (Fall 1987): 639–52.

    13. Janet H. Freeman points out that the narrator's direct addresses to her audience become more frequent towards the end of the novel. Freeman sees this change as producing a heightening of the text's self-conscious literary quality. See Janet H. Freeman, "Speech and Silence in *Jane Eyre*," *Studies in English Literature* 24, no. 4 (1984): 683–700. Melodie Monahan argues that certain aspects of the novel's conclusion, such as the illustration Jane uses to describe her sensation upon seeing Thornfield in ruins, render its resolution problematic. See Melodie Monahan, "Heading Out Is Not Going Home: *Jane Eyre*," *Studies in English Literature* 28, no. 4 (Autumn 1988): 589–608.

    14. See for example the scene in volume 2, chapter 9, in which Rochester expresses his desire to dress Jane in satin and lace and decorate her with jewels.

Jane refuses to submit to such a transformation and resists Rochester's chivalric attempt to transmute her into an angel.

15. Gilbert and Gubar, 359–60.

16. Ibid., 368. Helen von Schmidt concurs in the view of Bertha as Jane's double but sees her elimination as a greater loss to Jane. See Helen von Schmidt, "The Dark Abyss, the Broad Expanse: Versions of the Self in *Jane Eyre* and *Great Expectations*," *Dickens Quarterly* 2, no. 3 (Sept. 1985): 84–91.

17. The symbolic equivalence between Bertha and her brother is established through a chiastic crossing of stereotypical attributes of gender. Whereas Bertha is described as active and masculine, her brother has a "passive disposition" (213). He is "submissive" to Rochester and physically overwhelmed by Bertha (213).

18. For a discussion of the significance of the Bewick text, see Jane W. Stedman, "Charlotte Brontë and Bewick's *British Birds*," *Brontë Society Transactions* 15 (1966), 36–40.

19. Bodenheimer offers a different reading of this passage. She argues that Jane and Bertha are associated with the third story because both are imprisoned in their own passions. As the novel progresses, it moves away from this form of storytelling, which improperly conflates the roles of heroine, teller, and audience. See Bodenheimer, 156–57.

Helen Moglen studies the mythologizing impulse in the novel, arguing that its conclusion is an "interweaving of wish and fact . . . experience and convention." See Helen Moglen, *Charlotte Brontë: The Self Conceived* (Madison: Univ. of Wisconsin Press, 1976), 107; a portion of the book is reprinted in the 1987 Norton edition of the novel, pp. 484–91. In a similar vein, Barbara Hardy and G. Armour Craig discuss the tension between the novel's religious, providential resolution and the development of Jane's self—what Hardy calls her rational intelligence and Craig describes as her transcendence. See Barbara Hardy, "Dogmatic Form: Defoe, Charlotte Brontë, Thomas Hardy, and E.M. Forster," in *The Appropriate Form* (London: Athlone, 1964), 51–82; a portion of the essay is reprinted in the 1971 Norton edition of *Jane Eyre*, 488–96. See also G. Armour Craig, "The Unpoetic Compromise: On the Relation between Private Vision and Social Order in Nineteenth-Century Fiction," in *Self and Society in the Novel*, ed. Mark Schorer (New York: Columbia Univ. Press, 1956), 30–41; reprinted in the 1971 Norton edition of *Jane Eyre*, 471–78. Terry Eagleton analyzes the text's mythologizing tendencies and links them to Jane's (and Brontë's) conflicting desires for assimilation and independence. See Terry Eagleton, *Myths of Power: A Marxist Study of the Brontës* (New York: Barnes and Noble, 1975); excerpted in the 1987 Norton edition of the novel, 491-96. My study could be seen as an exploration of the ambivalence subtending the desire for mythical and religious resolutions of conflicting impulses.

Five
Domesticated Irony in Theodor Fontane's *Frau Jenny Treibel*

1. Theodor Fontane, *Sämtliche Werke* (Munich: Carl Hanser, 1962), sec. 3, vol. 1, 238.
2. Ibid., 239.
3. Ibid.
4. Richard Brinkmann would disagree with a reading of *Verklärung* that emphasizes its formal aspects. See Richard Brinkmann, *Über die Verbindlichkeit des Unverbindlichen* (Munich: R. Piper, 1967), 40.
5. Fontane, *Sämtliche Werke,* sec. 4, vol. 3, 147.
6. Ibid., sec. 3, vol. 1, 241.
7. Ibid.
8. Ibid., sec. 4, vol. 3, 177–78.
9. For a discussion of the role of subjectivity in Fontane's aesthetic theory and literary texts see Wolfgang Preisendanz, *Humor als dichterische Einbildungskraft. Studien zur Erzählkunst des poetischen Realismus* (Munich: Eidos, 1963), 214–41, and Dieter Kafitz, *Figurenkonstellation als Mittel der Wirklichkeitserfassung* (Kronberg: Athenäum, 1978).
10. Readers of Fontane owe much to Lukács's essay "Der Alte Fontane," in which he examines the relationship between Fontane's life and his works. Lukács reads *Frau Jenny Treibel* as an unmediated historical depiction of the bourgeoisie during the *Gründerjahre* and derives the text's political message from the conditions it mimetically represents. In order to produce this reading, however, Lukács must exclude the material from the text that resists his interpretation. While every reading proceeds through selection and exclusion, the agonistic nature of Lukács's analysis is manifest in the way he justifies his exclusions: he devalorizes the excluded elements on the grounds of their aesthetic inferiority. For example, he writes:

> Es sind verhältnismässig einfache Fälle, wo Fontane sich von seiner Virtuosität in der Führung des Dialogs hinreissen lässt, wo deshalb ein an sich geistvolles Gespräch zum Selbstzweck wird und aufhört, Motor der wesentlichen Handlung, der weiterführenden Beleuchtung zentraler Konflikte zu sein. So zum Beispiel . . . infolge ihrer disproportionierten Weite—die an sich witzige Kontrastierung von Berliner und Hamburger Bourgeoisie in "Frau Jenny Treibel" usw.

There are relatively simple cases where Fontane allows himself to get carried away by his virtuoso command of dialogue and where an inherently meaningful conversation is carried on for its own sake and ceases to be the motor of the essential action, a further illumination of the central conflict. So, for example . . . owing to its lengthiness—the contrasting of the Berlin and Hamburg bourgeoisie in *Frau Jenny Treibel,* which in and of itself is witty, etc.

Georg Lukács, "Der Alte Fontane," in *Deutsche Realisten des 19. Jahrhunderts* (Berlin: Aufbau-Verlag, 1951), 289–90, my translation.

In suggesting that certain dialogues are superfluous in terms of what he sees as the novel's primary referential significance, that is, the objective conflict it depicts, Lukács cannot possibly consider that the text's "excesses" may comprise a critique of the idea that the text represents objective, extratextual conflict. Lukács's cursory dismissal of passages from the novel replicates one of Jenny's characteristic practices. She calls anything she doesn't agree with "*Unsinn*" [nonsense]. Moreover, the gesture of identifying what is essential and then excluding the remainder seems particularly at odds with Fontane's, and for that matter Lukács's, awareness of the work of art as an organic totality. What Fontane wrote about Freytag's *Soll und Haben* pertains to his own work as well: *"das Fortfallen der kleinsten und unscheinbarsten [würde] als eine fühlbare Lücke empfunden werden . . . so organisch ist alles ineinandergefügt"* [the abolition of the smallest and most invisible element would be experienced as a notable gap, so organically is everything interwoven] (Fontane, *Sämtliche Werke,* sec. 3, vol. 1, 297).

Lukács's writings from 1931 on seem in many ways to reverse the claims of his earlier essays on literature. For example, the concept of totality appears to undergo an extreme displacement: whereas in *Die Theorie des Romans* it pertained to a structure of consciousness, in his later writings, such as "Erzählung oder Beschreibung," the concept of totality is identified with objective social reality. The question of mediation between the subject and objective reality no longer appears to be an issue for Lukács.

11. David Turner, "Fontane's *Frau Jenny Treibel*: A Study in Ironic Discrepancy," *Forum for Modern Language Studies* 8, no. 2 (April 1972), 134. See also Hanni Mittelman, *Die Utopie des weiblichen Glücks in den Romanen Theodor Fontanes* (Bern: Peter Lang, 1980), 84. Mittelman writes that there is no tension between Jenny's desires and social ideology. For a discussion of Fontane's view of the bourgeoisie see Katharina Mommsen, "Bourgeoisie und Sozialdemokratie," in *Gesellschaftskritik bei Fontane und Thomas Mann* (Heidelberg: Lothar Stein, 1973), 39–45.

12. The correspondence between Fontane and Schmidt is strengthened by the fact that Fontane based the character of Corinna on his daughter Martha. For a discussion of relevant biographical material, see "Zur Entstehung," in the Ullstein edition of the novel, 198–204, as well as Charlotte Jolles, *Theodor Fontane* (Tübingen: Metzler, 1983), 89. See also the letter Fontane wrote in June or August of 1883 to Frau Anna Witte regarding Martha and a suitor, Rudolf Schreiner, on whom the character Leopold Treibel is based; the letter can be found in "Auf den Spuren des Leopold Treibel," *Fontane Blätter* 2, no. 7 (1972): 519–21.

13. Theodor Fontane, *Frau Jenny Treibel oder "Wo sich Herz zum Herzen find't,"* ed. Walter Keitel and Helmuth Nürnberger (Frankfurt: Ullstein, 1974), "Briefliche Zeugnisse," 206, my translation. English translations, when not my own, are from Theodor Fontane, *Frau Jenny Treibel,* trans. Ulf Zimmerman

(New York: Frederick Ungar, 1976). Bracketed page numbers refer to the Zimmerman translation.

14. My translation.

15. For a discussion of the history of the Social Democratic Party and the *Verein für Sozialpolitik*, see Hajo Holborn, *A History of Modern Germany* (New York: Alfred A. Knopf, 1986), 3:285–91.

16. Cited in Thomas Mann, "The Old Fontane," in *Essays of Three Decades*, trans. H. T. Lowe-Porter (London: Secker and Warburg, 1947), 303.

17. The editor of the German text points out that this quotation echoes Aristotle's discussion, in chapter 9 of the *Poetics*, of the superior value of poetry over history. See page 232 in the Ullstein edition of *Frau Jenny Treibel*.

18. For a discussion of the symbolism of closets, see Sigmund Freud, *Die Traumdeutung*, in *Gesammelte Werke,* 18 vols. (Frankfurt: S. Fischer Verlag, 1940–68), 2:364 (English ed.: *The Interpretation of Dreams,* in *The Standard Edition of the Complete Psychological Works of Sigmund Freud,* ed. James Strachey et al., 24 vols. [London: Hogarth, 1953–74], 5:359).

19. Mary Ann Doane, "Film and the Masquerade—Theorising the Female Spectator," *Screen* 23, no. 3–4 (Sept.-Oct. 1982): 81–82.

20. See Sigmund Freud, "Fetischismus," in *Gesammelte Werke,* 14:309–17 ("Fetishism," in *The Standard Edition,* 21:147–54).

21. Nicolas Abraham and Maria Torok, *L'Ecorce et le Noyau* (Paris: Aubier Flammarion, 1978), 224. All translations from this text are my own.

22. Ibid., 224.

23. Ibid., 262.

24. Ibid., 262–63.

25. Jacqueline Riviere, "Womanliness as a Masquerade," in *Psychoanalysis and Female Sexuality* (New Haven: College and University Press, 1966), 213.

26. Walter Müller-Seidel sees Corinna as the main representative of the cult of English culture and concludes that the novel depicts the theme of Anglophilia positively, since Fontane based the character Corinna on his own daughter. We would note, however, that Corinna is not the only figure who represents the English bias. In fact, she explicitly denies that she knows much about English politics and history. Helene, on the other hand, is a self-proclaimed Anglophile. She chooses to raise her daughter in as English a manner as possible. Given that Helene is a highly ironized figure, the homage to England is no more absolute than any other viewpoint in the novel. Indeed, Fontane seems to ironize the concept of debating such a point in the first place. See Walter Müller-Seidel, *Theodor Fontane: Soziale Romankunst in Deutschland* (Stuttgart: J. B. Metzler, 1975), 317.

27. The word *Ungescheitheiten* comes from *gescheit,* which means intellectually sharp and itself comes from *scheiden,* to cut or split. *Ungescheitheiten* thus literally means something that is undivided or unsplit. Interestingly, the related word *Scheide* means both a sheath and the vagina; Corinna's longing for *Ungescheitheiten* may also be read as a desire to escape sexual determination. See Jacob and Wilhelm Grimm, *Deutsches Wörterbuch* (Leipzig: S. Herzel, 1899).

28. Bettina Plett points out that Corinna is named after an ancient Greek poetess, Corinna of Tanagra, who was believed to be a contemporary of Pindar. See Bettina Plett, *Die Kunst der Allusion: Formen literarischer Anspielungen in den Romanen Theodor Fontanes* (Cologne: Böhlau Verlag, 1986), 116.

29. For a discussion of Leopold's weakness see David Turner, "Coffee or Milk?—That is the Question: On an Incident from Fontane's *Frau Jenny Treibel*," *German Life and Letters* 21, no. 4 (July 1968): 330–55.

30. Doane, 83.

31. See for example Karl Richter, *Resignation: Eine Studie zum Werk Theodor Fontanes* (Stuttgart: W. Kohlhammer Verlag, 1966), 115. Norbert Frei views Corinna as an exception to what he believes is the general function of the woman in Fontane's novels as the *"Modell und Paradigma für humane Existenz Möglichkeiten."* Norbert Frei, *Die Frau als Paradigm des Humanen* (Königstein: Hain, 1980), 147.

32. Alan Bance, *Theodor Fontane* (Cambridge: Cambridge University Press, 1982), 136.

33. The English translator drops the third line in which *deceived* appears, sensing but unable to account for its overuse.

34. In keeping with this reversal of the assumptions of mimesis—language as representing a pre-existing reality—the events of the novel are presented as the fulfillments of a series of prophesies uttered by various characters. Schmidt and Corinna predict the entire plot before it unfolds; when Jenny pays her first visit to Corinna, Corinna suggests that Leopold might bring home a professor's daughter as his fiancée; after the dinner party, when Marcell and Schmidt are discussing Corinna's coquettish behavior, Schmidt says, *"den Ausgang der Sache kenn' ich. Du sollst sie haben, und du wirst sie haben, und vielleicht eher, als du denkst"* (80) ["I know the end of the affair. You should have her and you will have her, and perhaps sooner than you think," 81]. Corinna's prophecy about the engagement of Marcell to Hildegard comes true, and Schmidt even predicts that Leopold's phlegmatic nature will prevent him from following through with his intentions to marry Corinna: he jokingly suggests that Leopold would never have the courage to elope to Gretna Green; then, in a letter to Corinna, Leopold writes that he is thinking about eloping with her to Liverpool, which he says is two hours from the Scottish border (i.e., Gretna Green). This plan never materializes.

35. Grimm and Grimm.

Six
Orality, Aggression, and Epistemology in Walker Percy's *The Second Coming*

1. Walker Percy, *The Second Coming* (London: Panther Books, 1980), 123. Further references to this work appear parenthetically in the text.

2. Jac Tharpe, *Walker Percy* (Boston: Twayne, 1983), 112.

3. Patricia Lewis Poteat, *Walker Percy and the Old Modern Age* (Baton Rouge: Louisiana State Univ. Press, 1985), 163.

4. John Edward Hardy, *The Fiction of Walker Percy* (Champaign: Univ. of Illinois Press, 1987), 187.

5. Marc Kirkeby, "Walker Percy: He Can See Clearly Now," interview, *L.A. Times,* 3 August 1980, 52; reprinted in *Conversations with Walker Percy,* Literary Conversations Series, ed. Lewis A. Lawson and Victor A. Kramer (Jackson: Univ. Press of Mississippi, 1985), 190–92.

6. Ted R. Spivey, *The Writer as Shaman* (Macon, Ga.: Mercer Univ. Press, 1986), 147.

7. From the title of a collection of Percy's essays: Panthea Reid Broughton, ed., *The Art of Walker Percy: Stratagems for Being* (Baton Rouge: Louisiana State Univ. Press, 1979). Broughton notes that she takes the concept of the stratagem from Percy's essay "The Loss of Creature." See her Introduction, xvii, xv.

8. Doreen A. Fowler, "Answers and Ambiguity in Percy's *The Second Coming,*" in *Walker Percy,* ed. Harold Bloom (New York: Chelsea House, 1986), 115–16. Note that even Fowler, who has reservations about the novel's conclusion, shares one assumption with those readers who believe that the novel does end happily, namely, that Percy's writings are meant to be read as guidebooks.

9. Fowler, 122.

10. Ibid.

11. Ibid., 120, 122.

12. Ibid., 121.

13. Ibid., 122.

14. Ibid., 118.

15. Ibid., 121–22.

16. For a stunning reading of the relationship between madness and interpretation in Percy's *Lancelot*, see Jerome C. Christensen, *"Lancelot:* Sign for the Times," in *Walker Percy: Art and Ethics,* ed. Jac Tharpe (Jackson: Univ. Press of Mississippi, 1980), 107–20; reprinted in Bloom, 103–14.

17. The line "only the violent bear it away" alludes as well to Flannery O'Connor's novel of that title, and suggests that a certain violence may be inherent in Percy's attempt to insert himself into a genealogy that would designate O'Connor as his literary foremother.

18. The performative quality of naming is allegorized in the text when Will is in his garage: "In a word, no sooner had he opened the Mercedes door and stepped out than a rifle shot was fired from the dense pine forest nearby, ricocheting with a hideous screech from the concrete floor at his foot to a thunk in the brick of the inner wall. A vicious buzzing bee stung his calf" (18). The stinging bullet was shot by a deer poacher who regularly trespasses on Will's property. The vicious stinging bee is literally, as the first line indicates, "in a word," specifically in the name of the poacher, which is Ewell McBee.

19. Nicolas Abraham and Maria Torok, "Introjection – Incorporation: Mourning or Melancholia," in *Psychoanalysis in France,* ed. S. Lebovici and D. Widlöcher (New York: International Universities Press, 1980), 4.

20. Abraham and Torok, 6.

21. Will's fantasmatic reconstruction "reads" Abraham and Torok's theory in an interesting way; it suggests that incorporation is not only a neurotic aberration of introjection but its founding moment as well.

22. I thank Jerry Christensen for pointing out the implicit masochism of these images.

23. Percy has said, "I wanted Allie to start off afresh with language. It was an experiment." Ben Forkner and J. Gerald Kennedy, "An Interview with Walker Percy," in *Delta* (Montpellier, Université Paul Valéry) November 1981, 1–20; reprinted in Lawson and Kramer, 226–44.

24. Robert H. Brinkmeyer, *Three Catholic Writers* (Jackson: Univ. Press of Mississippi, 1985), 168.

25. Hardy, 187.

26. The theme of incest was anticipated in the passage discussed earlier in which Allie experiences a spontaneous revelation, a moment of "suddenly knowing" that the exhibitionistic pleasure she took in going by the book with Sarge was the same pleasure she experienced in making good grades for her father.

27. *The New Dictionary of American Slang,* ed. Robert L. Chapman (New York: Harper and Row, 1986).

28. By "screen memory" I am referring to a memory, the vividness and insignificance of whose content indicates that it is standing in for and deflecting from repressed material. See Sigmund Freud, "Über Deckerinnerungen," in *Gesammelte Werke,* 18 vols. (Frankfurt: S. Fischer Verlag, 1940–68), 1:531–54 (English ed.: "Screen Memories," in *The Standard Edition of the Complete Psychological Works of Sigmund Freud,* ed. James Strachey et al., 24 vols. [London: Hogarth, 1953–74], 3:299–322).

29. Walker Percy, *The Message in the Bottle* (New York: Farrar, Straus and Giroux, 1975), 3.

30. Percy, *The Message in the Bottle,* 64.

31. Ibid., 72.

32. Ibid., 69.

33. Ibid., 283.

34. Ibid., 285–86.

35. Ibid., 285. In his essays, Percy acknowledges his indebtedness to the existentialists. The influence of existentialism is apparent in Percy's vocabulary. For a discussion of Percy's philosophical origins, see Robert Coles, *Walker Percy: An American Search* (Boston: Little, Brown, 1978).

36. This same movement of splitting can be traced in the distribution of topics in Percy's theoretical writings. His individual essays never address the ambivalence of metaphor as such. Instead, they address either the generative power of metaphor or the reifying effects of discourse.

37. See Poteat, as well as the following essays in Tharpe, *Walker Percy: Art and Ethics:* Charles P. Bigger, "Walker Percy and the Resonance of the Word," 43–54; Michael Pearson, "Art as Symbolic Action: Walker Percy's Aesthetic," 55–64; and J. P. Telotte, "Charles Peirce and Walker Percy: From Semiotic to Narrative Strategy," 65–79. See also Weldon Thornton, "Homo Loquens,

Homo Symbolificus, Homo Sapiens: Walker Percy on Language," in Broughton, 169–91.

38. Fowler, 120.

39. Percy, *The Message in the Bottle*, 29.

Conclusion

1. Helene and Joséphine's dependence upon seeing and being seen perhaps accounts for the coincidental emphasis upon the waist as the sign of femininity *par excellence*. In both texts the womanly contour is defined by and ornamented with a pink sash: Marguerite wears a bright pink belt and tells Joséphine to change her faded one, while Lizzi wears a pink-colored scarf.

Index

Abraham, Karl, 127, 159, 201 n. 21
Adorno, Theodor, 4, 5
Analysis, literary: and madness, 151
Aristotle, 1, 4, 198 n. 17
Ästhetik (Lukács), 183 n. 5
Auerbach, Erich, 3, 4, 184 n. 9
Augustine, Saint, 8
Autonomy: of the novel, 9–10, 12, 29; of novelistic subjectivity, 33

Balzac, Honoré de, 5, 6, 11, 51, 56, 57, 58, 80, 88, 91, 190 n. 8
Béguin, Albert, 51
Benjamin, Walter, 4, 5
Berg, Maggie, 193 n. 7
Bergson, Henri, 11
Bernstein, J. M.: on autonomy of the novel, 10; on Lukács's use of Schlegel, 187 n. 16; on totality, 9
Bewick, Thomas, 110
Boccaccio, 13
Bodenheimer, Rosemarie, 195 n. 19
Brontë, Charlotte, 5, 6, 94
Brooke, Thomas, 103
Brooks, Peter, 52, 184 n. 8; 190 n. 16

Carroll, David, 183–84 n. 7
Cassirer, Ernst, 175
Castration: fear of, 71, 139; female, 66, 127; and primal scene, 45, 47. See also Medusa; *Recherche de l'Absolu, La*: castration (fragmentation) in
Chef-d'oeuvre inconnu, Le (Balzac), 55
Christensen, Jerome C., 201 n. 22
Cloacal theory: Freud on, 82
Closure, formal, 27, 112, 142–43, 184 n. 8

Cognition: as creator, 21; and deformation, 20, 35; and irony, 23, 28
Comédie humaine, La (Balzac), 180; *Études philosophiques* in, 55, 93; *La Recherche de l'Absolu* in, 52

Daemonic, the, 22–24, 28, 29
Death, 6; and cognition, 20; as theme in *Jane Eyre*, 98–101, 107–10; as theme in *La Recherche de l'Absolu*, 81, 83, 86–88, 93; as theme in *The Second Coming*, 154–55, 159–64, 168–71
Decameron (Boccaccio), 13
"Delta Factor, The" (Percy), 172–73, 178
de Man, Paul, 10–11, 90, 188 n. 22
Desire: ambivalence of, 65, 66, 71; and identification, 45–46, 47; imitative, 43; and judgment, 15–16; maternal, 126, 128; of novelistic subject, 19, 30, 31; and projection, 25; and reading, 89; renunciation of, 66–67; transgressive, 36–37
Dictung und Wahrheit (Goethe), 23
Dieckmann, Herbert, 183 n. 3
Doane, Mary Ann, 126
Dostoevsky, 13
Doubling, authorial: in *Frau Jenny Treibel*, 114, 116, 133; in *Jane Eyre*, 108, 112
Drei Abhandlungen zur Sexualtheorie (Freud), 38

L'Education sentimentale (Flaubert), 11
Einheit, 35, 39
Epic, the: as distinct from the novel, 4; and fetishism, 33–34; as presub-

Epic, the *(cont.)*
    jective, 28, 30; significance of, in *Die Theorie des Romans*, 2–3, 7–10, 12, 14, 18, 28–34; and transcendental topography of the mind, 7
Erlebte Rede, 116
Ernst, Paul, 13
Essay, the: compared to the novel, 13–14, 18; and constitution of identity, 14–18, 29; desire in, 16; irony in, 186–87 n. 15; judgment in, 15–17; method of, 14; search in, 13; style of, 13; subject in, 19

Fantasy, logic of, 159
Fargeaud, Madeleine, 51, 52, 88
Femininity: as established through phallocentrism, 45–46, 66–67, 74, 76, 89, 127, 129–30, 135–36, 138; and fetishism, 127, 128, 130; as image, 69, 70, 73, 80, 126, 127–28; and masochism, 69–70, 74, 128; and maternal desire, 126, 128
Fetish/fetishism, 33–34, 85; the child as, 128–30; and identification, 130; logic of, 130; and mimetic narrative, 180; and realist aesthetic, 179
Flaubert, Gustav, 11–12
Fontane, Theodor, 5, 6, 113; on bourgeoisie, 117; political views of, 118–19, 145–46
Fool of Quality, The (Brooke), 103
Form, narrative: genealogy of, 2–3, 6, 10–12, 18, 28–34
Fowler, Doreen, 149–51, 177, 200 n. 8
Frankfurt School, 4
Frau Jenny Treibel: Oder "Wo sich Herz zum Herzen find't" (Fontane), 179, 180; aesthetic debate in, 119–20; authorial *porte-parole* in, 114, 116, 133, 197 n. 12; breakdown of mimesis in, 145; conceptions of identity in, 115, 146; domestic arts in, 123, 124–25, 133, 134; femininity in, 126–30; irony in, 114, 121–23, 142, 145–46; narrative as empowerment in, 133–34, 135–37, 139; totality in, 124, 132, 138

Freeman, Janet, 194 n. 13
Freud, Sigmund, 4, 6; on Medusa, 66–67; on relationship between taboo and obsessional neurosis, 35–50, 189 n. 3

Gaze (perceiving), 75, 76, 201 n. 1; and desire, 77–78; and intersubjectivity, 65, 66, 69, 70, 72, 144, 179; and power, 137–39
Geneviève, Saint, 53
Gibson, Andrew, 184 n. 10
Gilbert, Sandra, 95–97, 108
Goethe, 1, 11, 22, 23, 26, 113
Gothic tradition, 5, 94, 95
Gubar, Susan, 95–97, 108

Halliwell, Stephen, 184 n. 10
Harari, Josué, 51, 52, 57, 58, 190 n. 16
Hardy, John Edward, 148, 166
Hegel, Georg Wilhelm Friedrich, 2, 11, 12
Heilman, Robert, 192 n. 4
Heine, Heinrich, 115
Historiography, 12
History of British Birds (Bewick), 110
Holborn, Hajo, 118
Homer, 8, 32

Icarus, 150
Identity, conceptions of, debated in *Frau Jenny Treibel*, 115. *See also* Identity-constitution; Irony: as principle of non-identity; Subjectivity, novelistic
Identity-constitution: and ambivalence, 98, 162, 163, 176; and death, 70, 158, 160; feminine, 130; male, 66–67; and mimesis, 4, 5, 33, 35, 77, 89, 179, 181; as positioning, 80, 81, 86–87; in relation to the fetish, 33–34, 85, 130, 180; as representational process, 70, 81, 83, 87–88, 160, 168, 173; and totality, 4, 14, 15–17, 18, 19, 29, 33, 69, 72, 73–74, 83, 87, 89, 179–80; violent,

108; in the "Wolf Man" case, 45–47, 129. *See also* Femininity
Imitatio, distingished from mimesis: 1, 183 n. 3
Imitation, logic of domination inherent in, 43–44; and self-consciousness, 42
Incorporation, 159, 163, 201 n. 21
Introjection, 127, 159, 201 n. 21
Irony: and cognition, 20–21; as daemonic, 22–24, 28; in essay, 186–87 n. 15; in *Frau Jenny Treibel*, 114, 121–23, 142, 145–46; Kierkegaardian, 3; and narratorial presence, 150; as principle of non-identity, 22, 26–27; as revised by Lukács, 20; Romantic, 3, 26; in *The Second Coming*, 150; as structural principle of the novel, 3, 19–29, 93, 180; as subversion, 152; voiceless, 178

Jameson, Fredric, 185 n. 3
Jane Eyre (Brontë), 5, 180; achievement of selfhood in, 96, 97, 98; Bertha/Jane identification in, 108–12, 193–94 n. 11; bird imagery in, 110–11; breakdown of mimesis in, 95, 107; death in, 98–101, 107–10; images of inscription in, 98, 100, 108; madness in, 110, 112; narrative as power in, 103–6; telepathy in, 95, 96, 103, 106–9, 110
Jay, Martin, 185 n. 3
Jesus Christ, 172–73
Jésus-Christ en Flandre (Balzac), 55
John the Baptist, 193 n. 10
John, Saint, 172, 193 n. 10

Kafka, Franz, 164
Keller, Gottfried, 115
Kierkegaard, Søren, 3
Knowledge: and aggression, 152; and orality, 153–54. See also *Second Coming, The*: search for knowledge in

Lacan, Jacques, 17
Language: and consciousness, 173; figural, 8, 90. *See also* Metaphor; Naming
Last Gentleman, The (Percy), 147
Lenin, Nikolai, 183 n. 5
Libido, organization of, 38–39
Lukács, Georg, 4–6, 180; on the essay, 13–18; on *Frau Jenny Treibel*, 115, 196–97 n. 10; on genealogy of narrative form, 2–3, 6, 10–12, 18, 28–34. Works: *Ästhetik*, 183 n. 5; *Die Seele und die Formen*, 13, 186 n. 15; *Die Theorie des Romans*, 2–5, 35, 179–80
Lyons, John D., 4

Madness: and literary analysis, 151–52
Masochism: ambivalence of, 162; and constitution of identity, 45–47, 69–70, 74, 167; as distinguished from sadism, 156–57; of naming, 158, 164; in *La Recherche de l'Absolu*, 69–70; and self-denial, 108; as symbolic suicide, 160
Masquerade: and femininity, 126–27, 130, 136; as threatening, 180
Méconnaissance, 17–18
Medusa: Freud on, 66–67; images of, 77, 139; myth of, 76, 83
Melmoth reconcilié (Balzac), 55
Metaphor: as constitutive process: 175–77. *See also* Naming
"Metaphor as Mistake" (Percy), 174, 177
Mimesis: ban on, 43; circumscription or breakdown of, 5, 28, 107, 145, 180; conditions for, 2, 7; and the daemonic, 24; defined in terms of its object, 1–2, 5–6; and desire, 77; distinguished from *imitatio*, 1; during eighteenth century, 1; as enactive, 4–5, 184 n. 10; fear of, 36; and figural language, 8; during Renaissance, 1; and *The Second Coming*, 148, 151; subjectivity in, 181; and totality, 8, 33; and will to power, 48. *See also* Identity-constitution: and mimesis; Imitation

Mimesis (Auerbach), 3
Monahan, Melodie, 194 n. 13
Müller-Seidel, Walter, 198 n. 26

Naming, 157, 168, 169; as constitutive, 172–73; and creation of identity, 160; as gendered process, 163; and projection, 175; sadomasochism of, 157–60, 163, 164. See also Metaphor
Narcissism: and death, 93; and the establishment of difference, 67; and identity, 38–39, 46, 92, 129; and mimesis, 8; object of, 160; of obsessional neuroses, 38–40; and the other, 74, 161; and totality, 69, 85, 89, 179
Narrative: and struggle for power, 103–6. See also Form, narrative
Neuroses, obsessional: apparent altruism of, 37–38; as asocial structures, 36, 39; displacement in, 37; egoism of, 38, 42, 44; egoistic instability of, 39–40, 42, 44, 46; and fear, 37; and identification 45; as masochistic process of identity-constitution, 44–45
Novel, the: autonomy of, 9–10, 12, 29; and constitution of identity, 18, 29; as distinct from the epic, 2, 4, 27; as formal totality, 2, 18, 26, 27; history of, 6, 12; realist, 1; time in, 11; totalizing and detotalizing impulses in, 2–3, 4. See also Form, narrative; Irony; Mimesis; Subjectivity, novelistic

O'Connor, Flannery, 200 n. 17
Oedipal and pre-Oedipal stages, 45, 82, 83

Pamela (Richardson), 103
Peau de chagrin, La (Balzac), 55
Penal Colony, The (Kafka), 164
Percy, Walker, 5, 147; and existentialism, 201 n. 35; on language, 172–77, 201 n. 36. Works: "Delta Factor, The," 172–73, 178; *The Last Gentleman*, 147; "Metaphor as Mistake," 174, 177; *The Second Coming*, 5, 180; "Symbol as Hermeneutic Existentialism," 172
Phenomenology of Spirit (Hegel), 11
Pickrel, Paul, 193 n. 10
Plato, 150
Play: and imitative representation, 42; and wish-fulfillment, 41
Poetics (Aristotle), 1, 198 n. 17
Poteat, Patricia Lewis, 148
"*Préface des études de moeurs au XIXe siècle*" (Balzac), 58
Primal scene, 45–47, 66; projection in, 40–41, 43, 44, 46. See also Castration; Medusa
Projection, 25; and ego, 40–41, 46; and irony, 21, 26, 27, 28; masochism of, 44–45; naming as, 175; as narcissistic, 45–47, 67, 179; and oppositional thinking, 56; and realism, 76; relation to work of art, 47–48; as structuring *Die Theorie des Romans*, 30–32, 34; as structuring *Totem und Tabu*, 36, 46, 48–50; and unselfconscious representation, 45
Prosopopoeia, 90
Proust, Marcel, 12

"*Questions intéressantes pour les connaissances humaines*" (Balzac), 57

Rasselas (Johnson), 103
Reading: and control, 103–5; naive, 69–70; narcissistic mode of, 88–89
Realism, 5, 77; American, 5; critique of, 6, 181; and fetishism, 179; Fontane's theory of, 113–14; and projection, 76; subject in, 6, 77–79. See also Mimesis
Recherche de l'Absolu, La (Balzac), 179, 180; the Absolute in, 56, 58–63, 73, 84, 85, 87, 88; castration (fragmentation) in, 66–67, 69, 71, 73–74; death in, 81, 83, 86–88, 93; Flanders in, 52, 53; masochism in, 69, 70, 74; narcissism in, 56,

92, 93; pictorial representation in, 77, 80; science in, 52, 57–58, 190 n. 8; search for identity in, 63, 73, 92; structure of repetition in, 53–56, 93
Representation: and identity-constitution, 45–47; social versus asocial process of, 44–45
Revelation, Book of, 94, 173
Richardson, Samuel, 103
Riviere, Jacqueline, 126, 130

Sadomasochism, 43–44, 156–58, 163, 180
Samson, 111
Schlegel, Friedrich, 26, 187 n. 16, 188 n. 20
Schlenther, Paul, 117
Schopenhauer, Arthur, 29
Second Coming, The (Percy): conclusion of, 166; didactic appeal of, 149; incest in, 167–68, 201 n. 26; irony in, 150, 178; meaning of title of, 163, 171; as mimesis, 5, 148, 151, 173, 174, 177, 178, 180; naming in, 157–60, 163, 164, 168, 169, 173; sadomasochism in, 156–57; search for knowledge in, 149–53, 178; suicide/filicide in, 154–55, 159–64, 168–71
Sedgwick, Eve Kosofsky, 192 n. 4
Seele und Die Formen, Die (Lukács), 13, 186 n. 15
Self. *See* Identity-constitution; Selfhood; Subjectivity, novelistic
Self-consciousness, 13–14, 29, 93; ironic, 114. *See also* Identity-constitution; Selfhood; Subjectivity, novelistic
Selfhood, achievement of, 97; violent, 98. *See also* Identity-constitution; Subjectivity, novelistic
Self-irony: and image of ironing, 123–25, 132, 145–46; and knowledge, 121–23; standpoint of, 180; as structural principle, 142, 180
Self-reflexivity, 5, 25, 26, 34

Sexual difference, 45–47, 66. *See also* Narcissism
Spariosu, Mihai, 5
Spingarn, Joel, 183 n. 2
Spivey, Ted, 148–49
Sternheim, Carl, 115
Strachey, James, 189 n. 12
Subjectivity, novelistic: ambivalent, 3, 16–17, 19, 22; and cognition, 20; epic, 33; essayistic, 15–18, 33; and formal totality, 2–4, 15–16, 18, 19, 26; and heterogeneity, 138; ironic, 20–22, 28; not self-identical, 3, 17, 21, 27, 28, 181; productive, 2–3, 33; self-consciousness of, 14; and time, 28
"Symbol as Hermeneutic Existentialism" (Percy), 175

Taboo: egoism of, 38–39; on filicide, 168; as social structure, 36, 39, 40; violation of, 36–37
Tharpe, Jac, 148
Theorie des Romans, Die (Lukács), 2–5, 180; and fetishism, 33–34; genre of, 10–14; ironic structure of, 3; performative nature of, 19, 33, 35, 180; projection in, 30–34; significance of epic in, 2–3, 7–10, 12, 14, 18, 28–34; temporality of, 11; tone of, 10–11, 19, 30, 33; totality in, 2-3, 4, 7–10, 14–18, 26–27, 179
Time: and subjectivity, 28; in the essay, 29; in the novel, 11
Tolstoy, Leo, 11, 48
Torok, Marie, 127, 159, 201 n. 21
Totality: and bourgeois conception of self, 97; centrality of, in *Die Theorie des Romans*, 7–10; fantasy of, 124, 138; and fetishism, 33–34; image of, 18, 132, 138; as linguistic, 87; Lukács on, after 1931, 197 n. 10; and narcissism, 69, 85, 89, 179; and the novel, 2, 26–27, 179; social, 2–3, 184 n. 9. *See also* Identity-constitution: and totality
Totem und Tabu (Freud), 4, 5, 35, 37, 50; on obsessional neurosis, 36,

Totem und Tabu (Freud) *(cont.)* 37–38, 39–40, 41, 42–44, 48; on play, 43; on projection, 40–41, 43–48; relation to *Die Theorie des Romans*, 35–36; as structured by projection, 48–50; on the taboo, 36–37, 38, 39, 41–42, 43, 44
Turgenev, Ivan, 113
Turner, David, 115

"*Unsere Lyrische and Epische Poesie Seit 1848*" (Fontane), 113

Vannier, Bernard, 76
Verein für Sozialpolitik, 118

Verklärung, 6, 113, 120, 139, 143, 196 n. 4
"*Vorspiel auf dem Theater*" (Goethe), 113

Weber, Samuel, 4
Widerspiegelung, 183 n. 5
Will to power: and identity, 146; and imitative magic, 47–48; and work of art, 48
"Wolf Man," the, 45, 66
Wundt, Wilhelm, 189 n. 9